Anatomy
of the Slasher Film

Anatomy of the Slasher Film
A Theoretical Analysis

SOTIRIS PETRIDIS

McFarland & Company, Inc., Publishers
Jefferson, North Carolina

LIBRARY OF CONGRESS CATALOGUING-IN-PUBLICATION DATA

Names: Petridis, Sotiris, 1990– author.
Title: The anatomy of the slasher film : a theoretical analysis / Sotiris Petridis.
Description: Jefferson, North Carolina : McFarland & Company, Inc., Publishers, 2019 | Includes bibliographical references and index. | Includes filmography.
Identifiers: LCCN 2019017078 | ISBN 9781476674315 (paperback : acid free paper) ∞
Subjects: LCSH: Slasher films—History and criticism.
Classification: LCC PN1995.9.S554 P48 2019 | DDC 791.43/6164—dc23
LC record available at https://lccn.loc.gov/2019017078

BRITISH LIBRARY CATALOGUING DATA ARE AVAILABLE

ISBN (print) 978-1-4766-7431-5
ISBN (ebook) 978-1-4766-3567-5

© 2019 Sotiris Petridis. All rights reserved

No part of this book may be reproduced or transmitted in any form or by any means, electronic or mechanical, including photocopying or recording, or by any information storage and retrieval system, without permission in writing from the publisher.

Front cover photograph by Jeff Thrower (Shutterstock)

Printed in the United States of America

McFarland & Company, Inc., Publishers
  Box 611, Jefferson, North Carolina 28640
    www.mcfarlandpub.com

Acknowledgments

My interest in slasher films goes back to my childhood. This love never faded and led to my PhD research, which this book is based on. First and foremost, I would like to thank my family and especially my mom who allowed me to see these "creepy" films from a very young age. I want to thank my best friends, Tania Nanavraki and Manolis Kapnopoulos, who were beside me during the challenging years of this research.

I would like to express my gratitude to Christina Adamou, my PhD supervisor, for her patient assistance and encouragement. I am indebted to Eleftheria Thanouli and Panayiota Mini, the members of my thesis committee, for their useful critiques of this research and their valuable support. My grateful thanks to Betty Kaklamanidou for her mentoring, her unlimited guidance, and her support through all these years. I would also like to thank my peer reviewers for their time and feedback. Finally, I should mention that this research was facilitated by a scholarship awarded to me by Onassis Foundation.

Table of Contents

Acknowledgments	v
Introduction	1
1. A Theoretical and Historical Approach to Slasher Films	5
Slasher Films: A Horror Subgenre	5
The Semantic/Syntactic Elements of Slasher Films	18
The Cycles of the Slasher Film Subgenre	34
An Epilog to the Theoretical and Historical Approach	45
2. The Classical Cycle of Slasher Films	47
The Normality of the Classical Cycle	48
The Other of the Classical Cycle	55
The Final Survivors of the Classical Cycle	60
The Victims of the Classical Cycle	64
An Epilog on the Classical Cycle	65
3. The Self-Referential Cycle of Slasher Films	67
The Normality of the Self-Referential Cycle	69
The Other of the Self-Referential Cycle	74
The Final Survivors of the Self-Referential Cycle	79
The Victims of the Self-Referential Cycle	84
An Epilog on the Self-Referential Cycle	87
4. The Neoslasher Cycle of Slasher Films	89
The Normality of the Neoslasher Cycle	90
The Other of the Neoslasher Cycle	105

The Final Survivors of the Neoslasher Cycle	112
The Victims of the Neoslasher Cycle	122
An Epilog on the Neoslasher Cycle	128
Conclusions	130
Appendix A: Films Referenced	135
Appendix B: Semantic Elements	141
Chapter Notes	145
Filmography	155
Bibliography	159
Index	167

Introduction

The horror genre is a term that covers a plethora of subgenres and film cycles. These films incorporate a wide range of narratives, from raw realism to purely paranormal narrations. Some of the most widespread subgenres of horror are the vampire film, torture porn film, paranormal film, possession film and splatter film. Of course, although this genre has existed since the birth of cinema, its systematic theoretical study began in the mid–1970s, about the same time that film studies were introduced to universities.

What makes these particular filmic texts a concrete genre is the fact that they are meant to scare the audience. In particular, the fear of death is an essential part of horror films, both in the sense of a natural process of the human body, and the eternal punishment of the immortal soul. This is represented by repulsive images of metaphysical or murderous situations. Another approach of the fears that are incorporated into the narratives of the genre is the cosmic fear.[1] Cosmic fear is a combination of fear, moral aversion and admiration. The curiosity and admiration of both evil and paranormal coexist with the human existence and are surrounded by an awe for our own world.

The expression of this particular cinematic genre can take many forms, depending on the type of each narrative. The slasher film subgenre, which will be the focus of this book, is one of the many forms of the horror genre. This subgenre is now defined by the widespread term "slasher," which was established in the mid–1980s. The prevalence of this term came from the widespread use of sharp objects by the murderers during the killings. Until then, other names have been used for the subgenre, such as stalker film, dead teenager, women in danger, psycho, slash-and-chop, stalk and slash, teeniekill and slice-'em-up films. The term slasher, of course, had been used in the past to describe either several film killers (e.g., *The Mysteries of Paris* [1935] and *Without Warning* [1952]) or real-life murderers (Vaughn Greenwood).[2] Of course, after the establishment of this particular subgenre, the term was associated only with these filmic texts.

The majority of the academic approaches to slasher films are usually spent on gender and sexual representations, and in this way, no one could realize the big changes of progress that happened to this subgenre over the course of four decades. The subgenre conventions and formula have changed over time and have evolved in line with the sociopolitical conditions of each period. The aim of this book is to fill this gap and analyze the whole subgenre.

A systematic study of the subgenre will show that there is great variation in its films over the decades. This book will shed light on the evolution of the slasher film and on its history, beginning in 1974 and reaching to the present day, under a narrative analysis through a semantic and syntactic approach. From this narrative analysis, it will be proved that there are four main semantic elements and three general syntactic categories, and that the subgenre has evolved considerably and can be divided into three film cycles: the classical (1974–1993), the self-referential (1994–2000) and the neoslasher cycle (2000–2013).[3] Of course, this research will be done systematically and methodically, and will be based on a film corpus from the whole lifespan of the subgenre. The research sample will consist of the films that were in the top 100 of the U.S. annual box office between 1974 and 2016.

More specifically, the first chapter will present the theoretical framework on which this research will be based. Employing a semantic and syntactic approach, there will be an identification of the four key semantic elements of these narratives that are present throughout the existence of the subgenre (Normality, the Other, the Final Survivor and the Victims), and a study of the changes of the narrative syntax, based on three main categories (the backstory of the Other, the connection of the Other with the Final Survivors, and the relationship of Normality with the rest of the three semantic elements separately) that lead to the differentiation of the three film cycles. These elements, based on the updated syntax, have changed in each cycle of the slasher subgenre.

The next chapters of the book will be devoted to the systematic study of each film cycle of the subgenre through case studies belonging to the corpus. More specifically, the second chapter will analyze the classical cycle and the characteristics that govern it. The classical cycle is known for its conservatism, the loose narrative connections between the backstory and the current events, while at the center of the representations gender and sexual identities play a key role in choosing who will be murdered. In this cycle, which is the beginning of the subgenre, many well-known franchises have been created and will be analyzed in the second chapter, such as *Halloween, Friday the 13th* and *A Nightmare on Elm Street*.

The third chapter will focus on the self-referential cycle and on the differentiation of the subgenre in the 1990s. Although some classical structures of the previous cycle have been maintained, self-referentiality and intertextuality have come to the fore, while permitting the remodeling of the syntax under a structure of trying to find the killer's identity. The case studies that will shed light on these changes will be films that belong to classical franchises, such as *Halloween*, so it will be easier to compare them with their classical texts. Of course, in this cycle there are also new self-referential franchises that will be analyzed too, like *Scream*.

Finally, the fourth chapter will refer to the neoslasher cycle, which began to emerge in the beginning of the new millennium. In neoslashers, there are strong narrative links between the backstory and the current events, and between the Other and the Final Survivors, while there is a constant effort to find the causes of the creation of evil, putting the Other at a central position in the narrative. In this chapter too, the case studies will concern films both belonging to famous franchises that were born during the previous cycles as well as new filmic texts that emerged during the new millennium.

The theoretical framework that will be introduced in this book will have innovative elements that will highlight issues that have not been analyzed, as its goal is to fill the gap in the academic community in regard to existing studies of slasher films. The systematic analysis from the birth of the subgenre to the present will provide a comprehensive study of the narratives of these films that will highlight the evolution of the structures and conventions of slasher films. The semantic and syntactic approach, as well as the historical analysis of the three film cycles, will be two important additions to the academic analysis of both the subgenre and cinematic horror in general.

1. A Theoretical and Historical Approach to Slasher Films

Slasher Films: A Horror Subgenre

Slasher films consist an integral part of the horror genre and have largely influenced American and global pop culture. Of course, before we go any further, first we have to define through genre theory what are slasher films. Based on acceptable facts regarding these films, the subgenre can be summed up by the following definition: slasher films are about a serial killer (not necessarily with human form), who, with the help of non-technological weapons, is spreading fear and death in a middle-class community by killing innocent people. At the end, the killer is defeated and the main character survives (or in some cases, more than one character).

Several critics argue that the subgenre's first influences are the works of horror that produced at Grand Guignol at the end of the 19th century.[1] Trying to identify the beginning of slasher films, we will realize that there is a controversy, with many of the academic community defending that *Halloween* (1978) is the first filmic text of the subgenre.[2] This is due to the fact that this particular text was the first to combine all the conventions that later became known as the subgenre's formula. The reason *Halloween* is mainly considered to be the beginning of the subgenre can also be found on a theoretical level. George Lakoff was the first to introduce the theory of prototype concept, in which he argues that categories have gradations of membership.[3] There are prototypical works that present a vivid set of properties and function as exemplary models in the center of the system, giving stability to the genre. Thus, the other texts draw data from these models, but show weaker qualifications. *Halloween* is widely considered to be the first text of the subgenre because it has all the features that were consolidated in slasher films, but that does not automatically mean that it is the beginning of it.

Four years before *Halloween*'s appearance, there were two filmic texts that, if thoroughly studied, will also be found to be part of the subgenre. In

1974 *Black Christmas* and *The Texas Chainsaw Massacre* were screened and launched the beginning of a new horror subgenre. Thus, in this book it is agreed that the subgenre began in 1974. Before 1974, there were some filmic texts that had some common elements with the subgenre's films, which have influenced them, but they do not have all the necessary prerequisites for them to be considered part of the total subgenre. The most important of these films is *Psycho* (1960).

In *Psycho*, in the role of the killer we have a boy next door. Norman Bates (Anthony Perkins) has a double personality (both his own and his mother) and kills women who sexually arouse him. The narrative of the film contains a murderer, victims and survivors, who in the end are proclaimed the winners of the narrative. There is also a primary violence against women who accept and embrace their sexuality. Of course, *Psycho* was created at a time when there was no systematic production of such films, so there was no concrete subgenre yet. Also, although it has several conventions, it is not fully compatible with the entire formula of the slasher subgenre. For example, it has a small number of killings and is lacking the sense of a widespread violence.

Hence, any filmic text produced before 1974 is an ancestor of the subgenre and not part of it. Before 1974 there was no extensive production of these films, so it cannot be considered as a historical period of the subgenre. If we needed to reference these particular films, we would call them as pre-slashers. Before *Psycho*, there are other pre-slasher films that are considered to be important influences of the subgenre, such as *Thirteen Women* (1932), *The Leopard Man* (1943), *The Bad Seed* (1956) and *Cover Girl Killer* (1959). Between 1960 and 1974, which marks the beginning of the subgenre, we have remarkable pre-slashers, such as *Peeping Tom* (1960), *Strait-Jacket* (1964) and *Berserk* (1967). These films helped to lay the foundations and create conventions, which led to the creation of the subgenre's formula.

Even though these films from 1974 until today constitute a cohesive subgenre, differences in filmic texts from different decades can be identified. At this point, the concept of the cycle of a genre/subgenre will be useful. According to Leger Grindon,[4] based on the definition of Rick Altman,[5] a cycle is a series of films of a limited period of time and linked by a dominant trend in their use of the genre's conventions. Although the slasher film subgenre seems to be possessed by distinct cycles, it has not been systematically studied under this approach. The majority of its academic analysis is usually spent on gender and sexual representations, leaving no attention to the tremendous evolution of their narratives that these filmic texts made over the four decades of the subgenre. The subgenre's conventions and formula have changed over time and have evolved, while the circumstances of each historical period influence these changes.

THE FILM CORPUS CREATION

The first step in an academic research, of course, is to identify and demarcate the analyzed material. But when we talk about filmic genres, things are not that simple. When referring to two or more films and placing them on the same genre or subgenre, we automatically accept that these films share some common elements. These elements may be part of the narrative or norms and conventions governing the films. The problem, however, is the equivalent of the chicken or the egg causality dilemma: first select the films that belong to a genre and then analyze their characteristics or identify the characteristics of a genre and then choose the films that can be part of it? Andrew Tudor has called it the "empiricist dilemma" as a circle in which films are first required to be isolated, for which a criterion is needed, but this criterion will emerge from the empirically common features of the films. The solution to the Tudor's dilemma is the common cultural consensus.[6]

From 1974 to present, hundreds of slasher films have been produced in the United States of America that shape, evolve, and/or reject conventions that share these filmic texts. To better strengthen this argument, the research began with the creation of a corpus of films that will be the foundation of this theory, enhancing it with tangible quantitative results.[7] Since the slasher film is a commercial subgenre, the film corpus is based on economic criteria. In particular, based on the Box Office Mojo website (www.boxofficemojo.com), the corpus includes all the subgenre's films that managed to be found in the top 100 American box office between 1974 and 2016. However, as the site's data start from 1980 and the subgenre appeared in 1974, all the information needed from the period between 1974 and 1979 is from the IMDb website (www.imdb.com).

As Christine Gledhill observes, genres are first and foremost a boundary phenomenon.[8] The choice of whether or not a film belongs to the subgenre in the creation of the corpus was based on three of the four genre classification methods set by Tudor in 1973[9] and analyzed by Janet Staiger in 1997.[10] Starting to watch the films, there was a particular pattern in my mind, in which the narratives should rotate around a killer, not necessarily human, chasing an innocent group of victims (the "a priori" method). In the a priori method there was a use of the family resemblance idea, which was first developed by Ludwig Wittgenstein.[11] Based on this idea, there is no rigid set of characteristics that defines membership in a category, such as a film genre, but there is a rigid set of essential traits that do not necessarily have to be all present in order to bring integration into the whole. Having some of these traits is enough to place a text as part of the family. As a second method, there was use of empirical evidence based on the viewing of the films (the "empiricist" method). Finally, there was a reliance on film summaries, promotional data, interviews with the creators, etc. (the "social consensus" method).

Based on the above, the original corpus created included 85 films. But then, by systematic readings of these texts, the number of films in the final corpus fell to 74. This was done for two main reasons. The first is that in some films, although they possessed some elements of the slasher film subgenre, some other filmic genres/subgenres prevailed in their narrative. Some filmic texts were identified as comedies (*Student Bodies* [1981]), some as science fiction (*The Faculty* [1998]) and some others as paranormal horror (*Deadly Blessing* [1981]). The second reason for removing films from the original corpus is that they belonged to a franchise based on the most famous pre-slasher, *Psycho*. During the subgenre's lifetime, two sequels (*Psycho II* [1983] and *Psycho III* [1986]) and a remake (*Psycho* [1998]) appeared, which were economic successes and could be incorporated into the final corpus. While *Psycho* influenced the creation of the subgenre, it is not part of it and therefore the entire franchise cannot be incorporated into the corpus. *Psycho* also influenced other subgenres of cinematic horror, such as the horror of double personality, urban horror, splatter, etc., so it would not be right to place it in a single subgenre just because it is considered to be its ancestor.

The final corpus of films (see appendix) consists of 74 film titles along with the first screening dates, the names of the directors, screenwriters and key actors, the production company that distributed the film and the total domestic revenue.

Based on the final corpus of 74 films, some preliminary conclusions can

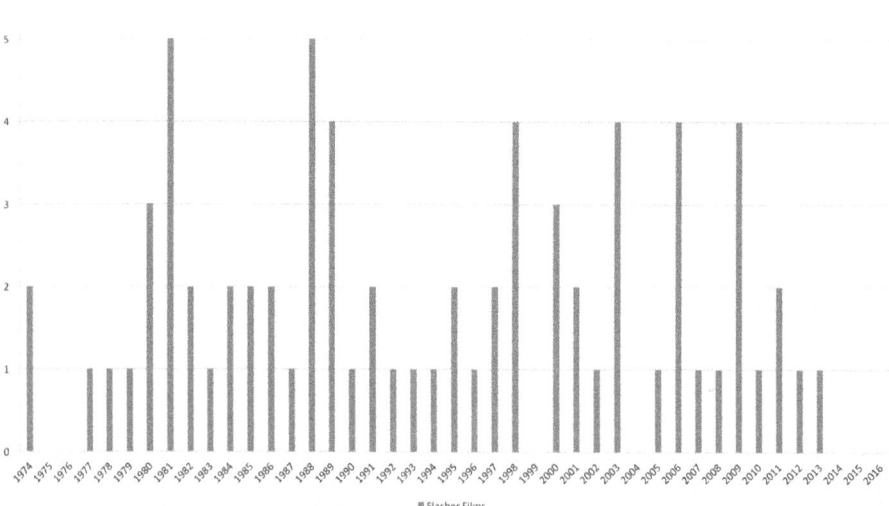

Number of slasher films in top 100 per year

be drawn. The first films of the subgenre appeared in 1974, but until the success of *Halloween*, the production of these films was not so systematic. In fact, for the next two years since the appearance of the first slasher films, no movie was economically successful. Until the late 1970s, only one filmic text per year is in the 100 most profitable films of the American box office. After *Halloween*'s first screening and during the early 1980s, we see a toss of the films at the top-100, perhaps due to the standardization of the subgenre's conventions. Of course, it is worth mentioning the fact that in the mid–1980s there was a fall due to the saturation of these films. Thus, films from the mid- to-late 1980s tried to differentiate themselves with various sophisticated themes or hybrid narratives, but they did not step away enough from the classical conventions that had been established. For this reason, there is a second upward trend in the late 1980s, but it did not last long.

The arrival of the 1990s finds the subgenre in a steady but negative course. At the beginning of the decade, almost every year, only one film managed to enter the annual top-100 and was usually part of a big franchise that had already established a loyal audience. At the mid–1990s, there is a sharp increase of films, equivalent to the 1980s, but has lasted for a few years, failing to escape beyond the 1990s. It is noteworthy that 1999 was the year when no slasher film managed to be considered a financial success and get into the top-100 of the domestic box office. Analyzing the narratives of these films in the 1990s, we notice that the conventions began to move away from the standardization of the 1980s, using primarily self-referential elements. Two thousand is an important year for the subgenre as we observe the closing of the 1990s film cycle with two sequels of well-known franchises—*Scream 3* (2000) and *Urban Legends: Final Cut* (2000)—but we also notice the beginning of a new cycle with *Final Destination* (2000).

The new millennium finds the subgenre flourishing and having a consistent presence with at least one movie in the top-100 domestic box office, while every two or three years, the slasher films go up to three or four per year. The only exception to this is the year 2004 where none of the films have been economically successful. The new period of the subgenre has completely distanced itself from the classical conventions of the 1980s and 1990s, creating a new form of narrative in which focus is no longer on the representation of violence but on the effort to identify its creation. Lastly, we notice that during 2014–2016 no slasher film managed to get into the top-100 domestic box office, but this can be justified by new forms of video-on-demand distribution services that are common among slasher films, but also the expansion of the subgenre on television, with examples such as *Scream: The TV Series* (MTV, 2015–today) and *Scream Queens* (Fox, 2015–2016).

The contribution of this book is that I propose that there are three main cycles in the lifespan of the slasher film subgenre: the classical cycle, the self-referential cycle and the neoslasher cycle. The classical cycle starts from the birth of the subgenre in 1974, and reaches until 1993, the self-referential cycle ranges from 1994 to 2000, while the neoslasher cycle begins in 2000 and exists until 2013. This separation is based on quantitative analysis of the subgenre, but also on the systematic analysis of these narratives. As we will see below, in the present study the genres and subgenres will be treated as entities that contain evolutionary abilities. The concept of film cycles is a key point to this claim. Each of the aforementioned periods functions as a subgenre cycle that brings different narrative conventions to the fore. Film cycles are usually influenced and associated with specific film studios and/or creators, while in the post-studio era this association could be among film franchises or sequels.[12] Observing the analyzed data of the film corpus, we see that certain distribution studios or creators of a specific period are repeated among the filmic texts and seem to influence the course of the subgenre itself. For example, Paramount appears to be quite a distributor in the classical cycle, while New Line, although existing in the classical and self-referential cycle, is established in the neoslasher cycle, where it distributes the majority of the period's films. Of course, in order to better understand the subgenre's differentiation from cycle to cycle, we need to analyze extensively the characteristics of the filmic texts.

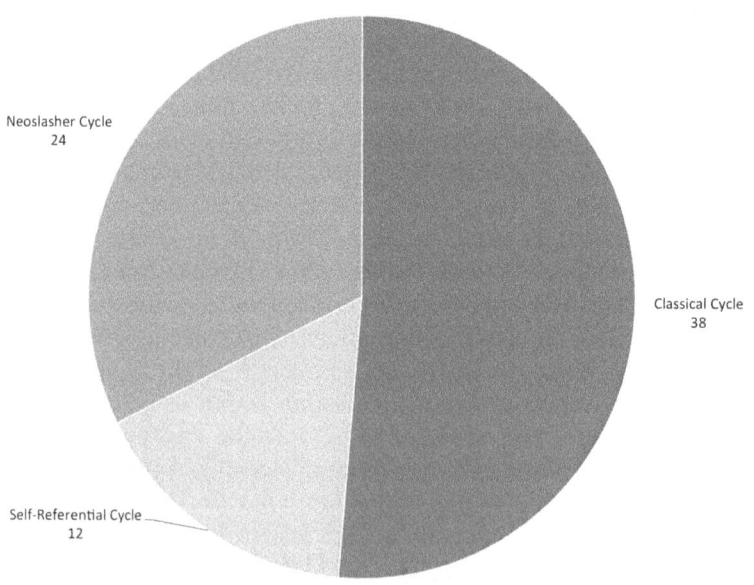

Number of films of the Corpus per cycle

The Theoretical Approach of the Slasher Film Subgenre

Based on Grindon, ideally, film genre history integrates formal analysis, thematic interpretation, and social considerations.[13] The cinematic genres are quite complex, and every definition of each genre is co-created by all those who use the term—from viewers and creators to production studios and the media. According to Steve Neale, the nature of a genre's evolutionary process is manifested as an interaction between three levels: the level of expectation, the level of generic corpus, and the level of the "rules" or "norms" that govern both.[14] Neale refers to the expectations and assumptions of viewers when they go to the cinema, which interact with the actual films during the viewing as well as the elements that are incorporated and reproduced over time, creating a coherence in film genres. According to Neale, the genres are not only created by the filmic texts, but also by these expectations. Therefore, any new film is a variation to a pre-existing collection of data that is available at any time in the life of the genre, and includes only a selection of them.[15] In the present study, the genres will be treated as dynamic texts that are constantly developing and adapting their conventions to the circumstances, because they are better understood when viewed as evolutionary processes.[16]

Apart from genres, the aforementioned principles, as one can imagine, apply also to subgenres, such as slasher films. At this point, we have to point out that the present study will not deal with the general theories of horror, but will specialize in the theoretical framework that has been set for the slasher films. This will be because the horror genre is a huge umbrella that covers different filmic texts, and their narratives often contradict with each other. It is worth noting that in the book by Noel Carroll, *The Philosophy of Horror: Or, Paradoxes of the Heart*, one of the most important studies of the horror genre, slasher films are left out due to the definition of the genre, as Carroll believes that the monster is a prerequisite of storytelling and cannot be replaced by a human form.[17] Based on this example alone, it is clear that engaging in theories that target the entire genre will make it difficult to specialize the research.

Regarding the academic studies of slasher films, we can see that the majority of the academics that dealt with this particular subgenre talked about various types of elements of the narrations of the filmic texts. The most systematic and widespread studies of the subgenre are made by the following three researchers: Carol J. Clover, Vera Dika and Adam Rockoff. As we will see below, all three studies have a very small sample of filmic texts on which they are based, while the years that are being analyzed are not the whole lifespan of the subgenre, basing the research in the early years of the subgenre and reaching up to the 1980s.

The most well-known study of the subgenre belongs to Carol Clover and is contained in *Men, Women and Chain Saws: Gender in the Modern Horror Film*, in which she develops the Final Girl theory. Clover defines the subgenre as "the immensely generative story of a psycho killer who slashes to death a string of mostly female victims, one by one, until he is subdued or killed, usually by the one girl who has survived."[18] Clover's analysis deals with the filmic texts of 1970s and 1980s and its limited range of study concerns sexual and gender representations. It also analyzes the perspective of the viewer of these particular films according to their gender.

Clover talks about two phases of the subgenre. The first is from 1960 to 1974, which contains filmic texts that are not considered slashers, but have quite common narrative elements with slasher films, and the second from 1974 to 1986 in which the subgenre's formula evolved and flourished. The film that is considered to be the point of change of the two phases is *The Texas Chainsaw Massacre*, followed by several slasher films that standardized and reproduced the subgenre's conventions, thus creating a narrative formula.

According to Clover's analysis, there are six important elements of the subgenre: the killer, the terrible place, weapons, victims, the Final Girl and shock.[19] The killer is usually a man and quite often has disturbed sexual behavior. The archetypal form of these killers is Norman Bates from *Psycho*, who killed any woman that sexually aroused him. Clover uses the theory of sexual punishment and applies it to the entire subgenre, speaking of a punisher who attacks those who are sexually active. The killer, even though he is dominated by human characteristics, often possesses some superhuman elements.[20] One of his main superhuman features is the fact that most of the time he cannot be defeated or murdered, leaving an open ending to the narrative with a sense of an invincible and all-powerful evil that exists in our society. Finally, the killers are a constant element of the narrations between the sequels.

The most characteristic element of the killers is the weapon that they use. Each franchise of the subgenre can be identified by the weapon. Michael Myers on the *Halloween* movie series uses a knife, Leatherface on *Texas Chainsaw Massacre* a chainsaw, Freddy Krueger on *A Nightmare on Elm Street* a blade glove and so on. As Clover says about the choice of weapons, "the emotional terrain of the slasher film is pretechnological."[21] In the filmic texts of the classical cycle, it is unusual to find a weapon that is advanced by technological means. The way victims are murdered is through hammers, knives, axes or other types of blades. This is in the same context with Clover's general approach to sexual punishment, since these weapons are phallic symbols and the murders can be perceived as an allegory of the penetration itself as part of a sexual act.

According to Clover, victims are most of the time teenagers, although she sets the victim's starting point on an adult character, Marion Crane (Janet Leigh) on *Psycho*. The basic form of the victims remains the same, as "Marion is first and foremost a sexual transgressor,"[22] or otherwise, the character that with her sexual activity and behavior defies the rules of the society. The difference between Marion and the other victims of the classical cycle is that they belong to both biological sexes. However, sexual transgression is part of their identity, which leads to their defeat. In these films, every character that smokes, drinks alcohol, uses drugs, or has sex has to die. The victims of the classical films can belong to both genders, but there is a substantial difference in the way their death is represented. Clover states that boys die not because they are boys, but because they make wrong choices (either sexual or behavioral). Also, their murders are usually quick and often seen from a distance or happening off-screen.[23] On the other hand, the murders of women are filmed at a closer distance, with more graphic detail and longer time.[24] This differentiation in the representation of victims' murders is based on the fear of male audiences about castration. As we shall see below, the fear of castration is represented in the classical cycle by the victory of the Final Girl over the male killer who is usually possessed by asexual and/or homosexual characteristics. Barbara Creed states:

> The horror film's obsession with blood, particularly the bleeding body of woman, where her body is transformed into the "gaping wound," suggests that castration anxiety is a central concern of the horror film—particularly the slasher sub-genre. Woman's body is slashed and mutilated, not only to signify her own castrated state, but also the possibility of castration for the male.[25]

Of course, that does not mean that the character that will survive will be a man. Although the majority of the victims are women, only one character will survive in the classical cycle and, according to Clover, this character will be a girl.

In addition to the killer, an important element in Clover's study is the Final Girl, who manages to stand out from the crowd and become the survivor of the film. This particular term is the best known regarding the subgenre and it was created to characterize and describe the female character who survives and defeats the killer. According to Clover, there are two types of endings in these narratives: the Final Girl will either find the power to delay the killer enough to survive, or kill him.[26] After *Halloween*, when the subgenre began to grow and stabilize, the Final Girl turned into a more active character that could face the killer without any help from the community. From the beginning of each narrative, the Final Girl is represented as the main character, while her sexual behavior is distinguishing her from the other adolescents of the filmic text. From her appearance to her character, she is possessed by virginal characteristics, which, if compared to the other characters of this particular film cycle, stand out because of their rarity in the narrative. Other characteristics of the Final Girl are that she is smart and watchful to the point of paranoia.[27] So, although she is smaller in size and physically weaker than the killer, she manages to defeat and sometimes even kill him.

The analysis of the above elements of Clover's work is based on the representation of genders and the sexual behavior of the main characters. The killer does not have entirely male characteristics, as the identity of the Final Girl is not entirely feminine. Although in the classical cycle, the killer is almost always a male character, his masculinity is quite limited: ranging from virginal or sexually inactive features to transgender or transsexual characteristics.[28] On the other hand, the Final Girl is a female character with pretty masculine features and male interests.[29] So, while the two main characters of every classical slasher film seem to be exactly the opposite of each other, they have something in common: their sexual oppression. Linda Williams, in her analysis of the female look in cinema, states, "[The woman] not only sees a monster, she sees a monster that offers a distorted reflection of her own image."[30] Jean Loth shares this opinion too, who states that film monsters should be regarded as embodiments of women's virginal sexual fantasies—a cross between fear and desire.[31]

The way these two characters exhaust their sexual energy is different, but at the same time similar. The killer does it through the killing of the victims, while the Final Girl does it through the castration (literal or metaphorical) of the killer himself, and thus the Final Girl turns into what the killer once was. As Clover says, "When the Final Girl stands at last in the light of day with the knife in her hand, she has delivered herself into the adult world … she is what the killer once was; he is what she could become should she fail in her battle for sexual selfhood."[32] Clover's view is in line with Walter Evans's approach, in which he parallels the monster attack with the sexual act.[33] The attack is usually done by night in people of the opposite gender (in this case, in the Final Girl) and after that the perpetrator feels remorse and shame while the victim turns into a new offender.

The book of Clover is treated as the "holy book" of the subgenre, as the author is one of the first members of the academic community who dealt with the analysis of this particular subgenre, and every text written about slasher films has a reference to her theory. Although it is a very in-depth and thorough analysis, her theory has a limited applicability, as this tool was created on the basis of a corpus of films containing only filmic texts from the 1970s and 1980s and does not take into account the differentiation of the films of the decades that followed. Slasher films have developed and evolved quite a lot since then, and Clover's theory can hardly be applied to modern filmic texts. Thus, her theory is a characteristic example of a study of this specific period of the subgenre, but it cannot be used for a generalized analysis of the whole subgenre because of its great evolution. As we will see in the present study, the subgenre began to move away from the punishment and/or reward of sexual behaviors, which contradicts Clover's theory.

The second most important analysis of the subgenre was made by Vera Dika and based on a structuralist approach of the filmic texts (Dika refers to them as "the stalker films" thus giving an alternative name to the subgenre). The chronological extent of the filmic samples under analysis is even more limited than Clover's, as the film corpus of this theory contains filmic texts only from 1978 to 1981. Hence, the application of this theory is limited to the first cycle of slashers and does not even cover the whole cycle, as it deals with the films that were screened during the aforementioned four years. Dika, too, bases her approach on gender and sexual elements, and, like many other theorists, recognizes *Halloween* as the beginning of the subgenre.

The purpose of Dika's analysis is to define the subgenre's films as concrete works that share a distinctive combination of narrative and cinematic elements.[34] In the narrative analysis, it presents a time structure divided into two parts.[35] The first part deals with an event that happened in the past and is usually a traumatic experience of the killer. The actions of the first part are:

Past Event
The members of a young community are guilty of a wrongful action.
The killer sees an injury, fault or death.
The killer experiences a loss.
The killer kills the guilty members of the young community.

The victims mentioned above are the first victims of the narratives and are usually part of the first sequence of the filmic texts. Dika continues the analysis and states that whatever the actions of the past are, "the opening sequence always presents a woman's death and/or an image of her mutilated body."[36] Most of the time, the killer is portrayed as the witness to a woman's injury or death.

According to Dika, the second part of the structure of these particular films relates to the narrative's present. In this part, the killer returns to take revenge from the guilty groups or their symbolic replacements. The killer chases and slaughters young victims and the female protagonist comes out of the crowd and confronts him. The narrative functions that constitute the second part of the structure proposed by Dika are the following:

Present Event
An event commemorates the past action.
The killer's destructive impulse is reactivated.
A seer warns the young community.
The young community takes no heed.
The killer stalks the young community.
The killer kills members of the young community.

The heroine sees the murders.
The heroine sees the killer.
The heroine does battle with the killer.
The heroine subdues the killer.
The heroine survives but is not free.

Through these 15 actions (four from the past and 11 from the present event), Dika creates a structuralist guide for the period of the subgenre that she is studying. It is worth noting that this guide is not fully implemented by all the filmic texts she examines, as there are variations. For example, based on her theory, Dika denies that *When a Stranger Calls* (1979) is part of the subgenre, even though this particular film is commonly accepted as a slasher.

In addition to the proposal of a structuralist guide, Dika talks about specific key elements of the narratives found in every classical slasher. The first and foremost element is the killer who is either off-screen or wears a mask for most of the film.[37] In this way, the process of manipulating the identification of the audience allows for the exchange of empathies between the killer and the female protagonist of the narrative. The heroine is another key element, which is close to Clover's term "Final Girl." The last element based on Dika's theory is the victims. These three elements are part of the youth community, to which the adult community (consisting of parents, teachers, psychiatrists or police officers), which has no power to change the facts, is in opposition.[38]

Dika's structuralist approach, even if is very detailed, is about a small amount of filmic texts in comparison with the whole subgenre, and is even more limited in scope than Clover's theory. This theory is a basis for approaching the classical cycle and analyzing the first subgenre's conventions. Both of Dika's and Clover's theories, relate to specific filmic texts and cannot be applied to the entire subgenre.

A third approach to the narrative elements of the subgenre is the one that Adam Rockoff made. In his book *Going to Pieces: The Rise and Fall of the Slasher Film, 1978–1986*, Rockoff gets the data set by Clover and Dika and moves the analysis one step further. Rockoff mentions seven categories of elements: the killer, weapons of choice, special effects, setting, the past event, the Final Girl and subjective point of view.[39] Of course, as Rockoff's analysis is a transformation of the above-mentioned theories, it covers only the first films of the subgenre and does not entirely apply to films of the new millennium.

In this book, a theoretical approach for the overall analysis of the subgenre and the identification of its evolutionary course over the decades will be created. To achieve this goal, Rick Altman's theory about narrative analysis will be useful. Altman, agreeing with the view of the evolution of film genres and their influence over the course of time,[40] spoke about two approaches, which according to him can be used in combination: the semantic and the syntactic approach. The semantic approach refers to a list of common elements that exist in the filmic texts (such as characters, shots, locations, etc.), while the syntactic approach refers to specific constitutional relationships, based on how the elements are placed on the narrative by means of the particular fundamental structure of the genre.[41] Examples of the syntax of the subgenre itself are the connection of the Other with the Final Survivor, the relationship of the victims with Normality or the contrasting representation of the Final Survivor with the victims. The semantic approach emphasizes the structural elements of a genre, while the syntactic gives a basis on the way in which the narratives are structured. Of course, the boundaries between semantic and syntactic elements sometimes blur, and the choices of each scholar have an impact on the analysis and the aesthetic approach of the genre under study.[42]

Altman speaks of a combinational approach that includes both the above-mentioned approaches to cover and analyze more aspects of the genre as opposed to an analysis based on either the semantic or the syntactic approach alone. The semantic approach has less explanatory power and is applied to a wider range of films, unlike the syntactic approach, which sacrifices the broad scope of its application for the benefit of the isolation of certain explanatory structures of the genre.[43] Using Altman's combinatorial approach, we can maintain a balance in the subgenre's analysis between a generalized semantic approach and a more targeted syntactic analysis.

At this point, it should be noted that Altman in a future text expanded the theory by adding a third part to his theory: the pragmatic approach. Through pragmatic analysis, Altman wanted to cover the links with the institutions around a genre, but also its audience. In simple terms, Altman's new theoretical proposition on a semantic/syntactic/pragmatic approach aims at studying film genres in relation to their production and acceptance,[44] which incorporates into the discussion all that Neale has suggested and mentioned above. The present study, however, will use the original form of Altman's theory without the additional third part that was added later. This is because the present study will be purely structural and narrative, and will not enter into issues of production or acceptance of the slasher film subgenre. Also, worth mentioning is that the pragmatic approach has not thrived at present in film theory, and there are not so many samples of this analysis.

Having in mind all the aforementioned theories regarding the subgenre, Altman's theory, and elements derived from the film corpus, this study will attempt a semantic/syntactic analysis of the subgenre based on the 74 films of the corpus. The four semantic elements of slasher films remain the same throughout the life of the subgenre, and the main cause of its division into cycles is the change of the syntax. Whenever the subgenre reaches a dead-end based on the expectations of the viewers, it adjusts its syntax and redefines the expression of its semantic elements.

The Semantic/Syntactic Elements of Slasher Films

The Semantic Elements of the Subgenre

As mentioned, there is no unified theory that covers the subgenre's lifetime and can be applied to all filmic texts, regardless of their period. Considering this particular void, this analysis will create a list of semantic and syntactic elements that targets the films of the entire subgenre and not just a group of them. These elements will be a useful theoretical tool, and their study will further help separation of the subgenre into cycles. The approach of the slasher films and the creation of a list of semantic and syntactic elements will be made in such a way that there will be a generalized grouping between these narrative elements. An analysis based on the details and not on the general framework of the narrative could create a list of dozens of semantic and syntactic elements, many of which would resemble each other, and instead of facilitating the analysis of the subgenre, would make it even more difficult to apply the theory. If there are many semantic and syntactic elements that often overlap each other, the analysis will be consumed by non-significant details about whether the filmic texts are similar or different, and thus the larger image of the narrative form of the subgenre will be lost. For this reason, the semantic elements are four umbrella-terms, which came out after the systematic reading of the corpus films and using Altman's semantic/syntactic approach.

More specifically, the semantic elements are Normality, Others, Final Survivors and Victims. As we will see in the analysis below, in these aforementioned elements are incorporated some other terms, such as the location, the weapon, point of view (POV) shots, but they are not significant and self-sufficient to constitute individual elements. Through these groupings, the approach of the subgenre is further improved and the theory created in this study becomes more useful.

Normality

In every slasher film, there is a choice of people as to who will be murdered and who will survive. If we study the filmic texts in-depth, we will see that these choices are not random and rely on some rules that change over time. These rules form the basis of Normality, which varies according to the needs and fears of the society in question. This code is closely related to the notions of Normality and Other, which Robin Wood mentions in his theory, saying that any person who does not obey the rules of society must either be eliminated or changed on the basis of the rules of the community.[45]

Sophie Freud's definition of Normality is useful in expanding this reasoning further.[46] Freud speaks of three different concepts on which Normality is based. The first speaks of a statistical average, or better, a statistical model that is not based on actual data but on a widely accepted situation (e.g., I had a normal childhood). The second concept of Normality is based on a particularly positive value of life and not simply the absence of physical or mental dysfunction (e.g., right to happiness). Finally, the third concept of Normality refers to conventional behaviors based on current community standards of a supposed majority of people. Although the three concepts seem quite useful, the present research will focus more on the third. The code is essentially the aforementioned conventional behaviors, which agree to build Normality.

Every society and its every representation has its own rules and laws. Each member of the community is seemingly free to choose whether to follow these rules or not, always with the fear of punishment because of a possible divergent behavior. With this as a basis, we can separate people into two general categories, those who obey and those who violate the rules. As a result, we have people who are rewarded for their obedience to community code and people who are being punished because they break this code, creating a sense of the absence of a gray zone. Generally, horror films are based on Normality, which promotes the general perception of the period in which the film was produced, what is "right" and what is not. Slasher films are not an exception to this general rule of the whole genre and use Normality as the cornerstone of their narratives.

An example of the Normality of slasher films is the punishment of the sexual act of the classical cycle (1974–1993). In this case, Normality is strictly linked to the sexual behavior of the characters of the film. Any person who deviates from what society thinks is right ends up dead, while the survivors of the filmic text have virginal characteristics and an aversion to the sexual act. It is commonplace in horror films to disturb Normality with an underlying erotic complexion. For this reason, the genre has been targeted by both feminist and queer (lesbian, gay, bisexual, transsexual) communities.[47] The woman in general was represented as the victim and very rarely had an active role in the narration of the film. This view is also in agreement with the psychoanalytic theory, which states that the view of the female body causes concern to the man due to the lack of a phallus and a potential castration, thus creating the background of the punishment of sexuality.[48] Sexual punishments are found in *Halloween* and *A Nightmare on Elm Street* (1984), films closely related to the subgenre and the classical cycle. Of course, although sexual behavior and identity is the main part of the Normality of classical films, it does not include only this, but also other divergent behaviors such as extensive drug use, alcohol consumption, and violation of social laws.

Every society represented in the narratives of this particular subgenre is governed by specific rules, which constitute the Normality. The proper functioning of Normality, based on the obedience of its members to the rules, creates a level of smooth functioning of society itself. Based on the rules, viewers distinguish the people who make up the majority of the social fabric and form Normality. Based on this term of Normality, we can identify the sociopolitical situation in which a society is situated, and thus look in depth at the limits set by its rules. To further clarify the term, an example from the subgenre's classical cycle will be used. In the classical films, Normality is closely related to the society of the adults, who are the exact opposite of teenage characters. Adults do not drink alcohol, do not deviate regarding their sexual behaviors, and do not help the youth community that is under attack. The main purpose of Normality is to maintain its intactness and eliminate people and/or ideas that do not obey and do not serve the rules set out in the community code.

Part of Normality, which is often mistakenly considered to be a separate element of the narrative, is also the place where the events occur, the location in which the actions of narration are progressing.[49] The location is an important part of the whole genre of horror and aims to create a feeling of fear for viewers. Medieval castles, remote residences and sites close to nature are now interlinked with the horror genre, which is closely linked to its Gothic roots. Naturally, slasher films rarely "honor" these Gothic influences, as the action is placed in familiar landscapes for an average citizen of a western civilization. An important film of the whole horror genre regarding moving the location from a Gothic style to something most familiar to the viewer is *Psycho*, a pre-slasher film. *Psycho* brought terror from paranormal and gothic locations to the city, with the mother's home displaying a Gothic style to better portray the realism of buildings in northern California, as there were plenty of similar homes there.[50] As Douglas Gomery says, *Psycho* made the usual world of Fairvale, in California, where the film takes place, the center of horror.[51] In this way, the audience felt greater fear because the story was closer to the realm of the average viewer of that period.[52] Viewers were not accustomed to such locations, and this increased the fear created by the film.

The slasher film subgenre remained loyal to the bases set by *Psycho* and very rarely uses as a location a gothic environment, unlike other horror subgenres such as vampire films. In general, the location in which the narrative of a slasher film evolves is characterized by isolation. This is whether we are talking about a home or even a city. Characters must be unprotected and cut off from the rest of the western culture. On the one hand, we have a location that has references to western culture, but on the other hand, it is cut off from its whole. By creating a familiar environment for every viewer of the western culture through its Normality and impregnating it with the element of isolation, the levels of fear and identification with the characters grow. It could be argued that this approach of the subgenre's location is based on the concept of Sigmund Freud's uncanny, explaining that the things that we will perceive as the most terrifying are so because we were once familiar with them.[53] With this term, he spoke of the simultaneous feeling of intimacy and threat manifested through the same person, object or event.[54] This is precisely what happens with the location where the action of slasher films evolves, since the fact that it is familiar to the viewer also creates a greater threat, resulting from the very feeling of intimacy. Thus, the location functions as a supplement to this semantic element, becoming part of Normality and giving it an intimacy that intensifies the feeling of fear and threat to the viewers.

Returning now to Normality, we understand that it significantly influences the other semantic elements of the particular filmic texts through its placement and interrelationships in the narrative. This relationship with the other semantic elements is an essential part of the syntax, as we will see below. Normality is one of the most important elements of the narratives of slasher films. On the one hand, we have Normality along with its code, and on the other, we have the fictional characters that do not obey these norms and are divided into two major categories: the Others and the victims. Wood, speaking of horror films, used the term "Other" to identify who is not part of Normality, that is, either the "monster" of the textual text or the victims. However, for the present study, the Others (monsters) and the victims are two completely different groups and have nothing in common except that they conflict with the establishment created by Normality.

Others—The "Monsters" of Slasher Films

When we talk about horror films, the first thing that comes to mind is the monster. This particular genre is closely related to the monster, which disrupts the community and is often the important point of reference for the public, regarding the recognition and categorization of a horror film. A typical example is the usual misunderstanding with the *Frankenstein* (1931) film. The majority of viewers have linked the name Frankenstein to the monster, although that name belongs to the scientist who created it.

The monster is usually a defining element of horror films, and there are several categorizations of the particular filmic texts according to the monster. One of these categorizations is by Charles Derry, who spoke about three major categories of horror films based on the monster: the Horror of Personality, the Horror of Armageddon and the Horror of the Demonic.[55] In the Horror of Personality, the Other is represented as a human being, the Horror of Armageddon deals with aspects of nature that are taking abnormal features, while the Horror of the Demonic represents the Other as a metaphysical being with demonic elements. Until the 1960s, the genre was largely loyal to its gothic roots, with the Other being influenced by the literary and cinematic archetypes of Frankenstein, Werewolf, and Dracula. In 1960 with *Psycho*, the plot began to be transferred to an urban location, and the monster was transformed into a human, with the extreme example of the shy boy next door.[56]

The monster can take various forms—metaphysical (vampire, werewolf, etc.), human (insane scientists, murderer, etc.) or forms related to nature (animals, extreme weather, etc.). Of course, in our everyday life, the term "monster" usually has a metaphysical and/or paranormal complexion and does not include the above-mentioned forms. Hence, to avoid confusion, only the term "Other" will be used in the present text, which is an umbrella-term that can cover all aspects of evil. But what do we mean when we refer to someone as Other?

A simplified interpretation of the term Other in relation to its human form comes from Kevin Thomas, who states that different groups of people can be classified as Others, since they are undoubtedly excluded from something or someone else.[57] Of course, this approach can be generalized and applied to our case too, where the Other does not necessarily have a human form. The terminology and the use of the word "Other" (with a capital first letter) was not accidental, as this term was formulated by important scholars, scientists and philosophers, including Georg Wilhelm Friedrich Hegel, Johann Gottlieb Fichte,[58] Jean-Paul Sartre,[59] Simone de Beauvoir,[60] Emmanuel Levinas,[61] Julia Kristeva,[62] and Jacques Lacan.[63] Of course, the choice of specific theoretical tools in this research through this great plurality of views on this term is made with the aim of analyzing and emphasizing the characteristics of this semantic element in the best way. Thus, the theories of Other in the present text are the ones best applied to the type of horror, but more specifically, to the subgenre under analysis.

Kristeva speaks about the abject, a terminology that refers to the human reaction to an imminent collapse in the light of the loss of distinction between subject and object, or between the self and the Other.[64] Wood, by using psychoanalytic theories, has the same point of view, and by defining society and its forms of oppression in the collective unconscious, a crucial question arises: what about those who do not keep up with the social constraints? Wood talks about the concept of the Other, which puts at risk the Normality of western society.[65] The Other, who can take various forms—from class and national to political and ideological—does not keep up with the rules of the bourgeoisie, so society either tries to reject him or make him conform to its own terms.

Lacan was a pioneer in the academic debate about the terminology of the Other, creating one of the most well-known and complex terms of his work. He made a distinction between the "little other," symbolizing him with a (from the French term autre), and the "big Other," symbolizing him with A (from the French term Autre).[66] The little other is the other who is not really other, but a reflection and projection of the Ego and is thus entirely inscribed in the imaginary order. On the other hand, "the big 'Other' designates radical alterity, an otherness which transcends the illusory otherness of the imaginary because it cannot be assimilated through identification."[67] In simple terms, Lacan spoke of two categories of Other, where in the first one there is a view of the self, while in the second the diversity prevails.

Starting from Lacan's big Other, Slavoj Žižek speaks of an Other who operates on a symbolic level and is the unwritten constitution of the society, a force that is present, conducting and controlling the actions of community members.[68] Žižek's approach to Lacan's theory of the Other speaks about an intangible entity that sets the operating conditions and rules of each society. As Žižek himself says, "when I violate a certain rule of decency, I never simply do something that the majority of others do not do—I do what "one" doesn't do,"[69] meaning that there are actions according to what this Other would do, or otherwise, this personification of the rules of society.

Of course, in this semantic element there is a contradictory condition: on the one hand the Other disturbs Normality, but at the same time tries to impose its code. Returning to Kristeva's view of the loss of distinction between the self and the Other, and bearing in mind Lacan's little "other" theory, which speaks of a view of the Ego itself, we see that the Other of the slasher films is a projection of a collective "Ego" of the society itself, under the veil of a different and contrasting form to the society, and through acts that mark the abject described by Kristeva. As Cary Morrison says, "[the monsters] reflect the deepest fears of a culture, mirroring those issues that confront us on primal levels."[70] The Other is in opposition to society, while reflecting and trying to maintain its code. Although the first reading of the Other refers to a frontal conflict with Normality, at second reading we see that Normality controls the Other and there is an indirect view within it in order to keep its code intact.

The form of the Other in the subgenre begins from the classical cycle as a standard element reproduced from one filmic text to another: a male killer, almost always white, who is most of the time asexual and/or has an aversion to sexual desire. It has been stigmatized by a traumatic event in the past and has become a "monster." In the narrative present, he chases and kills teenage characters who do not follow the code of the period. There are not enough classical texts that managed to escape from this convention. It is worth mentioning that out of the 38 films of the classical cycle, 34 obey the rule of a male killer and only four are differentiated; in two films there is a woman murderer, in one there is no one because the murders were a hoax and in the last one there is more than one Other. The best-known example of differentiation comes from the well-known franchise of the subgenre, *Friday the 13th*. In the first film in 1980, the killer was not the famous Jason that was established later on in the series, but his mother, Mrs. Voorhees (Betsy Palmer). Jason appears from the second film of the franchise. Hence, the killer of the first film is a woman, something very unusual for the classical cycle. Other film examples of the subgenre having a female as an Other are *Scream 2* (1997) and *Scream 4* (2011).

The standardization of the convention of the Other in the classical cycle is closely related to the standardization of the entire subgenre's formula. Since the birth of slasher films up to the 1980s, these films have been structured around the punishment of sexual and other deviant behaviors. As mentioned, sexual punishment is the biggest rule in the Normality of classical films. The white man, being at the top of the social pyramid, is the most obvious choice for the position of the "punisher." Incorporating the social hierarchy of western culture, the white man fills the position that the narrative seeks to punish people who do not obey the rules of the community, with Christopher Sharrett saying that these films are putting the Other to guard the sexuality of the young characters.[71] Of course, the Other is not part of Normality or its representative, but the active part of the enforcing code through the indirect projection of a collective ego in the process of abject acts that is the result of the distinction between the self and the Other.

When the classical cycle of the subgenre reached a dead end in the early 1990s and began the self-referential cycle, the audience saw a small shift in the representation of the Other and the way it is placed in the narrative. Since the reasons for the punishment of the victims and the sexual punishment in general have changed, the Other is moving away from the classical formula described above and new boundaries are set in the subgenre's conventions. Of the 12 films of the self-referential cycle—a cycle that is considered to be transitional—seven follow the rule of the male killer, while five differentiate—four of them increase the number of the Others per narrative, while one has a woman Other. In order to better understand this change of the Other in self-referential slasher films, we will see as an example one of the most famous films of the cycle, *Scream* (1996).

The main difference with the classical filmic texts is that *Scream* has two Others, which would be considered quite odd in an older slasher film. The main killer is Billy (Skeet Ulrich) and the secondary is Stuart (Matthew Lillard). The two Others do not kill those who deviate according to their sexual behavior, but follow a self-referential pattern of victim choice, killing according to a design based on conventions of classical slasher films, which marks the transformation of the previously known Normality and the evolution in the light of self-referentiality. Although there are some important deviations from the classical representation of the Other, neither *Scream* escapes the stereotype of the white male. The self-referential cycle takes a step forward and departs from classical conventions, but fails to cut them completely off. The neoslashers, the third cycle of the subgenre, manage to differentiate completely and create new conventions and conditions that will dominate the majority of the filmic texts.

The neoslashers of the early 2000s have narratives that are far away from any standard norm of the past, including the representation of the Other. With the help of the 1990s transitional cycle, neoslashers further break the strict rule of how to represent the Other. It is worth mentioning that, out of the 24 films of the cycle, half are completely different from the classical cycle, having paranormal, metaphysical, and/or mutant Others, and also more than one per narrative. Of the remaining 12 who follow the pattern of one male Other as a killer, 11 are sequels and/or remakes of classical films, which made them commit to the form of the Other. And in these cases, however, the Other, although rooted in the classical conventions, is represented through the prism of the neoslasher cycle. Well-known examples that break the classical representation of the Other are *The Cabin in the Woods* (2012), in which the Other is a mysterious company operating on the model of the capitalist system, the *Final Destination* franchise (2000, 2003, 2006, 2009 and 2011), where the Other is Death himself, *Freddy vs. Jason* (2003), where famous Others of the subgenre meet, *Jeepers Creepers* (2001), where the Other has monstrous characteristics in his appearance, and *Scream 4*, where the Other of the narrative is a woman and has all the characteristics of the Final Girl that Clover described. As we can see from a first look at this data, in neoslashers there is no standardized and stereotypical reproduction of norms as it existed at the beginning of the subgenre.

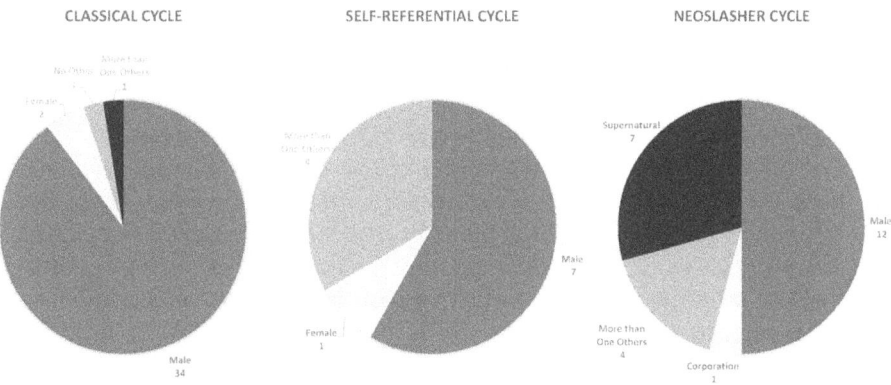

The representation of the Other per cycle

Within the Other, some other elements that several scholars have analyzed as autonomous semantic elements of the narrative can be incorporated. An example is the POV shots of the killer. Some scholars, among them Adam Rockoff,[72] speak of one more element of the slasher narratives, that of the POV shot through which we see from the perspective of the Other. But if one analyzes this element in depth, we will see that it is part of the representation and position of the Other in the narrative. This is in line with the views of Christian Metz and Jean-Louis Baudry, who dealt with identification of the viewer in cinema, a process that is divided into primary and secondary.[73] The viewer in the cinema sees pictures that have been shot in his absence, so the primary identification comes with the cinematographic camera. The secondary identification is happening with the characters of the film. So, there is a parallelism of Lacan's mirror stage[74] with secondary identification, where the viewer is in a stillness in the dark, as if in a dream state, and they see on the screen characters with whom they identify, like the infant in front of the mirror. In slasher films, there is an alignment of the mechanisms of primary and secondary identification, with the ultimate goal of the total identification of the audience with the Other as he acts as a familiar part of our own self.

The Others are an important part of the subgenre and several film franchises have been connected to the minds of viewers in the forms of their Others. Normality is disrupted by them, and they usually end up losing and/or dead, even though their actions are actually trying to enforce the code of Normality. On the one hand, there are the Others and on the other, there are the Final Survivors who, in the way they are represented, are considered to be the main protagonists of these particular filmic texts.

The Final Survivors—The Main Characters of the Film and the Way They Survive

After the Other comes his other half in every narrative, the Final Survivor. According to Patrick Jemmer, the general process of perceiving the Other is concretized through the creation of binary distinctions such as identity/difference, us/them, subject/object, in/out, certain/uncertain, true/false, male/female, Self/Other.[75] In the slasher film subgenre, the dominant binary distinction is that of the Final Survivor and the Other (as a personalized entity). Between the Other and the Final Survivor there is a two-way relationship, which is part of the Normality and the syntax and affects the characteristics and the identity of both. If we differentiate one semantic element, then the other's dynamics are differentiated, thus eroding its true position in the narrative. The narrative position of the Other in every particular filmic text becomes of significance only when it is perceived through its binary relationship with the position of the Final Survivor and vice versa. If the narrative fails one of the two elements, then it breaks the binary relationship and the power of the other element is also fails.

In a classical slasher film, two are the most important characters of the narration: the one who kills and the one who survives. As has been said, Clover analyzed the second category and named the character that survives "Final Girl." Due to the obsession of the classical cycle with sexual and gender representations, the character has almost always been a woman, with James Marriott states that gender expression tends to be at the heart of the relationship between slasher films and the Final Girl, something that underlines the killer's pathology.[76] Of the 38 films in the classical cycle, 31 have a purely Final Girl with all the features described by Clover and only three have a Final Boy or a Final Man. Finally, one film has two Final Girls, one ends up as a prank without victims and survivors, while in the last film the Final Girl dies in the end.

The Final Girl's convention in the wider context of the semantic element of the Final Survivor is differentiated and changes form when the self-referential cycle comes. As we have seen, until the early 1990s, the majority of survivors were one per narrative and almost always a female, something that began to change in the self-referential cycle. Out of the 12 films of this particular transitional cycle, none of them retains the Final Girl at its pure form, observing a generalized increase of the number of Final Survivors per film and/or the appearance of Final Women. Of course, even the Final Girls that exist in the self-referential cycle differ from the classical filmic texts, taking steps away from the virginal archetype.

One of the self-referential films that retain the form of the Final Girl is *Scream*. Even though we have a young girl again, she is not the only one who survives but has two main characters with her. The Final Girl is Sidney (Neve Campbell) and the other two characters are Gale Weathers (Courteney Cox) and Randy (Jamie Kennedy). The characteristics of the Final Girl set by Clover are separated into these three characters and no one has it all of them. Sidney is intelligent and energetic, Gale has masculine features in her behavior, something that is quite influenced by her profession (journalist), and Randy, the only male character that survives, has virginal characteristics.[77] Thus, we can see that Clover's theory presents some drawbacks in the analysis of filmic texts when the subgenre starts to disobey to the conventions of the classical cycle. Of course, the change in the representation of Final Survivors is even more important and radical when the transitional cycle of the 1990s ends and the subgenre enters its third cycle.

The creation of the neoslashers almost happened concurrently with the events of 9/11. These events, according to Kevin J. Wetmore, reshaped gender politics by empowering women, while it also allowing gender to be ignored as a concern.[78] Thus, in neoslashers there is no rule about the sexual or gender identity of who will survive. In fact, out of 24 films, only seven have Final

Girl as the only Survivor (five of which are remakes or sequels of classical films), one has a Final Woman, and 10 have multiple Final Survivors of different genders. Finally, there is a new trend of five films where Final Survivors eventually die. Hence, Final Survivors in neoslashers can be a pair of characters, men, women, and in some extreme cases, no survivors at all. For example, in the films *A Nightmare on Elm Street* (2010) and *The Cabin in the Woods* we have a couple that survives, there is a Final Boy in *Final Destination* (2000) and in *Halloween II* (2009) we have no survivors as all of the main characters die. Due to this heterogeneity within the three cycles, this semantic element is called "Final Survivors," an umbrella-term that covers all the subgenre's cycles and all the characters that stay alive in their narratives. Of course, the term is used only for main characters that significantly affect the narrative and does not cover minor roles.

Apart from the gender of the Final Survivors and their number per narrative, there is also a significant change in their age. In the filmic texts of the classical cycle the Final Survivors are mostly teenage characters. The only adults of the classical films are passive in the progression of the narrative and constitute a small part of it. The Final Survivor of the classical cycle is a teenage girl who, by the end of the film, she is has been turned into an adult. As David Greven says: "the heroine of the slasher film undergoes a similarly rapid transformation, from adolescence to adulthood, through mayhem and death generally but specifically through a particularly and peculiarly gendered schema."[79] Over time, there is a change in this area, and it is no longer surprising if there is no teenage character in a slasher film. In particular, only four films in the third cycle are about teen activities and/or groups, while the remaining 20 films have removed this convention.

The Final Survivors along with the Others are a dynamic duo of the sub-

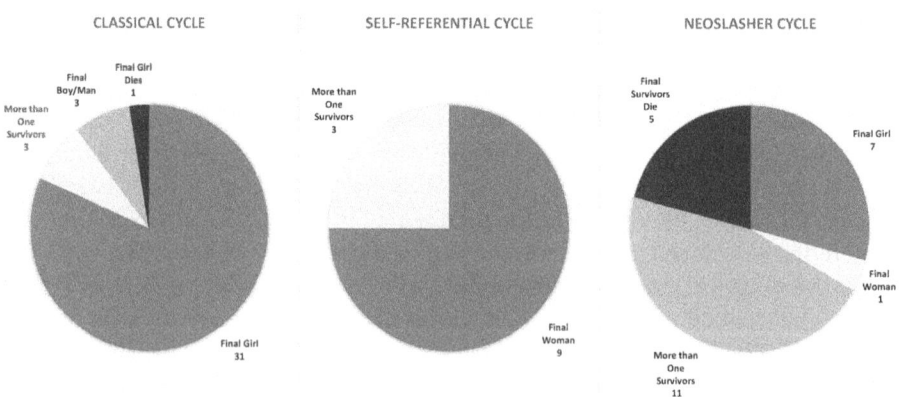

The representation of final Survivors per cycle

genre's narratives. When there is a change in one of the two, this automatically implies the influence of the second pole. Both of these elements have changed over the years and have actively participated in the differentiation of the subgenre into cycles. Final Survivors are an important element in the narratives of these films, because they affect and are significantly influenced by the Normality to which each film obeys. On the one hand, we have the characters that follow the rules of society depicted in the filmic text, and on the other hand, those who go against and are being punished for it.

The Victims—The Punishment of Breaking the Rules

Before proceeding with the analysis of the subgenre under study, we must examine the semantic element of victims in the light of the whole genre of horror, based on Wood's theory of Normality. We have a society (each horror subgenre identifies it according to its own conventions), which is disturbed by an external factor, the Other. These two elements are the essence of the genre and are characteristics of each of the individual filmic texts. An element that is found in all horror films, but usually without being recognized by the viewer, is the victims.

Victims form an important part of the Normality and at the same time deviates from its rules. Each narration of horror films imposes the punishment and violent treatment of a particular group of people, in order to increase the prerequisite feelings appropriate to the viewing of these films. Simply put, in order to scare the viewers, something that is the point of this kind of storytelling, there must be characters that the audience will be identify with until they end up dead or seriously injured. Regardless of subgenres and film cycles, this is a pattern that is an essential part of almost every horror film. Of course, because the existence of the victims is so self-evident in these films, it is often not given the appropriate attention.

The semantic element of victims has been around since the birth of the slasher film subgenre and has been analyzed in both academic studies of Clover and Dika. Victims are closely linked to the three above-mentioned semantic elements. The code that dominates the represented society and forms the Normality sets some rules to which its members must adhere. The Other is the one who will apply the punishment to those who do not obey. Through the narrative comes the reward for the members of the society that obeyed, and thus the element of Final Survivors is created, but there are always members that do not come into complete harmony with Normality. These members are the victims, which, as is logical from the above analysis in relation to the other elements, are the exact opposite of the Final Survivors. Victims are among the first characters that the public is urged to identify with, and although there is no time to develop, it is usually achieved through the common cultural identity with the viewers (a western, middle-class society).

In order to make the victim's position in the narratives of slasher films clearer, there will be once again a use of the classical cycle as an example. The Normality of the majority of classical films has been heavily influenced by the fear of sexual behaviors, which stems from the "family values" promoted by the conservative presidency of Ronald Reagan and prevailed in the American society of this period.[80] Most classical slashers are impregnated with this ideology on which the most crucial conventions are based.

Hence, the criterion by which the Other acts is the sexual behavior of members of society. The Final Girl with the virginal characteristics is being awarded be staying alive, while her friends which are also teenage characters, got punished. The specific members of the community make up the element of the victims of the narratives of the classical cycle. Of course, in individual filmic texts, there may be a number of victims who do not obey this general rule of the cycle, but these are taken into account on a case-by-case basis and by analyzing the particular film.

So, the victims of the classical cycle are made up of people whose expression of sexuality is in conflict with Normality. Of course, although the main characteristic of these victims is the expression of sexuality, there are other elements that make them deviate from Normality. Examples are the use of alcohol and/or drugs and the violation of laws. However, the general impression has prevailed that in classical films the characters are being punished only for their active sexuality, which is not entirely right, as this behavior is a part of the Normality of these particular films. This general principle of identifying victims was systematized through the standardization of the formula in slasher films until the late 1980s when the classical cycle came to an end.

The relationship between the victims and the rest of the narrative is very narrow and, as is logical, changing cycles drastically affects the specific characters of slasher films. Removing punishment of active sexuality means a change of Normality and thus a direct influence of the representation of the three basic groups of characters of a slasher film (Others, Final Survivors, and victims). The self-referential cycle, being transitional, has been a catalyst in this differentiation, but, as mentioned above, the subgenre changed drastically in neoslasher cycle.

The neoslashers adopt a critical look and stop to represent the fear of sexuality of the 1980s. The basis of the neoslashers' conventions that will be analyzed below is that they built their narratives under a cause/effect structure. There is now a tendency for generalized narrative justification of the reason the victims are selected and there is no arbitrary connection of the Other with them. It is often justified by interpersonal relationships with the Other, which, based on the above-mentioned approach based on Altman's theory, is a change to the syntax of subgenre's narratives. In simple words, a new connection between two semantic elements is created in order to further

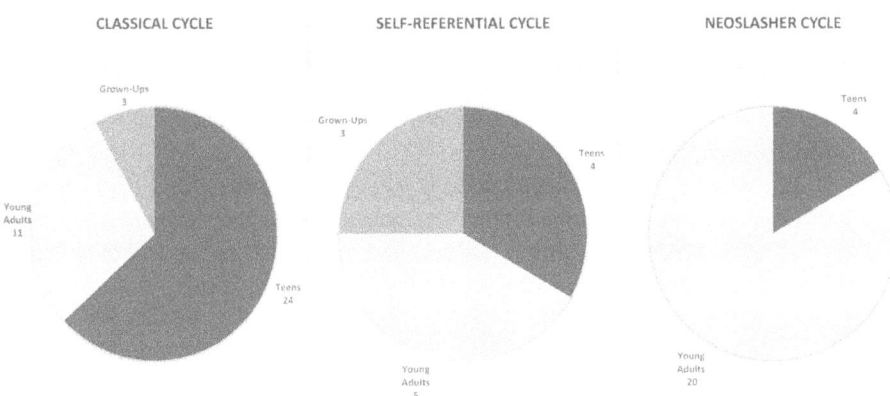

Victim representation per cycle

justify and structure the narrative. Finally, even the age of these characters has begun to change. While in the classical cycle, the majority of the films are about a teenage group, the self-referential cycle began to change this by offering other alternatives, such as young or older adults, while neoslashers consolidate their narratives around young adults, with only four films being about teen characters.

Although the two representative features through which the horror films are recognized are the Other and the Final Survivors, the victims are an integral part of its narratives and exist in every film of the whole genre.

The four above-mentioned categories (Normality, Other, Final Survivors, Victims) are the most important semantic elements of slasher films. Of course, we are talking about elements that are wide terms and, as we have seen in their analysis, there are other sub-elements in them. The four semantic elements in the slasher film subgenre can be found in all three cycles, but the relationships between each other and their expression in the narrative differ according to the cycle to which the film belongs. The discovery of these elements was mainly based on their application to the entire subgenre and with the aim of making this theory an important tool in the analysis of all slasher films.

THE SYNTAX OF THE SUBGENRE

After the emergence of the basic semantic elements under wide definitions, the systematic study of the syntax of these narratives follows. The semantic elements themselves cannot be the main source of a subgenre's analysis, but their basic functional interactions and placements in the narrative must be identified, as the evolution of the subgenre is located in the way they are placed in the narrative. Thus, based on the evidence derived from the films of the corpus, the syntax of the subgenre is divided into three major categories: The backstory of the Other, the connection of the Other with the Final Survivors, and the relationship of Normality with the rest of the three semantic elements separately.

In almost all slasher films, there is a reason why the Other does these murderous moves. This may range from something simple (the victims and the Final Survivors disturbing his by invading his "personal" space) to something more complex that involves interpersonal and/or family relationships with the other characters. This reason for the acts of the Other takes the form of a backstory in the narrative syntax. In all three cycles of the subgenre, the backstory of the Other exists in order to justify and reinforce the emotion of fear that the narrative itself attempts to create in viewers. Dika herself, in her structuralist analysis, gave a great attention to the backstory of the Other by dedicating the entire group of actions of the Past Event to it. Of course, Dika talked about the linear, narrative continuity of these actions in the filmic text, while the backstory of the Other under the narrative's syntax takes a different form.

Regarding the backstory, it is not necessarily implied that the Other's past should be represented on the screen, but it is more a set of actions that made the Other what he is in the narrative present. These actions can be represented, given as information or even implied. Examples of the backstory can be found in filmic texts of all subgenre's cycles. For example, in *Halloween*, Michael's backstory is established at the beginning of the film, at which a younger Michael kills his sister, and in *Friday the 13th* the backstory of Mrs. Voorhees is revealed at the end where the audience is informed about the drowning of her son, Jason. Of course, although the audience is informed at specific points in the film about these actions that have led the Other to murder, all the narrative is structured around them, and thus the syntax of the entire text is affected. The form of the backstory of the Other documents the reason for killing and thus affects both the Normality that he will serve and the type of victims he will chase. Hence, we see that this category of the syntax influences the interaction of the Other with Normality and the victims.

The second category of subgenre's syntax refers to the relationship of the Other with the Final Survivor(s). As discussed above, Clover systematically analyzed the connection of the Other with the Final Survivor, but it was confined to aspects of gender and sexuality. Although gender identity was at the core of the subgenre in the classical cycle, the following decades have moved away from this convention and brought other links to the forefront. Nevertheless, the relationship between the Other and the Final Survivor has remained at the heart of the slasher film syntax, leaving intact the significance of the binary created by these semantic elements.

The connection of the Other with the Final Survivor can take various forms. Their relationship may range from being totally unknown to being connected by the events and the backstory of the Other (*The Texas Chain Saw Massacre* [1974], *Friday the 13th* [1980] and *A Nightmare on Elm Street* [1984]), or they have a family connection (*Halloween* [2007] and *Texas Chainsaw 3D* [2013]) or even a sexual relationship (*Scream and Valentine* [2001]). This syntactic connection of the two semantic elements is very important for the narrative, as the whole story of every filmic text is based on this quirky quest for assassination-survival. As we will see later on separating the subgenre into cycles, this binary had several changes with the narrative syntax being shaped according to the characteristics of each cycle.

The last category of the syntax of slasher films is the relationship between Normality and the other three semantics separately. Although Normality is an element determined on the basis of a sociopolitical context, the elements of Others, Final Survivors, and Victims are personified within the narrative. Thus, the characters embodying them are directly affected by Normality. Each Normality is governed by a code upon which its foundations are based. This code contributes to the expression, positioning and interaction of the characters that express the other three semantic elements.

The classical Normality of the 1970s and 1980s has been constructed as conservative, sexually puritanical and vengeful to its infringers due to this code. Hence, the expression of the Other (who will hunt and why), the victims (why they are murdered) and the Final Survivors (which rules they obey and who survives) are directly affected. More specifically, in the example of the classical cycle, the Others chase those who violate the norms of conservative Normality, the victims are those who violate the rules through their sexual and social behavior, while the Final Survivors are the ones who obey the rules as a virginal behavior model.

Through these three categories, the syntax of the slasher film subgenre is structured. The semantic elements combined with the narrative syntax structure the identity of the subgenre. Although the semantic elements remain stable throughout the subgenre's lifetime, as we will see below, the syntax changes from time to time and leads to the creation of a new film cycle within the subgenre. Although the three general categories of the syntax analyzed above remain the same, new interconnections and expressions of the syntax are observed, prompting the subgenre to start a new film cycle. As Altman himself observes, the term "genre" is accepted in Hollywood more as a semantic, with the specific elements conferring stability and determination on the genre itself, while, with regard to the process of the creation of a genre, these semantic elements build different patterns of links until one becomes commonly accepted and the others are destroyed.[81] In simple terms, what is argued is that the semantic elements are stable and present throughout the life of the subgenre, but what changes from cycle to cycle is the expression and form of the three categories of the syntax of slasher films.

The Cycles of the Slasher Film Subgenre

By locating and analyzing the four semantic elements and mapping the syntax, the claim based on the film corpus of the subgenre on dividing the films into three cycles becomes even clearer. An important factor in subgenre's differentiation is the change of the syntactic structure of the filmic texts and the redefinition of the semantic elements within the narrative. Slasher films are a subgenre created with specific semantic elements, most of which are borrowed from the horror genre that they belong to. Within about four decades, slasher films have experimented and are experimenting with how their narratives relate and interact with these elements.

A film genre is not something that serves a purpose, but multiple things that serve multiple purposes for multiple groups.[82] By extension, the goals and the groups to which it is addressed may change over time. Thus, the first cycle of slasher films, impregnated by its conservatism, chose a way of linking narrative elements under the prism of punishing sexual and divergent behaviors in a context of social conservatism, promoting the notion of "family values." In the 1990s, the syntax of these films was dramatically influenced by of self-referential elements that existed in the pop culture of the period, thus creating the second cycle of the subgenre, which, as we will see below, adapts the narrative based on a whodunit structure and emphasizes the exposure of the mechanisms of the narrative itself. At the end of the self-referential cycle and the beginning of the new millennium, the syntax changed once again, signaling the beginning of a new cycle of the subgenre (neoslashers), where the widespread justification of violence by focusing the narrative to the Other come to the fore.

The semantic/syntactic approach of the slasher film subgenre helps to illuminate several aspects of the structure of the particular filmic texts and opens the way for a more organized and systematic study of them. Seeing Altman's theory with a more open mind and through the genres' approach that developed above, we realize that the differentiation of the narratives of the filmic texts from cycle to cycle is documented and it is easier to compare them.

Having analyzed the subgenre as a whole and having isolated the basic elements of slasher films and their narrations, the subgenre's cycles can now more easily be defined. In this way, it will be a better justification of the changes that have taken place. Hence, an overall and total analysis of the subgenre, based on theoretical and historical approaches, will be completed.

The Classical Cycle of Slasher Films—The Beginning of the Subgenre

After the first films of the subgenre and their great success, slasher films began to be produced systematically. The period from the early to the mid–1980s is important for the subgenre because its formula has been created and systematized. Several well-known franchises were created, with *Friday the 13th* and *A Nightmare on Elm Street* to be some of the most famous. By the end of the 1980s, the slasher film subgenre was recognizable throughout the North American film industry, the media, and the audience itself, as everyone talked about the new conventions that made it stand out.[83] The Normality of the classical cycle is middle class and conservative, with adolescent characters having divergent behaviors and the Other being used as a means of compliance and enforcement of social norms, ultimately to be punished himself. The only character of the classical cycle that is considered a "winner," because she follows literally the moral and social rules without contradicting the Normality, is the Final Girl.

The three general categories of the syntax were formulated in such a way as to strengthen this conservative form that began to take the subgenre during its first years of life. More specifically, the backstory of the Other in classical films has two main features: firstly, it has an event that usually involves sexually active or socially deviant behavior (for example, Michael's sister in *Halloween* has sex shortly before being killed; *Friday the 13th*'s Jason was drowned because of the reckless campers who had sex without paying attention to the helpless child) and secondly, the connection with the current events is narratively loose (the current victims are rarely directly related to the event of prehistory). Thus, there is a connection of cause and effect under the veil of conservative structures, such as the relationship created between sex and death.

Coming to the second category of the syntax, the Other with the Final Survivor are linked through their sexual identities. As we have seen, Clover has found out quite common elements among them, even if the narrative wants to show them as two completely opposite characters. Finally, the relationship between Normality and the other three semantic elements is structured in such a way as to establish a code that serves a conservative Normality that does not allow the free expression of sexual and other behaviors.

As is generally the case in cinema, the Normality of the subgenre is based on the society in which the film was produced. The classical cycle begins in the mid–1970s and blooms in the 1980s. So, in order to better understand the community of the narratives of these films, we must first look at the implications of the sociopolitical conditions in which the subgenre was born and developed. The 1980s are a conformist period for the United States. In 1980, Ronald Reagan was elected president of the U.S., and the country went into a more conservative sociopolitical period. Reagan served as president from 1981 to 1989, when many classical slasher films were produced. William J. Palmer writes that the social history of the decade is a sequel, the "Fifties II."[84] Both decades, 1950s and 1980s, politically supported style over essence regarding crucial social problems. The main problems of the American social history were explored and spread to a mass audience through films.[85]

Reagan allied with conservative religious groups, such as Moral Majority, a forerunner of the Christian Coalition.[86] The central idea behind the political beliefs of these groups and of Reagan himself was family values, which according to Harry Benshoff and Sean Griffin was basically an anti-feminist, anti-Gay program to keep white, heterosexual men in power within the nuclear family and at the top of the socio-cultural hierarchy.[87] One of Reagan's most famous political acts was the budget cut in social programs and the number of members of the government. These conservative ideas and actions characterized the majority of American society's political backdrop of the 1980s, in which the slasher subgenre was in its classical cycle.

However, we must also take into account another social factor. In 1981, the New York Times published an article on a new, recently recognized disease, AIDS (acquired immune deficiency syndrome), which was then referred to as GRID (gay-related immunodeficiency).[88] AIDS is a sexually transmitted disease, and one of the immediate effects of the outbreak of the epidemic has been the rise of concern regarding sexuality.[89] Many politicians with right-wing beliefs and religious leaders used AIDS as a "proof" of God's revenge on homosexuals.[90]

The interaction between Reagan's conservative ideas and the AIDS epidemic was one of the main influences of the punishment of sexual acts in classical slasher films of that time. The narratives of these particular films refer to teenage characters who have unprotected sex. In the 1980s, AIDS usually led directly to death, which was adapted and became a subgenre's convention. The Normality of these particular films is based on America's middle-class community, and the image of the Other is influenced by its main sociopolitical concerns. At that time, society was trying to link AIDS to homosexuality. Clover argued that although the killer of the classical cycle is male, he usually has homosexual or transgender characteristics. Thus, the image of the Other of the classical cycle is not only based on the fear of AIDS but also on the form and sexual identity in which the society of that time was trying to throw its responsibilities. If we look at the narratives of classical films of the subgenre, we will come up with a generalized description in which a homosexual or asexual figure kills sexually active, heterosexual teenagers because they do not obey the rules of conservative society. Sexual intercourse between homosexuals had been linked with death, not just of themselves, but also of heterosexuals through a possible sexual intercourse with a carrier. Hence, homosexual, asexual and/or transgender killers became a widely used stereotype, which the viewers perceive as a narrative cliché.[91]

The classical cycle of the subgenre lasted until the early 1990s. The subgenre, through the stabilization of its formula and its classical conventions, became so predictable that it led to a period of decline. Although at the end of the 1980s we see an explosion in the production of the slasher films who managed to get into the top 100 box office (in 1988 five films and in 1989 four films), the first years of the 1990s are distinguished by a great fall, each year having only one movie, with the exception of 1991 when there were two. At the beginning of the 1990s, the only slashers that were produced were sequels of famous franchises and various new films made through videotapes, unable to find national distribution.[92] There was an immediate need to renew the subgenre and redefine its formula. Under these conditions, the subgenre entered its second cycle.

The Self-Referential Cycle of the Subgenre—Slasher Films in the 1990s

The films of the classical cycle started to decline due to the high degree of predictability and the need for renewal began to come to the fore. Film genres operate in such a way that they are adapted to survive on the film market. Altman mentions that during some periods genres can operate under prescribed forms, while at other times in their history they are redefined and reshaped into unrecognizable new forms.[93] The answer to the predictability problem of slasher films was the element of self-referentiality through parody, which began to exist in the subgenre in the early 1990s.

Slasher films, as well as the whole horror genre, belong to the pop culture of the American society, which in its entirety was self-referential at the time. Self-referentiality refers to the process in which films bring to the forefront their production process, the creator itself, the processes that govern them as texts, intertextuality, or their perception by the public.[94] The main element that became part of the subgenre and expressed its self-referentiality was the one of pastiche and/or parody.

Frederic Jameson, speaking of the first, states that "pastiche is, like parody, the imitation of a peculiar or unique, idiosyncratic style ... the imitation of dead styles, speech through all the masks and voices stored up in the imaginary museum of a now global culture."[95] An example of a pastiche of the pop culture of the 1990s, whose aesthetics influenced the slasher subgenre, is the MTV music channel, which became known for quickly cycling through unrelated images belonging to different styles.[96]

Of course, Linda Hutcheon's approach better suits the slasher film subgenre. Hutcheon is not talking about an empty parody like Jameson, but about a parody that incorporates and simultaneously provokes its mockery elements, usually through caustic and/or ironic approaches.[97] In simple terms, there is a dialogue between the old and the new, and through the parody something brand new is produced. It is a critical view of the old through a new prism. Self-referential slashers parody the subgenre so that it is not a simple reproduction of the classical formula, but a review of it through criticism.

Having all that in mind, we must also take into account intertextuality. As Robert Stam mentions, the purpose is to combine references to the most varied sources in a funny game with the viewer, whose narcissism is not flattered through the old-fashioned indirect identification with the characters but through the demonstration of cultural capital, achieved by the recognition of references.[98] For intertextual references, Noel Carroll used the term allusion and said that

> [it] is an umbrella term covering a mixed lot of practices including quotations, the memorialization of past genres, the reworking of past genres, homages, and the recreation of "classic" scenes, shots, plot motifs, lines of dialogue, themes, gestures, and so forth from film history.[99]

Here, it should be noted that the two concepts of self-referentiality and intertextuality sometimes overlap, but do not cease to be different terms. There is a plethora of self-referential and/or intertextual references to the subgenre. A purely intertextual example is *Scream*'s murderer's mask as it deals with another form of art. The killer wears a mask based on Edvard Munch's *The Scream*. Of course, this narrative can also be seen as self-referential if viewed from another angle, since its choice to place a mask onto the killer's face can be seen as a peculiar game between the film and the entire subgenre, because all the famous slasher films, such as *Halloween* and *Friday the 13th*, have killers with masks.

Regarding the three syntactic categories in this particular film cycle, they were structured in such a way that the narration exposed the medium itself, but also the until-then established conventions. The backstory of the Other was redefined in relation to the classical cycle, and the 1990s created self-referential slashers with a narrative structure that developed around the whodunit conventions. This term refers to works that are structured around a possible answer to the question "Who did the crime?"[100] While in classical films we see the Other from the beginning and we know the motives under which he kills, in the self-referential cycle we see a new syntax in which the identity, motives and thus the backstory of the Other that leads him to murder are revealed towards the end of the film. Such examples of films include *Scream, I Know What You Did Last Summer* and *I Still Know What You Did Last Summer* (1998) and *Urban Legend* and *Urban Legends: Final Cut* (2000). The new form of storytelling around the whodunit conventions in combination with the relationship of Normality with the other three semantic elements brings to the fore self-referentiality and the notion of parody. Hence, the connection of the Other with the Final Survivor changes its form and often reaches the exact opposite side compared to the classical filmic texts, establishing an erotic relationship between them (e.g., *Scream* and *I Still Know What You Did Last Summer*).

Self-referentiality, intertextuality and parody dominated pop culture in the 1990s and inevitably affected slasher films. The subgenre started to play with the conventions of the classical cycle through intertextual and self-referential elements embedded in its narratives. They played with the predictability and incorporated into the narrative hyperconscious characters who knew the classical formula of the subgenre and were trying to change it. As Valerie Wee says:

> [These films] are, thus, the product of filmmakers who recognize that the over-wrought, intense nature of the horror genre can no longer be experienced "straight" by an American teen audience which has become overly familiar with and increasingly derisive of the genre's conventions. Consequently, these conventions are filtered through a much more cynical, knowing perspective, one that allows the audience to engage and "interact" with the equally hyperaware characters on screen.[101]

While *Scream* of 1996 is usually considered the beginning of the self-referential cycle, the credits belong to another film by the same director, Wes Craven: *New Nightmare* (1994). *New Nightmare* is the seventh film of the well-known franchise *A Nightmare on Elm Street*, and it came into theaters a decade after the birth of the franchise. In this film, we see almost all the actors, producers and crew that worked in the first film playing themselves. Freddy Krueger escapes from the world of the film and comes to the real world, in which he chases the people who worked in the first film. Heather Langenkamp, the actress who played the Final Survivor in the first film, is the one who again faces and kills the Other. *New Nightmare* not only plays with the subgenre's conventions creating a peculiar pastiche, but also has self-referential elements of the filmmaking as a process. A typical example of that is when Craven appears in the film and says the only way Freddy can be defeated is by making a new film and being "captured" in its narrative.

New Nightmare did not have a great financial and revenue success, as it had a budget of $14 million and earned only $19.7 million worldwide.[102] The first and most famous self-referential slasher film is *Scream*, which made $173 million worldwide, with a budget of $15 million. Economic success and popularity are the two main factors that have made *Scream* the start of self-referentiality rather than *New Nightmare*. *Scream*, of course, is the beginning of a tetralogy, which again reinforced the popularity of the subgenre.

The *Scream* films are pioneering and innovative. Together with *New Nightmare* they introduced new elements of self-referentiality and intertextuality to the narratives of the subgenre. An example of this is the television advertising of the first *Scream*, which appeared in the quote "Someone has taken their love of scary movies one step too far."[103] Sarah Trencansky reports that "Wes Craven's 1990s version of the slasher, reveals the ethos that would become the dominant slasher type for this decade."[104] The subgenre began to move away from the punishment of the sexual act and desire and move towards a more self-referential approach to the formula. Another two very popular self-referential slashers of this decade are *I Know What You Did Last Summer* (1997) and *Urban Legend* (1998).

Thus, self-referential slasher films soon became the mainstream of the subgenre from 1994 to 2000. Of the 12 films of the period, only two can not be described as purely self-referential—*Halloween: The Curse of Michael Myers* and *Candyman: Farewell to the Flesh*. It is worth noting that both films are from 1995, a year between the not-so-successful *New Nightmare* and the most profitable slasher of all time, *Scream*, which sparked the self-referential trend in the subgenre. The subgenre changed the structure of its formula in order to be less predictable to its audience. Of course, there are still powerful influences from the classical conventions, but they are under the veil of self-reference, intertextuality and parody.

The self-referential cycle worked as a transitional phase and lasted for a short period of time compared to the other two cycles of the subgenre. At the beginning of the new millennium, slasher films began to change once again and the neoslashers appeared. Of course, in the new millennium, there are still some self-referential examples that continue and readapt the main feature of the second cycle of the 1990s, with the most important example being *The Cabin in the Woods*. Although transitional, the self-referential cycle is very important to the subgenre because it has helped these filmic texts to be driven in a new direction far from sexuality and punishment. Thus, the standardization of its conventions became a thing of the past for slasher films.

The Neoslasher Cycle—The Subgenre at the New Millennium

At the end of the 1990s, the slasher film subgenre was again in a decline, and critics reported that paranormal horror films, such as *The Blair Witch Project* (1999) and *The Sixth Sense* (1999) meant the end of the graphic violence of the slasher film.[105] It is worth mentioning that in 1999 no slasher film was able to get into the top-100 American box office. The self-referential cycle was a reaction to the standardization of the formula, but it was not strong enough to last for a long period of time. The new millennium, however, brought to light new conventions that once again differentiated the subgenre's syntax and the interplay of its semantic elements.

The slasher film subgenre, having been removed from the standardized and conservative conventions of the classical filmic texts with the help of the self-referential cycle, began to focus more on identifying the causes of the development of violence and terror rather than the graphic representation of unjustifiable violence. The backstory of the Other was structured in the narrative in a way that the Other came to the foreground as a main protagonist, and the narrative attempted to represent him as a three-dimensional character rather than a stereotypical one. While in the self-referential cycle there is a tendency to conceal the identity of the Other until just before the end of the film, the neoslashers treat the Others as the main representatives of their narratives by devoting to them a great amount of filmic time in order to justify their actions. This contradicts the classical cycle, in which, as we have seen above, there are conservative conventions in combination with loose narrative links between the past and the present. In the narrations of the films of the new millennium, the Other is at the forefront and the public is often forced to "go along" with him.

At this point, the concept of empathy might also be useful. This term, having its roots in ancient Greek language, can be translated as "participation in passion," that is, in simple words, our personal involvement in what someone else is suffering. Empathy is used by film theory to describe the emotional union of the viewer with the fictional characters. Albert Michotte was one of the first to deal extensively with the application of empathy in cinema, saying that it is when we observe someone else's actions and experience them in the same way, rather than understanding them at a mental level.[106] Empathy in the slasher film subgenre usually existed for Final Survivors through narrative development, or for victims through a common cultural identity with the viewers. In the third cycle of the subgenre the syntax creates the background to provide empathy with the Other and to justify the creation of evil within the narrative.

An example of this evolution comes from the *Halloween* franchise. In the first film of 1978, Michael (played as a child by Will Sandin, played by Tony Moran at age 23) kills without conscious reasons and incarnates the ultimate evil. In the 2007 *Halloween* neoslasher version, we see Michael (played by Daeg Faerch at age 10, played by Tyler Mane as an adult) as a child for almost half the film. We see his troubled family, his bad childhood and his problematic social environment. There is also a connection with the Final Survivor, Laurie (Scout Taylor-Compton), who is portrayed as his sister. So throughout the film, he chases her because of this relationship.

Through this example, we come to the second syntactic category of the subgenre, the connection between the Other and the Final Survivor. In this part of the syntax too there is a tendency to strengthen the causal relationship between the two characters, establishing interpersonal (e.g., *Prom Night*), family (e.g., *Scream 4*) or even love relationships (e.g., *Valentine*) between these characters. Of course, there are also some neoslashers that do not link the Other and the Final Survivor with some kind of relationship, but nevertheless the continuity of the narrative builds a cause/effect relationship established between them. Also, as there is a generalized tendency to increase the number of Final Survivors per filmic text, something that began from the self-referential cycle, there is often a breaking of the Other/Final Survivor binary that existed in classical filmic texts and a creation of new power relationships between the above characters. Finally, the third category of the syntax focuses too on an extensive justification of narrative connections, with Normality to be linked to more solid structures with the other three semantic elements. Of course, as in the analysis of the classical cycle, in order to better understand Normality and its interaction with the other elements, we have to take into account the sociopolitical conditions in which this film cycle was born.

In 2000, George W. Bush was elected president of the United States, and his presidency was quite similar to Reagan's in the 1980s. As Murphy Jarrett points out, "both bore strong ideological agendas of supply-side tax cuts and increased defense spending, and depicted the world in stark terms like 'the evil empire' and 'the axis of evil.'"[107] The U.S. once again entered a conservative period that, ideologically, was similar to the 1980s, while the concept of family values came back to the forefront. What struck Bush's presidency and forced society into hardcore conservative ideas was the War on Terror, which came as a direct result of the events of 9/11. On September 11, 2001, Islamist insurgents hijacked four commercial airliners and crashed them into the World Trade Center in New York and the Pentagon in Washington, D.C., killing almost 3,000 people.[108] These attacks have had a tremendous impact on American society and have played an important role in major changes in public security.

In the conservative 1980s, one of the main concerns of society was the AIDS epidemic. In the conservative 2000s, the main concern of public opinion was terrorism. At first glance, 9/11 and the AIDS epidemic have nothing in common. But if we analyze them in depth, both social concerns were catalysts for the rapid increase of conservatism and spread of fear and terror into the American society. By the time these events happened, nothing was the same, neither domestically nor globally. Both events can be perceived as a direct impact on Normality by way of an attack on the American society itself, which became united under a common opponent and targeted social and ethnic groups by placing them under the concept of the Other. Thus, although the two events are very different, if they are thoroughly analyzed, they are quite common both in the way they were dealt by society, but also in the way they have influenced it.

After 9/11, there was a crucial question about cinema, and more specifically, about horror films: how can the American audience see violent images having already experienced real terror? Kathy Smith points out that in the days that followed the attack, the audience was at the same time fascinated and terrified by the narrative that was developing, while the viewer had to realize that what he/she saw was not imagination but reality.[109] According to Žižek, for the overwhelming majority of the audience, the events of 9/11 were events on the television screen that reminded quite a lot of the set-up and aesthetic of Hollywood disaster films.[110] On the other hand, however, some critics saw horror films as the ideal means of representation of September 11 and everything that followed.[111] Several horror subgenres and film cycles dominated the post–9/11 landscape, such as marauding giant monsters, home-invasion films, torture porn films and a lot of remakes with a focus on xenophobia and revenge.[112] In this period of time, slasher films began to flourish again and the neoslashers came to the fore.

Seeing the film corpus under analysis, we realize that neoslashers are divided into two major categories: remakes and films based on an original screenplay. The first remake was *The Texas Chainsaw Massacre* (2003), which was followed by *When a Stranger Calls* (2006), *The Hills Have Eyes* (2006), *Halloween* (2007), *Prom Night* (2008), *My Bloody Valentine 3D* (2009), *Halloween II* (2009), *Friday the 13th* (2009) and *A Nightmare on Elm Street* (2010). Of course, the trend of remakes was widespread in several film genres, including the horror genre, with famous examples *The Wolfman* (2010) and *The Omen* (2006). Besides remakes, there are other films that belong to big classical franchises of the subgenre as sequels or prequels, such as *Freddy Vs. Jason* (2003) and *The Texas Chainsaw Massacre: The Beginning* (2006). Richard Hand and Jay McRoy point out that the horror genre has more sequels, prequels, and remakes from any other film genre.[113]

Kevin J. Wetmore reports that the remakes of the slasher films contain two elements: "a nostalgia for a time in which America was strong (or at least perceived as strong on defense and the promotion of sexual morality), and the fear and nihilism of the post–9/11 horror film, resulting in an uneasy balance."[114] The 2000s have several similarities to the 1980s in terms of political governance. The subgenre expressed this through the extensive remakes of the films of the 1980s. However, this nostalgia was affected by the post–9/11 fear. Marcus Nispel, the director of the remakes of *The Texas Chainsaw Massacre* and *Friday the 13th*, described slashers as modern folk tales meant to be told and told again, adding detail and embellishment as they grow.[115] This view can be used as a mean of support to the present subgenre's study. In simple words, the narratives are replicated again and again with the ultimate goal of changing the narrative syntax and adding the details that are imposed by each period of time through the formatting of Normality on the basis of the rules of the society in which the individual filmic texts are produced.

In addition to remakes, there are also original neoslashers, examples of which are *Valentine* (2001), *Jeepers Creepers* (2001) and *The Cabin in the Woods*. Also, during this particular film cycle, a new franchise was created, *Final Destination*, that became popular and counts to date five films.

Returning to Normality and its interactions with the other semantic elements, and based on the analysis of the films of the corpus, we see that the main features of the neoslashers are the sociopolitical comments, the fights between social classes and the clashes of working class with corrupt forms of power, while gender and sexuality representations are in the past. As Stephen Asma says, terror and monsters have always been politically useful,[116] and from ancient times until now, monsters are impregnated with political demonization and dangerous propaganda.[117] In the new millennium, the subgenre began to look in depth at how evil is created and the killers have more realistic motives and a more three-dimensional psychological structure, but always under the scope of social critique. Previously, there was a hierarchy in the way social classes, figures, and forms of power appeared. The protagonists were usually part of the middle class community, they were sympathetic, and the audience identified with them, as opposed to the representatives of the working class who were usually the Others. Neoslashers overturn this form of Normality by changing the syntax. Many times, we find the working class represented by the protagonists of the narrative (*Halloween II*, 2009), the middle class appears to be the bad side, forms of power to be corrupt or even sometimes to be the Other itself (*The Cabin In the Woods*). Within this setting, the expression of the Others has been completely changed in relation to their predecessors. This particular element has stepped away from the stereotypical rules of appearance and representation, and has retained only the essence of its purpose in narrative. Even the number of Others per filmic text is not constant in neoslashers. It may be from just an abstract concept or entity (in the *Final Destination* film series where the Other is death himself, so technically speaking, there is only the idea of the Other, which is expressed in the narrative, but which is not embodied in any character), to an entire company (*The Cabin in the Woods*).

Apart from the Others, the Final Survivors have also been differentiated through their placement in narrative and their interaction with Normality. Of course, there are several neoslashers with a girl for Final Survivor (such as *Halloween* and *Halloween II*). Simply, even these few examples have removed all the features that Clover has described. In the new millennium, narratives often have more than one survivor, regardless of gender, and sometimes the character with the characteristics of the Final Girl ends up taking the position of the Other. Under the general definition of Final Survivors, apart from Final Girls, we can find Final Boys (*Final Destination*) and Final Couples (usually not in love, but in the light of friendship or family—e.g., *Friday the 13th*).

The neoslasher cycle is very important for the subgenre, because it changes the classical and self-referential conventions and creates its own rules, which come in line with the new fears and agonies of society. Neoslashers redefine the subgenre through the new syntax and the change of expression and interaction of the semantic elements due to the syntactic change. Even the filmic texts that are either part of a classical franchise or remakes, adapt the conventions and norms of the story and the narrative structure under the scope of the syntax of neoslashers.

An Epilog to the Theoretical and Historical Approach

Slasher films have not been favored as a subject of analysis by the academic community, even by those who are concerned with the horror genre in general. Clover and Dika are the exceptions of the academic community that dealt with slasher films, creating two powerful and important theories about the subgenre. However, their application is limited to certain periods of time and does not cover the whole subgenre. Also, both theories are about specific areas, such as representations or structuralist structures, leaving a gap regarding a systematic approach to their narratives as a whole. This chapter attempted to fill this gap and bring to light unfamiliar aspects of the narratives of the particular filmic texts through an overall subgenre's approach.

A useful tool in the analysis of film genres is Altman's theory of semantic and syntactic approach. Through this theory and by defining the list of four semantic elements and the three syntactic categories, it is argued that the subgenre has changed three times. While the list of semantic elements stays constant regardless of the period, the syntax is readjusted, altering the narrative itself. This readjustment of the syntax leads to the creation and/or termination of a film cycle within the subgenre. Thus, on the basis of the constant list of semantic elements and the changes in the syntactic categories, we conclude that the historical evolution of the subgenre can be divided into three cycles: the classical cycle (1974–1993), the self-referential cycle (1994–2000), and the neoslasher cycle (2000–2013).

The next chapters of the book will be about case studies aiming at a better and in-depth understanding of the films. The theoretical and historical approach developed in this chapter will be more clearly understood and individual cases will be examined in accordance with the rules set out above. Through the analyses of Normality, the Other, the Final Survivors, and the victims, and in combination with the three categories of the syntax, It will be strongly justified that the subgenre underwent great changes while being influenced by each period, and consequently by the expectations of the audience. Having undertaken a thorough analysis of this theory and its implementation, the chapters that follow will deal with the three film cycles and how they formed.

2. The Classical Cycle of Slasher Films

The subgenre began to exist in 1974, while its systemic production and the creation of a concrete package of its classical norms reached its peak in the 1980s. After endless diversification efforts, the slasher film reached its first period of decay in the early 1990s. From the corpus of the 74 films on which this study is based, 38 belong to the classical cycle of the subgenre, which lasted from 1974 until 1993. Even if the classical cycle is one of the most analyzed periods of the slasher film and a lot of theories have been developed based on these films, it is crucial that it be revisited under the scope of the proposed theoretical framework of this book. As we saw in the first chapter, even Clover's and Dika's approaches aren't fully applied to the whole cycle and have limitations. The proposed framework of this book is to create a theoretical tool that can be applied in every cycle.

The form of the classical filmic texts is structured by the conservatism of the period, and the interconnections of the four semantic elements have been shaped in a way that promote the punishment of sexual or other socially deviant behaviors of the characters. As established in the previous chapter, what makes the subgenre predominantly differentiate from cycle to cycle is the change of its syntax. The semantic elements remained the same throughout the life of the subgenre, but their expression and interactions between themselves changed. For this reason, this chapter, as well as the other two that will deal with the next film cycles, will be structured around the analysis of the four semantic elements and their placement and expression in the syntax.

The 38 filmic texts of the classical cycle have several common traits, but because they cover a longer period of time than the other two cycles (20 years, while the self-referential cycle covers seven and the neoslasher cycle 14 years), we see a slight differentiation towards the end of this period, as the over-exposition of the classical conventions had occurred and the films were trying to escape the extreme conservatism that had dominated the narratives of this cycle. Both the first films of the classical cycle in the mid-1970s and the films in the late 1980s did not have such intense tendency to punish acts of sexual release, but they still retained the conservative complexion of the classical cycle.

The films selected as case studies in this chapter are based on commerciality and popularity criteria. Thus, the films to be analyzed are *Black Christmas* (1974), *Texas Chain Saw Massacre* (1974), *Halloween* (1978), *Friday the 13th* (1980) and *A Nightmare on Elm Street* (1984). The following analyses aim to highlight everything that was proposed in the first chapter about the classical cycle and the syntax that existed in the narratives of these films. At the heart of the narratives is the conservatism that rewards virginal and conventional behaviors that come along with Normality, while gender and sexual representations come to the fore. Finally, the narrative links of the backstory of the Other to the way the victims and the Final Survivors are chosen are usually loose and based only on gender and sexual criteria.

The Normality of the Classical Cycle

The classical cycle is fully dominated by its narrative structures, which are bringing to the fore conservative compositions of the semantic elements of the film. Thus, Normality is built on these rules. Classical Normality is characterized by the aversion of sexual expressions and behaviors, the conservatism of the adult generation, which contrasts with the youths, who are the main victims, and the punishment of any sexual expression and/or social delinquency.

The classical syntax regarding the expression of Normality was formed under the aforementioned conditions. The relationship of Normality with the other three semantic elements was established in such a way that their connections with the stereotypical, conservative identity of the subgenre of that period were imbued. In particular, the Other, guided by the established rules of Normality, chases and kills the transgressors, the victims are the ones who break the rules and thus end up dead, while the Final Survivors are the perfect examples of obedience of the rules and thus, at the end they manage to survive. In order to better understand these relations of Normality, we analyze two of the most famous subgenre's franchises that belong to the first classical texts of the cycle, *Halloween* and *The Texas Chain Saw Massacre*.

Halloween (1978) is one of the most famous franchises, not just from the subgenre, but of the horror genre in general. It consists of 10 films, which cover the lifetime of the subgenre. There are classical *Halloween* films,[1] such as the first film of the franchise, self-referential films, such as *Halloween H20: 20 Years Later* (1998), and neoslashers, such as the last two remakes of the classical films. Although the slasher film began with two earlier films—*Black Christmas* (1974) and *The Texas Chainsaw Massacre* (1974)—its systematic reproduction began with *Halloween* (1978). With this film, its director, John Carpenter, was established as a leading representative of the horror genre. At its initial release, the film was a sleeper,[2] earning $50,000,000 with a budget of only $300,000.

But, before there is an analysis of the social fabric of the narrative and the Normality of this particular filmic text, we have to look at the sociopolitical context of the time this film was produced. The 1970s had a significant impact on the society of the United States of America. According to polls, crises, political scandals and the growing suspicion of citizens have greatly reduced confidence in political and social institutions. Within this sociopolitical context, political and social organizations began to emerge from various minority social groups, such as women, African Americans and homosexuals, with the aim of redirecting political action.[3] The 1970s drastically contributed to the sexual liberation and empowerment of both women and homosexuals. Let's not forget the Stonewall riots that took place just before the beginning of the decade in 1969, seen as the beginning of the public debate on homosexual human rights. We also need to take into account the important victory of the newly established movement, which was the decision of the American Psychiatric Organization in 1974 to remove homosexuality from the list of mental disorders.[4] However, in the late 1970s there was a turn that began to hold conservative values, and as a result of this, Reagan's presidency came in the 1980s. There was nostalgia for the 1950s, and it was depicted in the aesthetics of the audiovisual media of the time. TV examples include *Happy Days* (ABC, 1974–1984) and *Laverne and Shirley* (ABC, 1976–1983), which represent the 1950s as a simpler period. In the cinema there are examples too, like *Grease* (1978), which renounces disco music and time, as well as all the values that govern it, for a purer period.[5]

Within this context of turning to conservatism, *Halloween* was created. The story of the film begins on Halloween night in 1963 when Michael (at age 6: Will Sandin, at age 23: Tony Moran) murders his sister, who just had sex with her boyfriend. Then, the film forwards to October 30, 1978 (one day before Halloween), the day of Michael's escape from the clinic where he was being kept. The rest of the filmic text deals with the horror that Michael spreads at Haddonfield, the town where the film is set, and his attempt to murder Laurie (Jamie Lee Curtis), a teenage girl and the protagonist of the film. Normality in the narration is depicted in the social fabric of Haddonfield. The society consists mainly of suburban residents, citizens of the middle class whose social and/or family activities are the complete opposite of those in the working class. The characters of this society can be divided into two major categories, adults and teens.

Based on the aforementioned sociopolitical context, this conservative complexion seems to be logical about the relations created by Normality with the other semantic elements. The adults of the film are almost absent. Few non-teenage characters appear on the screen and the majority of them for a very short time, so the audience does not fully comprehend their contribution to the narrative context. An example of this adult absence is the scene where Laurie, chased by Michael, goes to a neighboring house to ask for help. While the light is on and the human figure appears, the neighbor does not open the door to help her. Thus, the minimum representation of adults becomes negative. The two exceptions of adult characters that play an important role in the narrative are the Dr. Sam Loomis (Donald Pleasence) and Sheriff Brackett (Charles Cyphers), both of whom are figures of power.

Dr. Loomis is the embodiment of the rival awe of Michael Myers. He tries to do good and protect the entire city from the threat of the killer without any personal gain. He even compromises his physical integrity to save Laurie, a completely unknown girl for him. Michael is the personification of evil without obvious causes for his actions, so Dr. Loomis is in a sense the narrative counterweight of it. Sheriff Brackett is the only parent who has an active role in the narrative, so his dual identity gives him more power in the progression of the narrative. Nevertheless, it does nothing essential to stop the violence against adolescents, nor the murder of his daughter, Annie (Nancy Kyes). Of course, these two characters are an exception to Normality in a teen-centric film that is in line with the norms of the classical cycle.

The filmic text comes in harmony with the classical teen character convention of the subgenre. The teenagers of the film are portrayed as sexually active and have divergent behaviors, such as drinking alcohol and making use of drugs. Of course, those characters who meet these conditions are brutally murdered by Michael. Only Laurie survives and in her character the concept of the Final Girl fully applies. In addition, although there are murders that appear on the screen, we do not see any blood being poured. Violence and terror are transmitted to the audience more with a psychological connotation, rather than the form of abomination through the representation of gore scenes.

Thus, while the teens of a society are punished for divergent behaviors, the adults of the community, or in other words, the Normality, applaud this punishment through their absence and indifference, thus setting the narrative agenda of the filmic text. Michael plays the role of a substitute of a parent. As Kendall R. Phillips observes, "Meyers watches the teenagers of Haddonfield more closely than their largely absent parents, he judges their naughty behavior more severely, and he punishes with extreme prejudice."[6] In one view, the absence of parents is what "calls" Michael to take action and punish teenagers. This is directly linked to the conservative shift of American society in the late 1970s. Throughout the narrative, young people have divergent behaviors while adults, through their absence, allow the imposition of a conservative rhetoric and a call to return to "family values."

Halloween is an important film for the whole horror genre. It introduced and made some conventions known, which are now considered classical, such as the POV shots of the bad guy, the re-emergence of the monster after its alleged assassination, and the creation of a central female character that can protect herself from the monster.[7] But its reputation was built around the fact that it combined conventions, which were then typified and represented many times during the classical cycle of the slasher film, a cycle that was closely connected with the punishment of sexual act. Seven sequel films followed, reinforcing the name of the franchise and creating one of the most important film titles in the history of the cinema.

The second part of the *Halloween* film series appeared three years later in 1981. Until then, other films that standardized norms and conventions under the prism of the classical cycle of the subgenre appeared. For example, in 1980, one year before *Halloween II*, there was the beginning of another important slasher film franchise, *Friday the 13th* (1980). The story of *Halloween II* (1981) starts right from where the first film stopped. In fact, the first scene of the film is exactly the last scene of 1978. Michael escapes and goes free in the Haddonfield neighborhoods, while Laurie is transferred to the hospital of the area. At the same time, Dr. Loomis tries to locate and capture Michael with the help of the police. Michael (Dick Warlock) continues killing young defenseless teens until he arrives in the hospital where Laurie is in order to kill her. At the same time, Dr. Loomis learns that Laurie is Michael's sister, and he realizes he will chase her again, so he goes to help her. The film ends with Michael's defeat.

This particular film adds a new way of connecting the Other and the Final Survivor, since it introduces that that Michael Myers is Laurie's brother. The emphasis on some type of familial connection between the killer and the Final Survivor is not only a significant shift in the *Halloween* franchise, but the slasher film in general. This trait remained in the subgenre until today, with a lot of films trying to connect in some manner the Other and the Final Girl (for example all the films from the *Scream* franchise).

Of course, apart from that, *Halloween II* reproduces the classical conventions that have already been set, presenting in a similar way Normality and its relations with the other semantic elements. POV shots of the killer, young people with sexual impulses slaughtered in front of the camera and a virginal figure who will survive in the end are the narrative evidence that confirms the aforementioned argument. Laurie is again the Final Survivor under the veil of the Final Girl, as in the first film. Her characteristics remain and are again represented as the pure, virginal girl. Although there is a flirtation with one of the two stretcher bearers, Jimmy (Lance Guest), Laurie does not give in and devotes herself to trying to "defeat" the Other. Finally, Michael himself is represented as in the first filmic text, as the personification of evil that sows the terror through the representation of the semantic element of the Other. To summarize, the 1981 film follows the classical syntax that was also analyzed in the 1978 film, with the punishment of sexuality and conservatism at the heart of storytelling. The end much resembles the end of the first filmic text. Laurie is the ultimate winner with the significant help of Dr. Loomis, who, with the sense of self-sacrifice he had in the first *Halloween*, sets the room containing both him and Michael on fire.

The narrative syntax is formulated in such a way that semantic elements are placed and interact with Normality within this general context of the classical cycle. More specifically, there is a Final Survivor with virginal characteristics that stands out from the group of the victims, who are possessed by sexual impulses. The "punisher" of the narrative is the Other, an asexual man who acts as the instrument of enforcing the rules of Normality that has been established in the narrative of the filmic text.

The second case study is *The Texas Chain Saw Massacre* (1974). This franchise is an important and integral part of the slasher subgenre, having created and/or redefined several norms that govern it, through seven films.[8] Observing the years of creation of every film of the franchise and analyzing their structures, we realize that this film series was more established in the classical and neoslasher cycle. Finally, the *Texas Chain Saw Massacre* franchise has the most neoslasher filmic texts of any other classical franchise of the subgenre.[9]

The Texas Chainsaw Massacre, along with *Black Christmas* (1974), are two of the first films of the slasher subgenre. The two particular films were screened close enough, with *The Texas Chainsaw Massacre* premiering on October 1st and *Black Christmas* on October 11th.[10] The systematic production of the filmic texts of the subgenre began four years later, and thus, the particular films, although having several elements of the subgenre, did not fully comply with the classical norms that were standardized in the later slasher films. But before there is an analysis of the Normality of this particular text, we have to look the sociopolitical development of the United States of America during the production of the film.

The film was created at a time when youthful optimism and the utopian dreams of the 1960s began to dwindle, while Richard Nixon claimed the country's presidency with positive promises such as the rapid ending of the Vietnam War, law enforcement In a violent America and the restoration of the feeling of common sense in the United States federal government. Of course, Nixon failed to complete his election goals and eroded even more the world's belief in the government's scheme and state institutions.[11] Nixon's presidency lasted from 1969 to 1974, when he resigned from the presidential post, which was the first time this had occurred in the United States. As Richard Melanson notes, the American nation in 1969 was more divided than any other period after the civil war.[12] Nixon managed to end the Vietnam War, but the end of the war was not at all honorable, and the U.S. Army was faced with a defeat for the first time in history.

However, Nixon's presidency has made history for the notorious Watergate scandal, which, as David Simon says, contains essentially any type of politically divergent behavior.[13] More specifically, the scandal concerns the burglary of the Democratic Party offices on June 17, 1972, and the subsequent identification of the burglars in the White House, which was seen as a spying move just before Nixon's re-election. This story began to grow by leaking information about audio recordings of conversations from Nixon himself, which led him to resign in order to avoid the legal implications of the scandal.[14] Under these sociopolitical conditions, we can understand why the citizens were shaken by uncertainty and suspicion, with David Brian Robertson noting that Vietnam and Watergate have undermined faith in a strong presidency.[15]

Within this social and political context, the first film version of *The Texas Chain Saw Massacre* franchise appeared, as the production of this particular film began in July 1973 under the working title *Headcheese*.[16] The story is about five young people traveling in a van and meeting a family with cannibalistic tendencies, one member of which is Leatherface, the Other of the narrative. Young people begin to be slaughtered one after another by Leatherface and in the end only one character from the five survives, Sally (Marilyn Burns). Of course, neither Leatherface nor his family are being punished, since the film ends with Sally's escape. According to filmmakers, director Tobe Hooper and screenwriter Kim Henkel, *The Texas Chainsaw Massacre* was meant to make a comment on the "moral schizophrenia" of the Watergate era.[17] Todd Platts states that the despair of the status of the cannibalistic family reflects the representation of those who managed to fall out of the social safety net at a time when many lost their confidence in the government.[18]

There is a general acceptance by the academic community that this particular text is a distorted and at the same time perverse representation of the sociopolitical events of its production period, through a cannibalistic system incarnated by the unemployed, murderous family of workers of a former slaughterhouse.[19] Matt Becker, using Robin Wood's description of horror films as collective nightmares of society,[20] speaks of the great influence of national traumas on the horror genre, including the Vietnam War and the Watergate scandal, and the creation of apocalyptic films in response to these traumas.[21]

The Texas Chain Saw Massacre belongs to the category of apocalyptic films and its documentary style is an element that perfectly demonstrates its type of narrative. The presentation of the film as a true story, as well as the aesthetic choices reminiscent of documentaries, lead to a kind of peculiar mockumentary based on a Normality under post-apocalyptic conditions. The post-apocalyptic term refers to a world where, through a dramatic and unrealistic event that has taken place (in the case of this particular filmic text, the acceptance of cannibalism), society has changed radically in relation to the form we know it today. As Christopher Sharrett writes, the film is about a world that breaks into a primordial chaos, set in an archetypal wilderness where the preserved powers of culture are not active.[22] James Marriott explains that

> the film's archetypal structure is borrowed from fairy tales: this isn't far from Hansel and Gretel, with its children lost in the woods who find an attractive house inhabited by a fiend who kidnaps and wants to eat them. But while fairy tales tend to serve the function of preparing children for the rigors of adult life, and thus present a positive face for all their often considerable violence, Texas inverts their traditional values and presents an apocalyptic vision of unremitting negativity.[23]

Of course, in this post-apocalyptic Normality, what separates and shapes to a large extent the narrative code is the element of cannibalism governing the family of Leatherface. If we read the film under a sociopolitical perspective, we will see that cannibalism is an allegory that can be interpreted in a variety of ways. As Wood points out, "cannibalism represents the ultimate in possessiveness, hence the logical end of human relations under capitalism."[24] Clover states that the mechanization of industrial production and the impetus of the whole family to unemployment forced them to use their knowledge from the slaughterhouse working on human subjects.[25] Kendall Phillips also maintains the same position, saying that the mechanization of the industry has extirpated the family into poverty and turned its members into cannibals through a perverted logic of modern capitalism, that is to exploit others for profit.[26] In this case, people are literally presented as products for sale and consumption. Director Hooper emphasizes that "It's a film about meat, about people who have gone beyond dealing with animal meat and rats and dogs and cats. Crazy retarded people going beyond the line between animal and human."[27]

Such a condition, which is opposed to the basic and essential foundations of human civilization in general and presupposes the beginning of a post-apocalyptic Normality, is a fiery commentary in the times of Watergate and Vietnam. In the context of a post-apocalyptic society, the Other is necessarily created by the norms of Normality and its syntactic connections with the other three semantic elements. At a time when the "enemy" was outside the borders and the political leadership was playing power games, the *Texas Chain Saw Massacre* raised as a matter of representation the creation of Others within the country, with the main cause of creation to be a social problem created through a specific policy. The narrative of the film is taking place at a time when the country is dealing with external problems, while specific regions and social classes are plagued by unemployment, which leads to the appearance of cannibalism as a need for survival. Through the creation of this specific Normality, the narrative's syntax predicts that the victims will be chosen on the basis of the Other's primordial need to find food.

The classical cycle of the subgenre was stigmatized by the construction of a Normality under the punishment of sexual act and desire. Although *The Texas Chain Saw Massacre* is essentially the start of the classical phase, we notice a big difference in its Normality. There is no suspicion of penalizing the characters who are sexually active and, consequently, the rewarding of virginity is absent. Although there is a female character that covers the position of the Final Survivor, she does not manage to survive because of her virginal characteristics. The victims are selected on the basis of Leatherface's divergent behavior, with Sally surviving because she manages to escape with the help of a passenger car without creating a clear separation between her and the other teenagers.

Although the diversity, which contradicts the Normality of the filmic text, is expressed through the cannibalistic family, the narrative structure allows Leatherface to stand out and grasp the position of the Other. The murders are committed by him and the victims try to avoid him. His family functions as an intermediary link between reality, as it expresses an important functional unit of the capitalist system, and the post-apocalyptic nature of cannibalism. Leatherface is influenced by a real serial killer, Ed Gein, who has also inspired the creation of other film characters such as *Psycho*'s Norman Bates and Buffalo Bill (Ted Levine) from *The Silence of the Lambs* (1991).[28] But of course, the Other-Final Survivor binary in this particular filmic text is constructed in the same way as the rest of the films of the classical cycle, meaning the position of the Other is covered by a male character and the position of the Final Survivor by a female.

The Texas Chain Saw Massacre includes all the semantic elements of the subgenre and obeys to a large extent the syntax that was established in this period. The main difference, however, of the narrative structure and the expression of these semantic elements lies in the way of expression of Normality through which a post-apocalyptic reality is promoted.

The Other of the Classical Cycle

The semantic element of the Other is present throughout the life of slashers and provides a brand name for every franchise. Freddy Krueger, Michael Myers and Leatherface are some of the examples of Others who overshadow the franchise, letting Final Survivors change from film to film and get lost in oblivion. As discussed in the first chapter, the backstory of the Other in classical filmic texts concerns an event that usually involves sexually active or socially aberrant behavior, and its association with current events is narratively loose. The gender and sexual identities of both the Other and the rest of the characters is of utmost importance, because they play a central role on the narrative and influence the backstory of the Other. The classical cycle is characterized by the dominance of the white male in the position of the Other, which usually punishes sexually active teen girls. Of course, there are exceptions to this rule, most notably the first film of *Friday the 13th*, and the whole franchise of *A Nightmare on Elm Street*. Of course, although significantly different from the above general rule, the essence of conservatism and punishment of sexual and social delinquency remains at the center.

What differentiates *Friday the 13th* from the rest of the franchise films that followed, as well as from the entire subgenre, is the choice to put a female character as the Other of the narrative. The story of the film is about the murders committed by Jason's mother, Mrs. Voorhees (Betsy Palmer), as retaliation to the young campers. Years ago, Jason was drowned in the lake (or at least that's what the narrative of the first film claims) because of the negligence of two teenagers who were engaged in sexual acts at that time. So, Mrs. Voorhees kills young campers to avenge her son's death. The choice of a woman as an Other was something innovative for that period, but it was quickly removed from the franchise, since Jason took over. In the second film of the franchise he appeared as the Other and in the third filmic text had already taken his known form with the hockey mask, a form that keeps up to the present day.

Yet, this innovative choice of a woman as an Other had an element that did not help in that structural change that was meant to do. The film is known for the extensive use of the POV shots of the killer, as all the murders and scenes involving the killer, in addition to the final scene of the revelation, are shot in this way. Thus, the filmic text is structured around the audience's question of the murderer's identity, which is answered just about 15 minutes before the end of the film. So, although there has been a significant change in one of the basic semantics of the subgenre, the narrative structure is not quite different from other stereotypical representations of a white, male killer, because the female Other appears only for a short period of time. Finally, it is worth noting that in the classical cycle only this film and *Night School* (1981) have a female character as the Other of the narrative.

On the other hand, the originality of *A Nightmare on Elm Street* is that it experiments with new elements from other subgenres of horror and introduces the paranormal element into the core of the narration and the Other. Although older films, such as *Halloween*, gave supernatural elements to the

Other (extreme power, immortality, etc.), *A Nightmare on Elm Street* uses this convention to the fullest. Freddy (Robert Englund), the Other of the franchise, is a child killer who has escaped from the legal sanctions of his actions because of a technical, legal issue. Some parents isolated him in the place where the children went and burned him alive. However, Freddy, having powers equal to a mythical entity, chases and kills adolescents in the area in their dreams. In other words, the young generation of the narrative is at risk from the Other only when they are asleep. Kelly Bulkeley reports that this particular film does everything to recreate the sense of being trapped in a nightmare, with the elements of fear, incapacity and inability to predominate in narrative.[29] Even though this particular text is an important representative of the slasher film, it also has influences from other horror subgenres, and as James Kendrick notes, this film is the first example of a cross between slasher and possession film.[30]

Freddy is different from the majority of the Others in the classical cycle. If the Others of *Halloween* and *Friday the 13th* are analyzed, there is a common ground between them: they are both alive, chasing their victims by wearing masks and not talking at all. According to Gary Heba, "they do not show any feelings: no pleasure, no pain—they are simple murder machines, working more as props than as characters."[31] In contrast, Freddy is more talkative, "playing" with his victims, and his appearance does not contain any kind of mask. Of course, the biggest difference between him and the rest of the Others of the classical cycle is the fact that he's already been dead since the beginning of the film, placing him more in the Horror of the Demonic. Such a structure adds new elements to the subgenre, but without removing or differentiating the classical conventions of the 1980s. The representation of the Other as a white man continues, even in the face of the "dead" Freddy.

But besides the few examples that go beyond the rule, the standardization of the Other in the classical cycle was extensive with plenty of narratives to copy the pattern, such as *Prom Night* (1980) and *Visiting Hours* (1982). Out of the 38 filmic texts of the cycle, only four are differentiated from the general rule of the male Other disrupting Normality.

One distinctive example is *Black Christmas* (1974), which along with *The Texas Chain Saw Massacre*, set the foundation of the subgenre and introduced the classical cycle. David MacGregor Johnston notes that although John Carpenter's *Halloween* is generally believed to be the first, modern slasher, the subgenre is more accurately spotted on Bob Black's *Black Christmas*.[32] Of course, *Black Christmas* is a special case because its country of origin is not the United States, but Canada. Warner Bros. bought the distribution rights and introduced the film to the American audience; however, fearing the misunderstanding of the title due to blaxploitation,[33] they changed the title of the film to *Silent Night, Deadly Night*.

The story of the film is about a female sorority house whose members are terrified and murdered by Billy, a killer who the audience never sees in front of the camera. Finally, when it is known that the threatening phone calls come from inside the house, Jessica (Olivia Hussey), the Final Survivor, kills her boyfriend Peter (Keir Dullea), thinking that he is the killer. The filmic text ends with the real Billy in the attic. The open ending of the film reminds of the one from *Halloween*. There are other common elements between these two filmic texts, such as the POV shots of the killer, the scenes where the killer is stalking the victims and the extensive use of hand-held camera. The fact that Black Christmas started several classical conventions of the subgenre is now a widespread opinion, including the unknown killer's phone call, which was also used in *When a Stranger Calls* (1979).

Although these conventions deviate from the standardized form of the classical cycle without extensive punishment of sexual behaviors, it nevertheless has some important elements that formed the core of later classical filmic texts of the subgenre. The Other enters into a house inhabited by female students who most of them violate the rules of Normality. Girls who drink, smoke and swear are murdered one after another. But without rewarding virginal characteristics and "family values," the syntax of this particular narrative acquires a slight sense of accidental choice of victims, further reinforcing the second feature of the Other's backstory of loose narrative connections.

Although Billy is one of the first Others of the subgenre, he has several elements that have been maintained throughout the classical cycle. POV shots, victim chasing scenes, and open ending are some of the elements that create the Other in *Black Christmas* and place him harmoniously in the group of the classical Others. In this context, there is the development of the backstory of the Other without, of course, enough information to help the audience develop a full picture of the situation.

Finally, although there is no mask—a trademark of almost every Other of the subgenre—Billy never seems to be a human entity as a whole, continuing the tradition of the uncanny and the classical representation of the Other. His POV shots combined with the fragmentation of his image in the editing do not allow the viewers to see him in full, while seeing some details of him, such as his eye or his feet. So, we have exactly the same result we would have if Billy wore a mask: the representation of an impersonal and non-human figure.

Another example of a classical Other is coming from *Halloween*. Michael Myers of the classical text of 1978 occupies the position of the Other, who with his diversity threatens the Normality of the narrative, while punishing those who violate its rules. Although the character is a man, he is portrayed as asexual and with oppressed sexual impulses. The narrative of the film, and also Michael himself, are governed by realistic representations, but there are also narrative elements with supernatural essence. For example, despite the serious wounds and shots that Michael receives, nothing happens, and he manages to escape, while leaving an open ending to the narrative. It is felt that Michael is the personification of evil and that he cannot be defeated altogether, something that Dr. Loomis too claims in the film. Carpenter commented that

> it was all to make a new legend. There's something really creepy about the fact that evil never dies. It can't be killed. If as in the movie he really is just a force of evil, he's like nature. Well, in the end, he's back up again.[34]

Apart from the sense of invincibility, another element that makes Michael non-human is the mask he wears. Throughout the film, his face only appears twice. The first time is in the first sequence right after he murders his sister, where he is still young and his parents find him with a knife dripping with blood outside the house. The second time is in the end, just before his defeat and his later escape, where Laurie takes the mask off. Both times his face appears just before his defeat. In the rest of the film, we do not see his face at all, and thus the goal of personification of absolute evil is achieved. Regarding the mask, Carpenter notes:

> There's a very famous book I read years ago called *The Mask of Sanity*. It's about psychopaths. It describes in really incredible detail that they wear this mask, that to us they appear human, but underneath they're just machines. They don't have any regard for us. I was always chilled by that. So, it was kind of a literal interpretation. And that went along with *Halloween* of course. Everybody is dressed up in costumes. I had a choice between a clown mask, which would be obvious, and this one, which was really creepy.[35]

Therefore, the representation of the Other tries to incorporate evil into a human body. One last point regarding the Other of the classical cycle is the identification of the audience with him. According to J. Telotte, horror films usually achieve their goals by creating a sense of the fact that we are also involved in the spread of horror.[36] In *Halloween* this applies extensively and the most famous example is the first sequence of the film, which is also the basis of the backstory of the Other. The film starts with a scene where the six-year-old Michael watches his sister and her boyfriend make out, takes a knife from the kitchen, goes up to her room (after the intercourse and the departure of the young man), kills her and then goes outside, where their parents find the bloody knife in his hands. All this action is covered by a classical one shot, which is also a POV shot of Michael. As Kelly Connelly comments, *Halloween*'s opening scene further strengthens the incredible and sometimes destructive power of the male gaze.[37] Through the POV shot and the great power of the medium, the filmic text forces the viewer to identify with the Other/monster, as he/she watches the development of the story from his own point of view and thus creates a sort of peculiar protagonist. The audience "sees" through the eyes of the murderer and the power of the medium "facilitates" the identification with him. This point is in agreement with the opinion of Christian Metz and Jean-Louis Baudry and their most famous approach of primary and secondary film identification, an approach that was analyzed in the first chapter. The primary identification of the viewers is done with the camera, while the secondary identification comes with the characters. In *Halloween*, as well as in the majority of the classical films of the subgenre, we see a merger of the two identifications with the ultimate goal of further imposing the likeness of viewers with the Other.

Summing up, in *Halloween* of 1978, the Other is represented on the basis of his backstory as the epitome of evil, and the audience is forced to identify with him, and at the same time his actions can be considered arbitrary within the concept of absolute evil.

The Final Survivors of the Classical Cycle

Among the other formulations of the classical cycle of the subgenre, one of the most famous is the one of the Final Survivor. This semantic element was almost always covered by a young girl with virginal characteristics. More specifically, out of the 38 film texts of this particular film cycle, 31 have a Final Girl as the Final Survivor of the narrative. This choice is in agreement with the other gender criteria of the narratives, thus creating a conservative link between the Other and the Final Survivor in the syntax.

The Other with the Final Survivor create a binary based on gender characteristics and sexual identities. Both of them experience sexual oppression, but each one expresses it in a totally different way—the Other through the murders and the Final Girl through its sudden adulthood based on the process of dealing with the Other. Through the following examples, the basic structure of the Final Survival of the classical cycle, as well as its links to the Other and Normality through the syntax, will be identified.

One of the first completed Final Girls is Laurie from *Halloween*, played by Jamie Lee Curtis, an actress who has been described as the ultimate Scream Queen. Although in the first part of the film, through techniques such as POV shots, the audience identifies with the Other, as the narrative proceeds, this identification begins to diminish. The viewers start to identify with Laurie, the character that embodies the semantic element of the Final Survivor, because of the percentage of the narrative she covers, which is gradually rising. This change in focus helps to cognitively confuse the audience and develops anxiety. The viewer now knows less about Michael's position and moves, and this helps to create a sense of horror.

At this point, the term of feminism will also be useful. If we could give a general definition to feminism, then we would be talking about a collection of movements aimed at defining and consolidating political, cultural and social equality between the two genders.[38] Of course, even within the movement itself there was an evolution based on the prevailing sociopolitical conditions of each period, both in demands and in the victories of feminism. Thus, feminism is divided into three waves. The First Wave of Feminism dates back to the 19th and early 20th century and focused on claiming legal rights of gender equality, most notably women's voting rights. The Second Wave of Feminism began in the early 1960s and lasted until the 1980s, expanding the debate on equality into other areas such as sexuality, labor and reproduction. Finally, the Third Wave of Feminism, which began in the early 1990s and continues to this day, promotes further change in stereotypes, representation from the media and the language itself.[39]

Returning to the film's analysis, the Final Survivor is Laurie, a representation based on a fictional and real neoconservative environment towards the end of the second wave of feminism, namely from the late 1970s to the 1980s. *Halloween* opens the way for the creation of other characters with virginal characteristics such Laurie in classical filmic texts that followed.

Laurie and Michael are the two main characters of the film. The narrative begins with Michael, and as the film progresses, Laurie takes the lead, and becomes the big winner of the narrative by surviving from the killer. The two protagonists are a dynamic binary and share a common element, a repressive sexual identity. However, Laurie expresses her asexuality under the laws of Normality, as opposed to Michael, who expresses it by killing sexually active teenagers. Ideologically, sexual abstinence can be considered permissible for a girl, but not for a boy, which contributes to the punishment of the Other.

Laurie's asexuality, coupled with some other classical conventions, leads her to survival, allowing her to become the Final Girl. Steve Neale notes that "babysitting on Halloween night while her friends anticipate a night of sex, she is cast in the roles both of virgin and mother, two roles which are signified elsewhere as exempt from Michael's aggression. Of the four adolescent women who are attacked, it is therefore, logically, Laurie who survives."[40] Laurie, even at the most difficult time, prioritizes the children and tries to protect them first. Thus, this female character goes hand in hand with the needs of a male-dominated society and for this reason not only is she not punished but rewarded with survival.

But apart from being asexual, Laurie's character also has several masculine features. Her name is also male, for most of the film she wears a shirt and pants and she is also embodied by Curtis, an actress with androgenic features.[41] Laurie is energetic, strong, persistent and fearlessness, features that were usually connected with male characters. Thus, she fully agrees with the characteristics of the Final Girl: smart, virginal and active. Of course, as active as she is throughout the film, she does not save herself, but she is saved by Dr. Loomis, who shoots Michael. Laurie is considered to be one of the most important examples of the Final Girl, and the rest of the classical cycle of the slasher film have standardized her features and incorporated them into its narratives. Her capacity and energy did not only affect slashers but also the whole horror genre, allowing a female character to lead the narrative.

The Final Girl's convention has been portrayed and reproduced many times, with two other famous franchises serving as pillars of the subgenre and the specific expression of the Final Survivor. *Friday the 13th* and *A Nightmare on Elm Street* franchises are now in the pantheon of slasher films, and alongside with *Halloween*, they are the most celebrated films of the subgenre, having spread and expanded into all of the three film cycles. *Friday the 13th* is composed of 12 films (the original, 10 sequels and a remake),[42] while *A Nightmare on Elm Street* has nine films (the original, seven sequels and a remake).[43] Their success was not limited to cinema, but it also switched to other media, such as television, with the *Friday the 13th* (Syndication, 1987–1990) and *Freddy's Nightmares* (Syndication, 1988–1990), or material products such as posters, masks, etc., resulting in their transformation into a phenomenon of pop culture in the 1980s and 1990s.

Friday the 13th is one of the first samples of the subgenre's standardization during the classical cycle, as it came just two years after *Halloween*. The commonality in the two filmic texts is enough and the narrative structure has many similarities. Even the two Others of the franchises, Michael of *Halloween* and Jason of *Friday the 13th*, have quite common characteristics. As both Matt Hills and Steven Jay Schneider report, Michael and Jason are portrayed as relentless, impersonal, masked and outcasts.[44] Even the director of the film, Sean S. Cunningham, states that he knew *Friday the 13th* had to be fun, at least in terms that would create surprises for viewers, as did *Halloween*.[45] Within these changes to Cunningham's approach is the emphasis on special effects, as he hired Tom Savini, one of the most famous of his craft, with a salary of $20,000, twice as much as the most expensive actor of the film.[46] The scenes of murders are held by realism while the gore element dominates. Thus, the film differs from *Halloween*, which had chosen the element of suspense as a key component of his narrative. Apart from the different ways that are the aesthetic choices of the director, the two filmic texts have faithfully followed the classical, stereotypical conventions of the 1980s.

Andre Borges points out that the "the films, although not all got excellent critical reception, have become a cult phenomenon with devoted fans re-enacting scenes from the movies and producing their own fan made films."[47] The film closely follows the conventions set out by the pre-existing filmic texts and respects the basic rule of sexual punishment. It promotes the reward of virginity and abstinence from any sexual activity. The semantic element of the Final Survivor was incorporated into the narrative of the 1980 film through the stereotypical norms of the classical cycle of the subgenre. This character is called Alice (Adrienne King) and is in the standard of the theory of the Final Girl. Thus, the first *Friday the 13th* is a proof of the standardization brought by *Halloween*'s great commercial success.

Four years later, the decline of the subgenre began. At this time, *A Nightmare on Elm Street* appears and gives an air of rebirth and redefinition to the slasher film. Proof of the decline of the subgenre is the fact that the fourth film of *Friday the 13th* (1984) had the subtitle "The Final Chapter" and was intended to be the last film of the series. But the success of *A Nightmare on Elm Street* contributed to the creation of *Friday the 13th: A New Beginning* one year later and pushed the whole subgenre to flourish creating a revival essence within the classical cycle, which of course took a while, as in the late 1980s the final decline led to the introduction of the self-referential cycle.

The Final Survivor of this particular narrative was portrayed in accordance with the standards of a Final Girl. The punishment of the sexual act is pervasive, including Tina's murder (Amanda Wyss) immediately after her sexual intercourse with Rod (Jsu Garcia). There is a representation of violence against women, which does not contradict the general line that the subgenre has set. Craven argues that "certainly the horror film has traditionally shown a great deal of mayhem directed toward women, but on the other hand, I never felt that this was an inaccurate depiction of the violence that is directed against women in our society."[48] Of course, when this is not accompanied by a critical view, it confirms and perpetuates violence against women. The classical cycle of the subgenre happened at the same time as the second wave of feminism, characterized by dynamic and activist actions aimed at the much-needed equality—legal and social—between the two genders. Within this climate of claim for equality, there was a general confession of non-equal treatment of women, hence the director's own admission of violence towards them.

The character of Nancy (Heather Langenkamp), who, although related to the young Glen (Johnny Depp), has virginal characteristics in accordance with the syntax of the classical cycle. There is not even one scene to represent or imply the protagonist's sexuality. Thus, the audience of the 1980s, who had already watched several classical films, was not surprised to find that Nancy is the only character who manages to survive and face the Other.

However, in the evolution of the subgenre in the classical cycle, the expression of the semantic element of the Final Survivor evolved to a certain extent. Although the virginal characteristics of the Final Girl were retained, the character taking this position at *A Nightmare on Elm Street* became more energetic than previous texts. Nancy is the one who goes to find Freddy in his own world, trying to find a solution to how to stop the murders, and finally, she's the one who sets up traps and brings Freddy to the real world, which makes him vulnerable. In relation to *Halloween*'s Laurie or *Friday's 13th*'s Alice, it's a more active and sophisticated version of a Final Girl of the classic cycle. As Jonathan Markovitz observes, Nancy asks for help from males, but she still knows not to rely on it.[49]

In this way, a female representation that moves within the framework of the feminist arc, strengthens the dynamics of the Final Survivor and its influence on the evolution of the narrative itself. Of course, the film fails to differentiate itself sufficiently from the other classical filmic texts, as the punishment of sexual act and the reward of virginity remain fixed points in the connection of Normality with the semantic elements of Final Survivors and Victims.

The Victims of the Classical Cycle

The pattern of the punishment of any sexual and deviating behaviors has been established throughout the classical cycle, with the discriminative punishment/reward described above being directly linked to the semantic elements of the victims and the Final Survivors. In the classical cycle, Normality works in such a way as to reward the Final Survivors with their virginal and conservative characteristics, while punishing those who do not obey this pattern of behavior through the actions of the Other.

Of course, in order for punishment to be based on a divergent behavior, there must be some characters that will suffer it. These characters represent the incarnation of the semantic element of the victims in the slasher films. Victims in the classical cycle are usually teenage characters, engage in sexual activity, drink alcohol, and sometimes even do drugs—deviant actions in relation to Normality established in narratives. The examples are innumerable to confirm the above pattern, with *Friday the 13th* and *Halloween* being two of the most popular.

As Tania Modleski observes for the classical *Friday the 13th*, a group of young people gets together to oversee a summer camp and be killed accidentally whenever they have sex.[50] The subgenre was consumed throughout the 1970s and 1980s to represent murders of young characters with the ultimate aim of highlighting the conservative qualities of the Final Survivor/Final Girl.

Of course, in this franchise, the whole causality of the Other's backstory and the relationship of Normality with the victims is based on this classical motif of choice of who will be murdered and who will survive. The story begins when Jason is supposed to be drowned in the lake. This is because some reckless campers preferred to have sex rather than watch and help the unaccompanied child who was in danger. So, his mother, who is the Other of the first film, and also Jason himself, who becomes the Other of the whole franchise from the second film, kill unsuspecting teen victims who show similar behaviors to the first campers. We see that while this classical motif is placed at the center of the storytelling, it also preserves the characteristic of the classical syntax that speaks of a narratively loose link between the past events and the present acts of the Other. Although there is a conceivable connection between the victims and the backstory of the Other that led him to these deeds, this connection remains loose and relies on the standard conventions of that particular cycle.

Another famous example is *Halloween* (1978). The Other is referred to as the boogeyman, a word that is repeatedly mentioned in the filmic text to characterize Michael. The use of this word also helps indirectly link to the punishment of the victims, as, as Kendall Phillips says, "tales of the bogeyman have long served as a threat to unruly children who must conform to proper behavior or be menaced by these horrific figures."[51] The Other is the realization of this threat that is transmitted to children through fairy tales. Another obvious goal that serves the use of this word is the supernatural dimension that imparts to incarnate evil. In other words, the use of such a word puts more emphasis on the elements of the Horror of the Demonic rather than those of the Horror of Personality. In other words, there is a human entity with supernatural extensions designed to conform the young generation in accordance with the conservative norms of Normality.

And in *Halloween II*, young people are the victims, although the story in biggest part of the filmic text focuses on the actions in the hospital where Laurie is hospitalized after the attack on the first film. Nonetheless, the majority of hospital staff are represented by young people with intense sexual desires, which does not make the film different from the rest of the classical cycle. Such a narrative structure proves that the filmic texts of the classical cycle were willing to sacrifice the realism of the story in order to maintain the norms of the narrative's syntax.

An Epilog on the Classical Cycle

The slasher film subgenre began to exist in 1974, thus starting the classical cycle of these films. The classical cycle has the longest duration and most of the filmic texts compared to the other two cycles, while during that period important elements of the narrative created and followed the subgenre up to the present day. Through the above analyses based on the fixed semantic elements of the subgenre and the emphasis on the syntax of the classical cycle, we can understand that during this period, the subgenre suffered a standardization of its narratives around stereotypical and conservative representations.

More specifically, the classical syntax was modeled on the conservative form established by the earliest filmic texts and evolved over time, while the emphasis of narratives revolves around gender and sexual identities that come to the forefront of these films. Finally, there is a loose connection between the narrative events and, more specifically, between the backstory of the Other and the present actions. In simple terms, the link and relationship of the Other with the victims, but also with the Final Survivor, is often not sufficiently justified or even not at all. All the characteristics of the semantic elements and the connections between them are impregnated by the above features and they build the classical syntax of the subgenre, which emphasizes the conservatism and the "family values" that prevailed at that time in the United States of America. The stereotypical characters of the classical narratives gave a hint of stereotypical structure as a reflection of the reality of the period.

Of course, over time, the saturation of the particular formula and classical syntax began to occur, with the audience considering the structure to be predictable and looking for other perspectives in the subgenre. Towards the late 1980s several filmic texts attempted to escape the punishment of sexual acts, but they were unable to move away from the conservatism of this particular cycle. So, in the early 1990s, the slasher films began to fall in number, and almost every year only one managed to get into the top–100 box office in the U.S., with the exception of 1991 when two entered. In this way, the classical cycle came to an end and gave the baton to the self-referential cycle of the 1990s, the dynamic solution for the renewal of the subgenre.

3. The Self-Referential Cycle of Slasher Films

As the classical cycle came to an end, the subgenre began to separate the stereotyped representations of genders and sexualities that dominated the core of its narratives from the earliest films of the 1970s. Of course, these films obeyed the syntax of the classical cycle, and for this reason they are part of it. The full separation from these conventions, which marked the beginning of a new cycle, came in 1994 with *New Nightmare*. This particular film is a milestone for the subgenre because it expressed as a whole the tendencies of renewal that was trying to show the end of the classical cycle and was the beginning of a new cycle that, although it existed for a short period of time and was a transitional phase between classical and neoslasher films, constitutes an important part of the formatting of the slasher film. The self-referential cycle lasted from 1994 to 2000, and included 12 films based on the corpus under study.

Before there is an analysis of the basic differentiation of the syntax between the classical and the self-referential cycle, we have to examine the penetration of the self-referential element into the subgenre. As we saw in the first chapter, the second cycle of the subgenre is characterized by the self-referential elements and intertextuality incorporated in the narratives under the prism of a peculiar parody of the classical slashers. Self-referentiality aims to bring to the forefront of the narratives the process of producing the films, the question of their creative status, their intertextual influences or their perception by the audience. The 1990s saw the subgenre hold a high level of self-consciousness, bringing to the forefront its classical conventions, and through their mockery, managed to break and overcome them.

Regarding now the syntax formed in the second cycle of the subgenre, we understand that it took steps away from the conventions of the classical cycle. During the first cycle of the subgenre, the syntax of classical films is structured around a conservative form through gender and sexual identities. The connection between the Other and the Final Survivor, as well as the relationship of Normality with the semantic elements of the Other, the Final Survivor and the victims, is made in such a way that conservative comments about the gender identity and sexual behavior of each character come to the forefront of the narratives. Of course, all these connections were made through a loose narrative connection between the backstory of the Other and the present events, as well as the individual links of the semantic elements. Thus, all three basic categories of the syntax were structured around the umbrella of conservatism. The second cycle of the subgenre began to subtract the basic elements of this conservatism and to use self-referentiality and intertextuality as techniques of overcoming it through parody.

The syntax of the self-referential cycle is based on the preservation of some classical structures, but by using the parody element, it integrates them into the narratives of these slashers through their self-referentiality. Kara Kvaran reports that the slashers of the 1990s show their success in the game they create with the already known subgenre rules.[1] Through these changes and by redefining the three basic categories of the syntax, the narrations of self-referential slashers now take on the structure of a whodunit and are in stark contrast to the narrations of classical films of previous decades. While the syntax of the classic films has a loose link between the backstory of the Other and the present events, the self-referential films of the second cycle have such a structure that usually the identity, and hence the backstory of the Other, appears at the end of the narrative. Others of the classical narratives are established from the beginning of the narrative, and their backstory is usually set on the first sequence of the film, before the main narrative story begins. On the other hand, the Others of the self-referential cycle are usually not revealed until the last minutes of the film, with the narrative rolling around the question of who does the murders and why.

The self-referential cycle lasted only seven years, of which one year, and more specifically 1999, no film did not make it into the top-100 American box office. With the exception of 1998 in which there were four films, the remaining years had only one or two films, which indicated that the saturation of the classical cycle was not completely overcome, and only the films that managed to differentiate were quite distinct to the audience. In 2000, the subgenre began to differentiate its syntax once again and, in fact, it is considered a year that overlapped the second with the third cycle. Of the three films of that year, the two are the last films of the self-referential cycle (*Scream 3* and *Urban Legends: Final Cut*), while the third is the beginning of the neoslasher cycle (*Final Destination*). Finally, because of the short duration, the few films, and the relation of its conventions with the classical films, the self-referential cycle is considered to be a transition stage between the first and the third cycle of the subgenre.

The films selected as case studies for this chapter were based on the criteria of commerciality and popularity, but also on a relationship between the examples analyzed in the previous chapter or those that will be analyzed in the following chapters. So, the films that will be analyzed are *New Nightmare* (1994), the first three films of the *Scream* franchise (1996, 1997 and 2000), *Halloween H20* (1998), *I Know What You Did Last Summer* and its sequel (1997 and 1998), as well as *Urban Legend* (1998) and *Urban Legend: Final Cut* (2000). Through these case studies, the differentiation of the subgenre in the second cycle will be made clearer on the basis of its new syntax. This will be done through individual analyses of the semantic elements of the narrative and how the three basic categories of the syntax were formed.

The Normality of the Self-Referential Cycle

The self-referential cycle of the subgenre tried to move away from the conservatism of the classical cycle by incorporating into the Normality of its narratives a hyperconsciousness about the conventions of these films. Paul Kahn states that these films work through a self-referential humor that aims to convey our fears.[2] The characters themselves, as well as the narratives of the films as a whole, know the classical structures in which the subgenre became known and try to overcome them by breaking the previously customary conventions of a slasher film. A major role in this turn of the subgenre was played by the change of the younger audience in relation to the audience of the classical cycle.

Of course, this was done through self-referentiality, a feature that gives its name to the whole cycle. By means of self-referentiality, the narratives of the cycle establish a Normality that exposes to the audience the production conditions of the subgenre's films, but also the process of how the public perceives these filmic texts. Thus, the Normality of self-referential films keeps some conventions of classical films, but through this hyperconsciousness that self-referentiality imparts to narration and characters, these classical conventions are redefined by building a new Normality that does not have in its core gender representations and conservative structures.

In this process, intertextuality also plays an important role. Several self-referential films intertwine with older films of the subgenre belonging to the classical cycle, bringing to their forefront standardized conventions. In this way, the Normality of the self-referential cycle compares and overcomes these classical conventions. Throughout this setting, the concept of parody appears. Several times, the narrative pattern takes a tendency to parody the first cycle and its conventions, trying to establish new dynamics in Normality, but also in its syntactic links with the other three semantic elements. Thus, although the Normality of the self-referential cycle has several elements common to that of the classical cycle, the new mechanisms create new features that affect the syntax itself.

A filmic example that can further shed light on the Normality of the second cycle and how its syntax was influenced by this semantic element is *Halloween H20: 20 Years Later* (1998). The film continues the central story of the franchise 20 years after the first film. Now, Laurie (Jamie Lee Curtis), the Final Girl of the first two films, is the headmistress of a private school, in which her 17-year-old son, John (Josh Hartnett), attends. Of course, due to Michael's (Chris Durand) attacks, Laurie pretends to die in a car accident and now lives under the fake name Keri Tate. On the twentieth anniversary of the first events, Laurie begins to have nightmares and visions that Michael has returned to kill her. Michael returns on the day of Halloween, and the private school run by Laurie is transformed into a horror stage where the final battle between the two will be played.

In this film, there are self-referential and intertextual elements, which also signify the differentiation of this Normality from the classical texts of the first cycle. Such examples are when Jimmy (Joseph Gordon-Levitt) wears a hockey mask like the one of Jason Voorhees from the *Friday the 13th* franchise, or when Molly (Michelle Williams) is in a class of the private school and sees the killer outside the window, which reminds the scene with Laurie from the first *Halloween* where she once again saw Michael. There are also elements linking the text to the most famous pre-slasher, *Psycho*. Janet Leigh, who played Marion in *Psycho*, plays in this film the secretary of the school, Norma. There is a scene in which she talks with the character embodied by Curtis, Laurie. In this dialogue, there is the phrase "If I could be maternal for a moment...," which is a reference to reality, since Leigh is Curtis' mother. After this dialogue, Leigh leaves with the same car from *Psycho*, while the music that plays in the background comes from the same film. Even the plates of the car are the same as those of Marion's second car.

Thus, the Normality established through self-referentiality and intertextuality creates a peculiar pastiche, which, through nostalgia, breaks the classical conventions and establishes new ones. The relationship between Normality and the other semantic elements is influenced and differentiated, creating new syntactic relations between them. The main feature of these new relationships is the lack of punishment for divergent behaviors and sexual expressions. While the Normality of the classical cycle—and hence of previous texts of the franchise—was structured around conservative ideas, the placement of self-referentiality at the center of Normality removed these conventions from the narrative. There are no teenage characters who are murdered immediately after drinking alcohol and/or having sexual intercourse, while the Final Girl is not a virgin, but as it will be analyzed below, a Final Woman who has fully entered into the adult world, whatever that may be.

Finally, the relationship between Normality and the Other has been affected. Intertextuality plays a major role in such lengthy cinematic franchises, as its steady characters evolve singularly through the filmic texts. Thus, while in the classical cycle and in the first *Halloween* there were loose connections between the Other and the Final Girl who helped in the creation of a conservative Normality, now there is Michael, whose acts are more justified than before. Of course, this is due to the backstory that has been built in previous films, such as his family relationship with Laurie established in *Halloween II* (1981).

Halloween H20 is an important example of the self-referential cycle, as it belongs to a big franchise of the subgenre that has filmic texts in all three cycles, and so it can better be identified the evolution of the syntax in its narratives. Of course, although its Normality possesses all the characteristics of the cycle discussed above, it is an exception to the general tendency of the structure of self-referential norms. The norms of the second cycle are usually created around the narrative structure of a whodunit, that is to conceal the identity and motivation of the murderer, and to develop the story about the question of "who does the crimes and why" until almost the end of the film. *Halloween H20* could not have such a structure, since the franchise killer is already known to the general public. Thus, Normality kept all the other features of the cycle around a narrative structure that resembled the classical cycle. A typical example of the whodunit structure of Normality is *Scream* (1996).

An interesting example of the self-referential cycle regarding Normality is the first filmic text of the *Scream* franchise. This film is the most commercial slasher film and is commonly referred to along with *Silence of the Lambs* (1991) and *The Blair Witch Project* (1999) as films that helped revive cinematic horror from his decline that was talking place in that period.[3] The story is about a series of teen killings from a murderer wearing the Ghostface mask and the subsequent pursuit of the lead female character, Sidney (Neve Campbell), to find his identity. In the end, it is revealed that behind the mask were Billy (Skeet Ulrich), Sidney's boyfriend, and his friend, Stu (Matthew Lillard). Billy justifies his actions based on the previous murder he reveals that he committed, the one of Sidney's mother who he murdered for revenge because she had an affair with his father. Just by telling the narrative facts, we realize that Normality is built around the whodunit structure, as the story is rotated by the riddle of who is under the mask of Ghostface and why he does these murderous acts. The whole self-referential cycle has adopted this narrative form, completely changing its syntax as compared to classical texts. Of course, this form will be extensively analyzed in the subchapter of the Other, as the backstory of the Other is the most important syntactic element that has been influenced.

Returning to *Scream*, we observe that this particular text builds on the norms of the self-referential slasher, the main feature of which is intertextual references and the reproduction of older styles. As Valerie Wee also observes, an important part of the aesthetics and content of the film is based on previous films of the subgenre.[4] Of course, as Fran Pheasant-Kelly says, although it simulates other films, at the same time it is opposed to them, and, although it is a copy, it has come to replace the original.[5]

Most of the intertextual relationships relate to older films and more specifically to classical slashers, while the intertextuality is mainly coming from the main characters of the film. One famous example that proves this claim is the opening sequence where the first victim (Drew Barrymore) is murdered. Barrymore plays a girl who is home alone, while the killer is in the yard and speaks to her on the phone, making her a movie quiz. The first wrong answer leads to the murder of her boyfriend and the second to the end of her own life. The fact that the biggest star of the entire cast is killed at the beginning of the film could be considered an indirect reference to *Psycho* (1960), one of the most famous pre-slashers. On the other hand, the sequence is based on the motif set by a classical slasher film, *When a Stranger Calls* (1979). Besides that, the verbal references of the victim and the killer to horror films are continuous. First of all, the victim is preparing to see a "scary movie" from her favorite genre, as she mentions herself. Also, the movie quiz, from which her boyfriend's life and her own is judged, is based on slasher films.

In this pattern, the whole movie continues, with the references to previous slasher films increasing. Victims already have a knowledge of the subgenre's formula and use it in order to manage to survive. References are even made to rewarding virginity and sex punishment, which seem to be based on Carol J. Clover's theoretical analysis. Indirect references to the theoretical study give the characters a kind of hyperconsciousness. They themselves participate in a slasher, but also know the conventions and clichés that govern it. Randy (Jamie Kennedy) talks about certain rules you have to follow to survive a horror film, examples of which are not to have sex or drink and do not use drugs. This hyperconsciousness leads to the peculiar feature of the narrative about blurring the boundaries of reality and fiction, as fictional characters behave as if they are part of the real world, while commenting on the fictional world itself. In this respect, Todd Tietchen reports that *Scream*'s audience remains quite uncertain about the boundaries of reality and fiction.[6] At this point, the interaction between the young generation of the narrative and the media is also linked. The killer murders in cinematic fashion with the precision of classical slasher films, while the mass media are awaiting the next murder, with the ultimate goal of commercial success. Evidence of this is the statement of Weathers (Courteney Cox), in the police's attempt to explain to her that Ghostface is still not considered a serial killer, to which she replies cynically: "we can hope, can't we?"

The confusion between reality and fiction becomes very distinct in two scenes towards the end of the film. The first scene is when police officer Dewey (David Arquette) walks into the house looking for the murderer. At the same time, *Halloween* is on television. While the policeman walks through the house, the audience hears the *Halloween* music as the natural sound of the film, as it comes from the television. John Carpenter's stressful soundtrack becomes the soundtrack of *Scream*'s murder scene, bringing the self-referential feature to the forefront.

The second scene is where Randy sits alone and watches *Halloween* on television. As he sees the final scenes on the screen, the audience sees the killer behind him. Randy is shouting at the TV: "Jamie, behind you!" referring to *Halloween*'s star, Jamie Lee Curtis. The confusion between fiction and reality on this scene is remarkable. A protagonist calls to a fictional character what the real audience wants to shout at him. What further confuses reality with fiction is the fact that the actor incarnating Randy is called Jamie Kennedy. So the phrase "Jamie, behind you!" is exactly what the audience is shouting at that time, once again stressing the scope of self-referentiality in the film. Yet, another aspect of this scene is that viewers see it after a while for the second time, through the monitor of the TV crew in the van, which is connected to a hidden camera inside the house. In this scene, we see Sidney along with the cameraman of the crew watching the action, shouting "behind you!" The scene ends with an ironic tone on the confusion of real and mediated images, as the cameraman is murdered, having come out of Van because he has forgotten the difference of 30 seconds between the reality and the monitor images. In fact, the image controller dies, because even he has confused the mediated image and the real violence.

The hyperconsciousness of the characters, as well as the cinematic narrative, promotes a confusion between reality and fiction. Andrew Syder emphasizes that

> most of our knowledge of the world derives from what we glean from the media's representations of the world; how we perceive and make sense of experience, then, is in significant measures controlled and conditioned by the media. The possibility that the world is actually quite different from its media representation is now a common social concern.[7]

Syder's statement is based on Jean Baudrillard's theoretical approach, about blurring boundaries of reality and the difficulties of isolating the real in the postmodern era.[8] According to Baudrillard, it is no longer a matter of imitation, duplicity, nor even parody, but of substitution of the real itself.[9] Of course, the separation of reality and fiction has begun to blur in the American society itself, exemplifying the election of former actor Ronald Reagan as president of the country, reaching the beginning of the 1990s with the Gulf War, who was described by Baudrillard as a creation for television.[10] Returning to *Scream*, we conclude that through the cynicism of characters, the film does not simply reproduce conventions, but re-shapes them, as it does with the connection of Normality with the Final Girl.

However, Sidney denies this role. First of all, she does not want her life to be parallel to a movie, saying to her boyfriend, "This is life. This isn't a movie." Sidney denies the position given to her by the syntax and instead of obeying the norms, she is fighting dynamically to change them. As a result, it can be described as an inverted form of the Final Girl. She is popular, has friends and a boyfriend, and breaks the stereotype of the virgin girl who survives.

Scream followed by *Scream 2* (1997), *Scream 3* (2000) and *Scream 4* (2011). According to Timothy Shary, the fact that only one year later came the sequel and within four years became a trilogy, testifies to the great success of the first *Scream*.[11] The next two films also belong to the self-referential cycle and continue the structure of Normality that was established in the first filmic text. *Scream*'s franchise, and in particular the first film, through its extensive commerciality, consolidated a new state into the subgenre where it transformed self-referentiality into the main component of slasher films of the 1990s. Its Normality is based on a hyperconscious characters, thus altering its syntactic links with the other semantic elements of the narrative.

The Other of the Self-Referential Cycle

The semantic element of the Other is decisive throughout the life of the subgenre, and the most important element of the syntax that has to do with the backstory of the Other. As we saw in the previous chapter, in the classical cycle, the Others are not represented in depth and are not presented with a three-dimensional character structure, since the links of the past and the narrative present are loose and do not rely on the cause/effect binary. Their backstory usually has no or very loose connections with the main events, while narration itself starts with these past events in order to consolidate the Other as a character. In the self-referential cycle, this structure changes, as there is a whodunit narrative consolidation. The backstory of the Other is not narrated until the end of the film because the viewers, as well as the main characters of narration, do not know the identity and motives of the Other.

In the majority of the second film cycle, the identity of the Other is usually hidden behind a mask and/or outfit that establishes it as a presence, but it removes its syntactic extensions around the element of his backstory. Thus, it drastically changes the whole of the syntax and this also appears in the expressions of the other semantic elements, with the main example of the

Normality analyzed above. But through this syntactic differentiation in relation to the classical cycle, there is a more solid association of events than the loose narrative connections observed in classical texts. There is a stronger connection between the backstory of the Other and the reason that kills the present victims, no matter if this link is usually revealed at the end of the filmic text. An example of this is *Scream*, where, until the revelation of who is hiding behind the mask, the audience and viewers do not know why Ghostface kills the victims and chases Sidney. But when the revelation is made and we see Billy as the main killer, he is fully justified with the new elements of his backstory because he is obsessed with Sidney.

This tendency to move away from the loose connections of the Other's backstory and the current narrative events is also observed in the very self-referential slashers that do not have a whodunit structure. Another example that comes from the previous subchapter is *Halloween H20*. Michael goes to the private school for a specific reason, as Laurie is his sister and through this connection is justified his persistence—let us not forget that he is the only member of his family who stayed alive and was not murdered by his hands. It is worth noting that this tendency to move away from the loosely connected narrative structures and present events was the step towards consolidating the powerful narrative connections of the neoslasher cycle as, as mentioned in the first chapter, the second cycle is a transitional stage between classical and neoslasher texts.

Returning to the analysis of the filmic texts, their selection was based on their whodunit structure, to bring out the full syntactic features of the cycle. Thus, the analysis will focus on two famous franchises of the subgenre that were created and they were only in the self-referential cycle, not having a film in either the first or the third cycle—*I Know What You Did Last Summer* and *Urban Legend*.

One year after *Scream*'s big commercial success, another self-referential slasher that followed the same structure that was established in the 1990s made its appearance—*I Know What You Did Last Summer*. The story is about four friends who hit a man with their car on a desolate road and in their panic they decide to throw his body into the sea. After the victory of Helen Shivers (Sarah Michelle Gellar) at a local beauty contest, Julie James (Jennifer Love Hewitt), Barry William Cox (Ryan Phillippe) and Ray Bronson (Freddie Prinze, Jr.) decide to celebrate it in conjunction with the American Independence Day of July 4th. The four friends go to a party and then decide to go to the beach. Barry, who is drunk, decides to let Ray drive them back, and then they hit an unknown man. After they throw the body into the sea, they decide not to ever talk about it. One year after the events, all four begin to receive threatening messages about the incident, and then the Other makes his appearance, hunting and killing them. Finally, is revealed that the killer is Ben Willis (Muse Watson), the man who they hit with the car and threw into the sea.

John Stephens refers to this film as a dark moral story.[12] It is worth mentioning that the screenwriter of the film, Kevin Williamson, is a writer who is very often found in the self-referential cycle; he wrote the screenplay of all the *Scream* films, but was also a co-executive producer on the *Halloween H20*. So, the formula of the story is kept the same, with the structure evolving as a classic whodunit and revealing the identity of the murderer with an element of surprise, since it is not someone who tries to take revenge for the unhappy man, but the man himself. Thus, while the narrative passes through various fluctuations, with the audience identifying with the protagonist and suspecting even her former boyfriend, Ray, in the end, all the necessary information is given about the backstory of the Other with the narrative ending just like an average film of the subgenre: the Final Survivors defeat the Other, but they do not kill him, with the last scene suggesting that he is still alive and determined to kill them.

Throughout this setting, the complete removal of the Other from the systematic punishment of sexual behaviors is achieved. In the classical period, many times even the backstory of the Other was associated with such behaviors, with *Friday the 13th* (1980) being one of the well-known examples, where the six-year-old Jason was drowned in the lake because of the careless campers who were making out. In this film, which also acts as an exemplary example of the entire self-referential cycle, neither the backstory of the Other nor the subsequent choice of victims use sexual behaviors of the characters as an essential component of their choice and murder. Of course, although the film makes a significant step away from the conventions that made the subgenre known since its birth, it still retains its stereotyped gender identities of the basic characters, with the Other being a male and with the basic Final Survivor being a female. The self-referential cycle stepped away from the punishment of sexual behaviors, but continued to retain the gender stereotypes, even though the Final Survivors, as we shall see below, grew in number per film, and we now find men who survive at the end—as in this film Ray survives too, creating a Final Couple.

This film was followed by a sequel one year later, titled *I Still Know What You Did Last Summer* (1998). The film follows Julie, the Final Girl of the first film, and we see her trying to leave behind her previous events and start her life from the beginning. Together with her university roommate, Karla (Brandy Norwood), they earn a trip of four people on a tropical island and decide to go with Tyrell (Mekhi Phifer), Karla's boyfriend, and Will (Matthew Settle). Within this setting, Julie again begins to receive threatening messages about the initial event of the first film. In the end, it is revealed that Will is Ben's son, the murderer of the first film who managed to survive, and that father and son were trying to take revenge on Julie. The two Others are defeated and Final Survivors are again proclaimed the Final Couple of the first film, Julie and Ray.

And the second part of this self-referential franchise follows the same narrative structures of the second cycle and revolves around the question of the identity of the Other. Here, of course, the backstory of the Other is partly known, as it was narrated in the first film. The new element of the narrative is that we have two characters that fulfill the semantic element of the Other, one being also the erotic interest of the Final Girl. Thus, it functions as an intertextual element regarding *Scream*, further expanding the self-referential mood of the narration.

In addition to splitting the semantic element of the Other into two characters and partially concealing the backstory of the Other until just before the end, this film does not evolve the new conventions, and faithfully follows the syntax of the self-referential cycle. In a nutshell, the narrative focuses on removing sexual behavior punishment and maintaining gender norms of classical storytelling, with the male Others chasing the Final Girl, until the boy saves her and together they are declared the Final Couple of the narrative. Of course, this tendency of the film's comradeship for the period of its production is also reflected by its own title, which Rick Worland describes as the laziest sequel title of horror film.[13]

A year after the first film of *I Know What You Did Last Summer*, another self-referential franchise of the subgenre made its appearance, which also consists of two films—the *Urban Legend*. The first film appeared in 1998 and involves a series of strange deaths associated with some urban myths. More specifically, the story revolves around Natalie (Alicia Witt), a charismatic student at Pendleton University. Natalie and her friends attend the Folklore class, taught by Professor Wexler (Robert Englund), who introduces students to urban myths, including the myth of a university that involves a psychopathic professor who murdered six students 25 years ago. Natalie, having links to all the victims, is the first to suspect there is a murderer on the campus, but no one believes her until it's too late. In the end, it is revealed that the murderer is Brenda (Rebecca Gayheart), Natalie's best friend, and she did so to take revenge on Natalie, who, through a youthful recklessness, was co-responsible for the death of Brenda's boyfriend in a car crash.

In this filmic text too we observe a narrative structure that faithfully follows the norms of a whodunit narration. Normality here is built around the question of who is the killer, and so the backstory of the Other remains hidden until the last scene, when the revelation that Brenda is the one who committed the murders occurs. The novelty of this narrative is that it chooses a female character to embody the semantic element of the Other. If we take a closer look at the film corpus, the last film slasher that only had a female

Other in its narrative was *Night School* in 1981, which is 17 years away from *Urban Legend*. Of course, one year before, *Scream 2* incorporated both a man and a woman as Others, while in the same year that *Urban Legend* came out, the *Bride of Chucky* has also a couple of Others.

The choice of a female character to fulfill the position of the Other of the narrative is something innovative and shows gradual removal from the stereotypical choices about gender identities. The self-referential cycle functions as a transition between classical texts and neoslashers. Two years before the third cycle begins, *Urban Legend* is an example of this gradual shift of the subgenre away from the conservative structures of the 1970s and 1980s. The film has a female Other and a Final Couple showing this progress of the subgenre, as this could not have been done with the classical syntax.

Finally, the Other's backstory itself helps to the creation of better links, comparatively to the loose connections of the classical cycle, without using sexuality as the main cause of the connection of events. At the end of the film, the audience learns that the Final Girl was co-responsible for the death of Brenda's boyfriend, and thus, a better causal pattern is created compared to the classical texts. Of course again, the cause/effect pattern is not fully present in the second cycle, but what self-referential slashers did was to lay the foundations to the consolidation and composition of strong narrative links to neoslashers.

Two years after *Urban Legend*, *Urban Legends: Final Cut* followed. In this filmic text, self-referentiality comes to the full with the story revolving around a film school and the protagonists being its students. More specifically, we are following Amy (Jennifer Morrison), a college student at Alpine University, who is trying to finish her bachelor film degree on urban myths. As the film progresses, the crew members die from apparent accidents. Amy begins to suspect that there are no accidents and finds out that a killer is behind them. In the end, it is revealed that the killer is Professor Solomon (Hart Bochner), who did so in order to blame Amy and steal Travis' (Matthew Davis) film—the first victim, in order to present it as his own. Solomon even justifies his choice of targeting Amy, saying her father was in the jury for the Alfred Hitchcock Prize regarding his graduate film, and Solomon was not awarded because of his vote.

The film follows faithfully the original text of the franchise and fully integrates the narrative and syntactic structures of the second cycle of the subgenre. *Urban Legends: Final Cut* is a classic whodunit slasher where the revelation of the killer's identity is a surprise, as the victims and the Final Survivors are teenagers and young people while the Other is their professor. Although the narrative takes a step back compared to the first filmic text by putting a man in the position of the Other, yet again it does not have sexually and/or gender-centered criteria. Even the backstory of the Other does not refer to such stereotypes of the classical cycle, but the justification is based on the effort of the Other for professional advancement through lawless acts. Thus, the Other has the form developed in the self-referential cycle: an impersonal entity hidden behind a mask and/or outfit while the revelation of its backstory is towards the end of the narrative, when the audience learns his identity and the motives of his actions.

The Final Survivors of the Self-Referential Cycle

In a typical slasher film, the Final Survivors are the protagonists of the narration. Even if the Other and his actions are the driving forces of the progression of the story, sooner or later, the Final Survivors take the lead of the narration and try to defeat the Other. As we saw in the previous chapter, during the classical cycle, the semantic element of the Final Survivor was fulfilled by a character with the features of the Final Girl, as identified and analyzed by Clover. In simple terms, the semantic element of the Final Survivor in the first cycle had two basic characteristics: first, it was fulfilled only by one character, and secondly that character was usually female with virginal characteristics. During the self-referential cycle, both of these characteristics began to be nullified, with the narrative going through the creation of new conventions around the syntactic connections of this semantic element.

First of all, in self-referential films there is an increase in the number of the characters that survive at the end. More specifically, of the 12 corpus films belonging to the second cycle, only three have a Final Survivor (*Candyman: Farewell to the Flesh* and *Halloween: H20*), while the remaining nine have two or more characters. By comparison, it is recalled that in the classical cycle, out of the 38 films, only three have more than one Final Survivor, so we understand that there is a huge difference regarding Final Survivors in these two cycles.

Also, the second feature too of the classical cycle regarding Final Girls began to go away. As Peter Hutchings says, these films, while retaining the idea of women as central characters, do not reminisce the isolation they had in older films such as *Halloween* and *Friday the 13th*.[14] Most films, even if they have an archetypal form within the classical Final Girl, incorporate other Final Survivors into the narrative, such as Final Boys, Final Couples or even four different Final Survivors, as in *Urban Legends: Final Cut*. And all these three films that have only one Final Survivor, although it is a female character, do not remind one of Clover's Final Girl in any way. In these films, the surviving female characters are now adults and have nothing to do with the frightened teenage Final Girls of the classical cycle, nor with their virginal characteristics. Thus, we see that the semantic element of the Final Survivor and the syntactic connections that govern it changed significantly between the first and the second cycle of the subgenre, enhancing with these changes the consolidation of the new syntax of the self-referential films of the 1990s.

By dividing the differentiations according to the two characteristics of the classical cycle, the first part of this subchapter will deal with the change in the characteristics of the female character that survives, while the second will deal with the increase in the number of Final Survivors. Thus, in this section there will be an analysis of the meaning of the Final Women in the self-referential cycle, with *New Nightmare* and *Halloween H20* as the main examples.

New Nightmare is part of one of the most profitable franchises of the subgenre, as well as the first film of the second cycle, by bringing the self-referentiality in the center of the slasher film. The differentiation from the classical cycle was so enormous that some scholars, with James Francis among them, consider *New Nightmare* not part of the subgenre.[15] Of course, the new wind that brought this film worked, with many critics to speak in favor of it compared to other filmic texts of the franchise, or even other horror films of the time.[16] The story takes place during the tenth anniversary of the first film of the franchise, *A Nightmare on Elm Street* (1984), and the main actress of it, Heather Langenkamp, is terrorized by Freddy Krueger (Robert Englund) who managed to enter into the real world. The only way to defeat him is for Heather to accept her fate as Final Survivor and face him.

Only from the outline of the story, we understand that the film is built around self-referentiality as it plays with the cinematic medium itself and blurs the boundaries between fiction and reality. Even the advertisement of the film promoted this pattern, stating that "this time the terror doesn't stop at the screen."[17] In the film, we see plenty of people working in the first film playing themselves, under the general convention that Freddy has entered the real world. Heather, the real actress who portrayed Nancy, the iconic Final Girl, is called upon to take the lead and be the Final Survivor, but no longer with the fictional features of the classical cycle that her character possessed. The fictional world of the 1984 film wanted her to be the Final Girl, but the real world of 1994 wants her to be the Final Woman. Heather may be Nancy, but she is no longer the teenage girl who stands out from the rest of the characters while her basic occupation is not being a student. The Final Survivor of this film is a famous actress who has been distinguished as a horror icon through a popular franchise, while at the same time she has managed to balance professional and personal life, by having a family too. Throughout this complex and demanding setting, she is called upon to face the Other of the narrative. This Final Survivor, which is a peculiar development of the 1984 Final Girl, has fully entered the adult world, whatever that may be. She does not expect the male figure to come to save her as was often the case in the classical cycle, especially in the early years of the subgenre, but she protects herself as well as her child. An example of the power of this particular Final Survivor is the fact that her husband, Chase (David Newsom), is murdered by Freddy, but she manages to stand on her feet and protect her family against the threat the of the Other. Heather is the first example of an adult version of the classical Final Girl with the characteristics evolving from the adult world, but again there are some intact conventions of the classical cycle, like being a mother figure.

Another example of the Final Woman in the self-referential cycle with a more sophisticated form and more distinct features is Laurie from *Halloween H20*. More specifically, in this example, the Final Survivor of the film could not be described as a Final Girl with the features described by Clover, but as an adult evolution of this cinematic archetype of the subgenre. Inside this self-referential Normality discussed above, Laurie is no longer the frightened, teenage girl waiting for a male figure to save her in the end, but a dynamic woman who has taken her life in her own hands. Even the fact that she faked her death and started her life from the beginning with a new identity shows how energetic of a character she is and how little she resembles the girl of the 1978 film, where Dr. Sam Loomis (Donald Pleasence) saves her from the Other.

Apart from this feature, however, Laurie has other expressions of her activeness as the narrative progresses. The culmination of it comes at the end where she manages not just to escape the killer, but to chase him and decapitate him. While Michael murders Will (Adam Arkin), Laurie manages to hit him with a fire extinguisher on his head and leave him unconscious. She, John and Molly run and get to the car, where Laurie drives to the main exit of the school. While they are ready to flee and escape the risk of the Other, Laurie decides to return and to cope with the threat that is chasing her. Thus, she sends the children away, closes the door of the exit and breaks the mechanism that opens it. Laurie goes inside the school where the final battle takes place between the Other and the Final Survivor. Finally, having stabbed Michael several times, Laurie steals his body to be sure she has killed him once and for all, but he revives, as he has done in all of the films. The film ends with Laurie beheading him.

The framework of activeness and adulthood also promotes non-virginal characteristics, as she has a love affair with Will, and she is not in complete contrast to the victims, since they are also not considered to be "sexual transgressors," as Clover names them. She also systematically consumes alcohol, which in the classical cycle was considered a deadly sin. An example of this is when Laurie is in town to have lunch with Will. When Will goes to the toilet, Laurie drinks the whole glass of wine and orders a second one from the waiter while telling him to rush in order to keep it a secret from Will. Even with Laurie's own response, the narrative states that this act is reprehensible but still does not remove the reward of survival from that character. Of course, within these contradictions with the classical cycle, the maternal figure is back in the spotlight with Normality to promote it. She is not just John's mother, but also a school headmistress, a parent figure that protects many children from the evil that comes.

Through these two film examples, a general observation is being made that in the second cycle of the subgenre the Final Girl matured and within the self-referential Normality, it began to have different interactions with the other semantic elements, while the binary Other/Final Survivor acquired new power relations.

In addition to the evolution of the Final Girl and its incorporation into the new syntax of the self-referential films, the second cycle has seen a large percentage of films that increase the number of Final Survivors in their narratives. A typical example of this is the two famous self-referential franchises, *I Know What You Did Last Summer* and *Urban Legend*. In both film and their sequels, there is not only one Final Survivor, but the semantic element is composed of more than one characters per narrative, with the most characteristic example of the Final Couple. More specifically, there is a Final Couple in *I Know What You Did Last Summer*, while in *Urban Legend* there is a Final Couple plus the guard of the university, an adult woman. The Final Couple is something that emerged during the self-referential cycle, as there were no such characters in the first decades of subgenre's life, but as it will be analyzed in the next chapter, it evolved and perfected in the neoslasher cycle.

In *I Know What You Did Last Summer* we see that the two Final Survivors, Julie and Ray, are a couple. Not only does the convention of virginal characteristics and aversion to sexual acts break, but the Final Survivors themselves come together in an erotic encounter, creating new syntactic rules among both with Normality and the Other. Normality does not regard the sexual behavior of characters as something foreign and reprehensible, so the Other does not punish these acts. So, for the second film cycle, it is not a strange event that an erotic couple fulfills the position of the semantic element of the Final Survivors. This franchise, determined to completely break the classical convention on virginity and punishment of sexual acts, opts for the pair to fulfill the position of the Final Survivors in the second film too that followed the next year.

Within this context, characters that survive have nothing to make them stand out from the other characters murdered by the Other. The narrative framework is part of a teenage community that functions as a nostalgic pastiche of the 1970s and 1980s slasher films, but at the same time, by subtracting the main convention of the classical cycle, the characters of all three semantic elements (Final Survivors, Others and Victims) acquire a more realistic form with specific motives. Many times, as in this film, these motives are simplistic and do not give a three-dimensional representation to the characters. But again, this is a sign of the functionality of the second cycle as a transition between the classical filmic texts and the neoslashers. Regarding the Final Survivor, the self-referential cycle is the intermediate stage between the conservative and loose narrative structures and links of classical films and the strong narrative links that place the focus on trying to find and represent the causes of the creation of evil. Julie and Ray are two characters whose representation has taken steps away from the concrete representation of the 1970s and 1980s, but still varies in the stereotyped range of subgenre's conventions, as it is the product of an intimate conversation between that film with its ancestors.

The representation of Final Survivors in *Urban Legend* does not differ at all. Here, in addition to the Final Couple, which has similar features to Julie and Ray, there is a form of power, Reese Wilson (Loretta Devine), that manages to be a Final Survivor. More generally, in a slasher film, it is not a strange fact for a character that is a symbol of the authority of Normality to survive. In the classical cycle, there are many examples—from Dr. Loomis of *Halloween* to Lt. Donald Thompson (John Saxon) from *A Nightmare on Elm Street*. The main difference with Reese of *Urban Legend* is that in the classical cycle, these forms of power did not cover the semantic element of the Final Survivor, but these characters functioned as representatives of Normality. As we saw in the previous chapter, the characters of the Final Survivors and the victims were almost exclusively covered by adolescent characters, while the adult community was a passive representative of Normality imposing conservative punishments on the younger generation. Reese, however, is part of the self-referential cycle, in which there are no strict age rules, nor a stereotypical and conservative Normality that must be represented by a form of power. Thus, the narrative works in favor of a triadicity in this particular semantic element, with Paul (Jared Leto), Natalie (Alicia Witt), and Reese being the Final Survivors of the film.

Reese, of course, also works as a link between the two films of the franchise, as the only basic character in both narratives, with the exception of Brenda, the Other of the first film, appearing for a short narrative time in the last scene of the second film. More specifically, the two films take place in two different universities and the viewers follow Reese who worked in the first and then moved to the other. So, Reese is a Final Survivor in *Urban Legends: Final Cut* too, together with a Final Couple, but also two other characters who survive in the end.

Through these two examples of the self-referential cycle, we notice that through the increase in the number of Final Survivors per narrative, two more stereotypical conventions of the classical cycle broke: first, erotic behavior and relationships may exist in the Final Survivors, and secondly, in conjunction with the above analyses of Final Women, Final Survivors may be older, but also forms of power, which was not part of the first cycle of the subgenre. Final Survivors are an important element of the narratives of slasher films, and although it began as a semantic element that is expressed and circulated under certain standardized conventions, the self-referential cycle removed it from this context and opened the way for the third cycle, whose syntax redefined the entire subgenre.

The Victims of the Self-Referential Cycle

The victims as a semantic element are an important part of the narrative, as their links to the other semantic elements greatly influence the form of the syntax of any cycle. From the punishment of the classical cycle to the narrative links of the neoslasher cycle, the victims are the ultimate recipients of these syntactic structures, and their death gives meaning in these conventions. The main component of differentiation of the second cycle is self-referentiality, which is impregnated in the syntax through the interconnections around Normality, and thus the expression and interaction of the victims has been differentiated in relation to the classical cycle. More specifically, the victims of the second cycle are characterized by the hyperconsciousness they possess because of the self-referential structure of Normality analyzed above, and in this way they have knowledge of how the narrative operates and the conventions that govern it. So, while trying to avoid old convention, the narrative creates new ones.

While the characters know the conventions that govern the narrative and have survival as their main goal, they try to change the events and overcome the conventions of the classical cycle. Of course, through these acts, they essentially contribute to changing the syntax from the first to the second cycle and to further emerge the self-referential element of their narratives through intertextual references. This, of course, was a natural consequence, since both Normality and the Other are governed by self-referential elements and thus, their connections with the victims are impregnated by this element.

Although the victims begin to differentiate themselves in the self-referential cycle by moving away from sexual punishment, one thing remains the same; the young age. As Wheeler Dixon reports, at the end of the 1990s, many films aimed at young audiences from 13 to 19, with many films belonging to the slasher subgenre.[18] Of the 12 films in this cycle, only three have adult characters: *New Nightmare* (1994), *Bride of Chucky* (1998) and *Scream 3* (2000). Of course, all three films are a continuation of well-known franchises with Final Survivors, whom also existed in previous films. So, since characters who fulfill the position of the Final Survivor have grown, it is logical for the victims to have this age too. But the general rule of the self-referential cycle is that victims are again teenagers and/or young characters.

As we saw in the analysis of Normality of the first *Scream*, this franchise was the most commercial film of the subgenre that place self-referentiality in its core and elicited the production of similar films at that time. The second film of the franchise came just one year after the first, following the main characters that survived. More specifically, the story is set two years after the events of the first film that happened at Woodsboro, and now Sidney and her friend, Randy, are students at Windsor College in Cincinnati. At the same time, Gale's book, referring to Woodsboro's events, has been adapted into a film called *Stab*, and in one screening two students are murdered. Gale goes to the university to cover the event, while Dewey, having learned the facts, goes to visit Sidney. Soon, there are other student murders, with Gale and Dewey discovering that someone is trying to imitate the killings of Woodsboro. In the end, it is revealed that under the mask of Ghostface were Mrs. Loomis (Laurie Metcalf), the mother of Billy, who was the murderer of the first film, with his death as the main motivation for revenge, as well as Mickey (Timothy Olyphant), the new boyfriend of Sidney, who did all this for glory through the media.

The victims are young, as the main set of the events is a university, while self-referentiality is evident in every aspect of the narrative. The boundaries of reality and fiction are even more blurred than the first film, as there is a film inside the film that depicts the events of the first *Scream*. The main victim who fully represents and integrates this self-referential tendency of expression and interaction of this semantic element in narration is Randy. As in the first *Scream* in which he managed to survive, Randy is the basic acquaintance of the narrative structures of the subgenre and tries to change the flow of the story as compared to how it would be under the conventions of the classical cycle. In the second film, he also takes into account the rules that govern a sequel film. Of course, he is murdered amid trying to change the narrative rules as he tries to delay the killer on the phone and find him on the university campus. Although Randy is murdered in the second film, it is worth mentioning that he manages to "turn back" in the third film through a video tape where he warns his friends about the possibility of a trilogy—as it happens— and about the new narrative rules that govern it. Randy is perhaps the only character to appear as a victim in two films of the same franchise, even through this peculiar way.

In this particular filmic text, self-referentiality is at the center of storytelling, and therefore in the choice of the victims, but at the same time retains some structures from the classical cycle, such as young victims, the university as a place of Normality and their choice based on their connections to the Final Girl. The third film of the franchise, however, is a better example of the penetration of self-referentiality into the second cycle.

Scream 3 came four years after the first film, in the year that came the transition from the self-referential to the neoslasher cycle. While self-referentiality has reached a point of decrease in the subgenre, *Scream 3* is an attempt at the extreme expression of the self-referential element in order to differentiate it from the past films, with Claire Perkins observing that the film magnifies even more the self-referential links of trilogy.[19] The story of the third film finds Sidney isolated in an unknown place with only Dewey knowing where she is. While *Stab 3* is filming, someone makes his appearance with Ghostface's mask and starts killing members of the cast of the film. So, Sidney goes to Hollywood to face the murderer, while she learns a lot about her mother's past and death. Shortly before the end, it is revealed that the killer is the director of *Stab 3* and Sidney's half-brother from a rape of her mother, Roman (Scott Foley). Sidney, together with the other two Final Survivors, Dewey and Gale, manages to defeat the Other, and in the end Dewey, after Sidney's help, shoots him in the head.

Self-referentiality is evident in the third film, with humor overcoming the brutal violence that existed in the first two films. The main feature of the intense self-referentiality is the fact that the murders of the victims are made in the shooting of a film based on the events of the first film, with the murderer killing the actors in the same order that they would die in the film. The narrative of a film in another film that was first introduced in the second filmic text of the franchise goes one step further and uses it as the primary justification of the choice of victims in a peculiar Normality that makes the boundaries of reality and fiction even more inconspicuous. An inventive scene that plays with this reality/fiction pattern is when the killer sends a script from a killing scene to his victims, and then follows it literally. There is an extensive revelation and projection of the filmmaking itself, while this technique is used as the main reason for selecting the characters to fulfill the role of the victims.

Of course, as mentioned, due to needs based on the film's own story, *Scream 3* is one of the few examples of the self-referential cycle involving adult characters as victims. The progression of the story, and also the fact that we are watching the same main characters in three films, leads to the fact that the victims have to be adult characters. However, the use of self-referentiality as a stripping of the filmic medium itself has also been used in *Urban Legends: Final Cut*, but retaining the characteristic of young victims.

As it was mentioned before, this film, which also appeared in 2000—the year of transition from the second to the third cycle, revolves around aspiring filmmakers trying to complete their graduation film. One film is about urban legends and one killer begins to kill the film crew according to urban myths. Only from the description of the story we understand that the film has more self-referential elements than the first text of the franchise, as it plays with the film's own conventions. It deals with urban myths, which is the main theme of the franchise, but also incorporates it through a peculiar narrative where we watch a film in which a film about urban myths is made, while the crew is murdered on the basis of urban myths.

As in *Scream 3*, the choice of victims is based on the structure of Normality and its interaction with both the Other and the victims. In the classical cycle, conservatism was at the heart of these syntactic links, and so the murders of the victims were made in accordance with their social behavior. In the self-referential cycle and in these examples, conservatism was replaced by the self-referential relationship of narration with the medium itself. Thus, victims are related to the filmmaking process and their selection is due to this relationship. In the first example, the victims are selected on the basis of their role in the fictional film, *Stab 3*, while in the second example the victims are selected according to their participation in the graduation film that their teacher tries to steal and present as his own.

Even the backstory of the Other helps this self-referential structure of choice of the victims. In *Scream 3*, the Other is the director of *Stab 3*, but also the half-brother of the Final Survivor. This is supported by the dual choice of killing these victims in this order. On the other hand, in *Urban Legends: Final Cut*, the Other is Professor Solomon, who, when he was a student, missed the opportunity to win the prize and is now trying to steal the best film of the year by killing the director and the crew so there are no witnesses.

Through the above case studies, it can be argued that self-referentiality has penetrated into all aspects of the syntax of the second cycle, with an important example of the choice of the victims. This expression can vary widely from film to film and ranges from intertextual references (*Scream 2*) to self-referential structures revealing the medium itself (*Scream 3* and *Urban Legends: Final Cut*), but the fact is that the narrative justification of the choice of victims on the basis of their social behavior is over, thus opening the way for the creation of the third cycle.

An Epilog on the Self-Referential Cycle

At the beginning of the 1990s, there was an intense saturation due to standardized conventions of the classical cycle that the subgenre had already been trying to eliminate since the late 1980s. The answer for the subgenre was self-referentiality. The new period began to move away from the classical conventions of the previous decade and create their own features that gave a fresh look to the entire subgenre. Although the second cycle lasted a shorter time compared to the first and third cycle, it was an important step into this transition between classical films and neoslashers.

The syntax of the second cycle had at its center self-referentiality and intertextuality, often under the veil of parody or pastiche. Maintaining classical structures and conventions from the first cycle that had their focus on conservatism, the self-referential cycle uses parody as the basis of its narratives, thus eliminating classical conventions and creating new structures from the point of view of self-referentiality. Of course, the most important element of the second cycle's syntax is the widespread use of a whodunit structure in the majority of films, the extensive search for the killer's identity until the end of the film. While in the classical cycle the identity and backstory of the Other become known from the very first scene of the filmic text, in the self-referential cycle there is a structure of concealment of the Other and its motives, up to the last sequence of the film. Thus, the whole structure of the narrative revolves around the question of who is the Other and why he kills the victims and chases the Final Survivors.

Of course, the second cycle had seven years of life and it quickly started to decline. At the top–100 American box office, slasher films did not exceed two per year, with the exception of 1998 where there was a production boom with four films, just before the second cycle came to an end. Two thousand is an important year for the subgenre, as there is an overlap between the second and the third film cycle. More specifically, while the self-referential cycle was ending with two films, the neoslasher cycle started with *Final Destination*.

The new syntax of the new millennium not only left behind the whodunit structure of the self-referential cycle, but put the Other and its backstory at the center of the narrative. More specifically, the third cycle took advantage of the self-referential cycle to move away from the loose narrative links of classical texts, giving space to neoslashers for strong narrative structures. Thus, the third cycle is characterized by the emphasis of narration on trying to find the causes of the creation and spread of evil. In simple words, while in the second cycle we had narratives that revolved around the mystery of who is the Other, the neoslashers have the Other at the center of attention—sometimes the narrative focuses more on him than on the Final Survivors.

The self-referential cycle, despite its small duration and its transitional character between the other two cycle, managed to stigmatize the whole subgenre and put new structures on its foundations. Its contribution is so important that many times we can identify self-referential elements that have been established in the subgenre, even in neoslashers. Of course, the syntax of the narratives from 2000 and on has changed radically, and a new cycle has started for the slasher film.

4. The Neoslasher Cycle of Slasher Films

At the turn of the new millennium and after the inactive for the 1999 subgenre, the slasher film began once more to come back to the fore. The year 2000 is characterized by the ending of the self-referential cycle with two films (*Scream 3* and *Urban Legends: Final Cut*), as well as the beginning of the neoslasher cycle with *Final Destination*. After the saturation of the self-referential cycle that functioned as a transition from classical texts to those of the new millennium, the subgenre's syntax began to change once again by creating new connections to the constant semantic elements of these narratives. The neoslasher cycle lasted from 2000 to 2013, and then began the decline of the subgenre and its commercial transfer to another medium: television.

The new subgenre's syntax in the third cycle is characterized by strong narrative structures, by placing the Other at the center of the story and the parallel effort to find the causes of the creation of evil. The backstory of the Other now comes to the forefront and takes a big part of the narrative, by creating a peculiar main character that has a lot of anti-hero features. While previously there was the Final Survivor as the key character of the narrative, in neoslashers this changes as the Other takes the lead of narration. Through this change, there is a widespread use of the cause/effect structure in all the aspects of storytelling, thus creating a stronger narrative relationship between the semantic elements that contrasts with the loose connections of the classical cycle. Hence, the connection of the Other with the Final Survivor, as well as the relations between Normality and the other semantic elements (Other, Final Survivors and victims), is clearly justified and narratively solid. Finally, while in the classical cycle there is a tendency of stereotypical gender representations, in the neoslasher period we see a tendency to represent social structures and classes.

The films selected in this chapter as case studies of the third cycle of the subgenre were made on two criteria: the first criterion is again the commerciality and popularity of these films, but the second criterion is their relation to the classical and self-referential filmic texts which were analyzed in the second and third chapters, as most of the neoslashers are remakes, sequels, or prequels of these films. So, the films to be analyzed below are *Final Destination* (2000), *The Texas Chainsaw Massacre* (2003), *The Texas Chainsaw Massacre: The Beginning* (2006), *Halloween* (2007), *Halloween II* (2009), *A Nightmare on Elm Street* (2010), *Scream 4* (2011), *The Cabin in the Woods* (2012), and *Texas Chainsaw 3D* (2013). These case studies aim to highlight the new structure of the third cycle and to strengthen the theoretical framework of this book.

The Normality of the Neoslasher Cycle

Within the context of changing the syntax in the neoslasher period, Normality changed radically in relation to the previous two cycles. The stereotypical gender representations of the classical period have already begun to be removed during the self-referential cycle, but in the neoslasher cycle are completely obsolete. The new Normality is based on representations of social classes and the emphasis of community structures on the basis of their opposing elements. Normality is built around the informal struggle of social classes and the attempt to prevail against each other.

Having analyzed Normality in the chapter about classical cycle through *Halloween* and *The Texas Chain Saw Massacre*, this subchapter will analyze the neoslasher versions of these franchises to consolidate the great evolution of the syntax around this particular semantic element. Finally, a single neoslasher that does not belong to a famous franchise, *The Cabin in the Woods*, will be analyzed.

The remake of the first *Halloween* film, with a budget of about $15 million, premiered in the United States on the last Friday of August 2007, one day considered by the American studios the last weekend of the summer, and despite the negative reviews, it secured a good box office position with $26 millions in the first three days of its screening. The time when this particular film comes out has many similarities to the period of the original film. Both in the late 1970s and in the mid–2000s, the United States was dominated by a conservatism and a shift into family values. Prior to 2007, the World Trade Center was attacked in 2001, and two wars were started: the war in Afghanistan and the war in Iraq. Terror and fear had spread to America and citizens were not feeling safe in their own environment. The presidency of George W. Bush has dramatically contributed to strengthening this conservatism.

Inside this sociopolitical context, *Halloween* (2007) appears. Although it is a remake of 1978's film, the story is quite different. The film follows the life of Michael Myers (age 10: Daeg Faerch, adult: Tyler Mane) and how he became a serial killer. Up to about the first half of the film, we see the first murders and his hospitalization in the psychiatric clinic, and then in the rest of the film we see Michael returning to Haddonfield to find Laurie (Scout Taylor-Compton). An element that is overwhelming in the film without even being in the original filmic text is the sibling relationship of Michael and Laurie. The narrative of the remake builds on this relationship, aiming at a more compact cause/effect story structure. Thus, although the film is divided into two equal parts, due to this narrative justification, there is a uniformity in its story.

These important differences between the original film and the neoslasher were also commented on by Joe Tompkins, who named the neoslasher as a reboot that is not a perversion of some original property but a discursive opportunity to breathe new life into an established franchise.[1] This new impulse can also be understood through the interpretation of the new neoslasher cycle. In the same manner, there are some statements of Rob Zombie, who states that his film can be compared to the reboot of the Batman film series, *Batman Begins* (2005)—keeps Wayne Manor, holds Batman, holds the suit, maybe keeps Alfred as a butler, but their placement and connections to the narrative completely differ.[2] In other words, it keeps some of the classical elements, but the way they are portrayed is totally different. Zombie talks about some stable semantics that get another expression in his film, accepting the change in syntax in the third cycle compared to the classical syntax used in 1978.

If one studies in depth the two parts of the film in connection with the concept of Normality, he/she will understand that each one represents a different social class that together form a peculiar Normality. The 2007 film begins with the Michael's family (mother, stepfather, big sister and baby) as main characters. The representation of the characters and the spatial structure of the story are structured in such a manner in order to claim that these people belong to the working class. The mother is a stripper, the stepfather is an alcoholic and unemployed, and his sister is provocative. Even the house is stereotypically represented, since it has a lot of damages and is dirty.

In complete contrast, the representations of the characters in the next half of the film are people belonging to the middle class. Their homes, jobs and occupations betray their social class and intensify the differences with the representation of Michael's family in the first half of the filmic text. Their economic freedom is in contradiction with the poverty recorded in the first half. The only link to the working class representation is the return of Michael, who spreads the fear in the middle class community.

So, the film focuses on a battle between the two classes. The middle class community lives the American dream in a utopia at the expense of the working class. But when the working class threatens this dream, the utopia is destroyed and the middle class is suddenly surrendering to the terror that covers real life. Generalizing this observation, we see that the American dream is a utopia that is maintained through the exploitation of the working class. Lastly, it is worth mentioning that the bourgeoisie is completely absent, as this filmic text does not involve any relative representation of character. This huge divide within Normality that separates the characters of the film, but also the two social classes in general, becomes more apparent in the representation of the two main characters, Michael and Laurie, or the Other and the Final Survivor.

Throughout this context, Dr. Loomis (Malcolm McDowell) makes his appearance much earlier and oversees Michael's progress almost throughout his stay at the institution. As mentioned, Dr. Loomis in the first film was Michael's counterweight. In the film of 2007, Michael's character is based on a realistic background and his actions are based on a cause/effect structure. So, Dr. Loomis too has been changed. In the first film, Dr. Loomis has accepted that Michael is the embodiment of evil and simply tries to exterminate him. In the 2007 film, Dr. Loomis tries to help Michael become normal again. He feels responsible for his failure and for this he helps the Haddonfield community and Laurie. In other words, this time, Dr. Loomis acts by personal motivation and not selflessly. He also has negative characteristics, as he exploited the whole story and made money by publishing a book and lecturing. An example of this is the scene where Dr. Loomis asks the police to intervene and Serif Brackett (Brad Dourif) accuses him of certain acts and the commercialization of a tragedy.

There is a general tendency in *Halloween* 2007 to create a cause/effect structure, while the characters become more realistic than the original film. There is no absolute evil or absolute good, and the sociopolitical state of the story is more realistically addressed by accepting possible upgrades and downgrades, which is closely related to the syntactic relationship of Normality with the other semantic elements. Based on this tendency, the connection between the first and the second half of the film is made, as Michael returns to find his little sister, Laurie, a peculiar Final Survivor, best suited to this realistic context established by this particular film through its Normality.

The syntax of the original film strives to introduce a metaphysical hint into a highly realistic environment, while its 2007 syntax abandons this idea and removes the metaphysical elements, both from the stylistic choices of narration and from the story itself. An example of this realism of the filmic text that touches the limits of gore is the representation of blood. While the original film does not shed a single drop of blood in front of the camera, in the 2007 film, the representation of blood is so intense and so realistic that it touches the limits of a splatter. In the rawness of *Halloween* 2007, the audience does not identify with the Other through techniques such as POV shots, but through the story. We follow Michael's steps, see where and how he lives, and then follow him to the institution that remained incumbent. While in the 1978 film, the whole action of the Other until its escape takes place in the first ten minutes; in the remake of 2007 it occupies about the first half of the film.

Bearing the above in mind, we understand that the 2007 neoslasher has nothing to do with the classical slashers built around a Normality of punishing sexual liberation of adolescents. In this particular filmic text, we have a Normality based on the cause/effect binary established through the struggle between the working class and the middle class. Michael, a member of the working class, takes on the role of the Other that disrupts the Normality of the middle class. Even for the first half of the film that the audience identifies with Michael, what we actually see is that Normality tries to conform the Other to its rules through a detention institution. When Michael escapes and there is no attempt to enforce the rules of society, the narrative prompts the viewer to identify with Laurie who, although started as a member of the working class, managed and developed into the social fabric. In the end, Laurie totally takes the lead of the narrative and is proclaimed Final Survivor by killing the Other. If compared with the norms of the classical slasher, the Final Girl succeeds and defeats the Other with immediate effect her violently adulthood. If, however, there is a neoslasher analysis, it is concluded that the middleclass exudes the working class in crime through marginalization and defeats it with the ultimate objective of maintaining the conservative norms governed by the new syntax. Although the two films (1978 and 2007) are based on the same idea and are similarly developed, they show the great evolution made by the subgenre and the comparison of them reveals the new features incorporated in the films of the new millennium.

The remake of *Halloween II* premiered two years after the remake of the first film, in 2009. In the course of these two years, several changes have taken place in the United States of America, as the financial crisis broke out in 2008 and the major recession began. Insecurity and fear became part of the everyday life of the working and middle class. As is logical, even though it is a remake, *Halloween II* has several changes from the original 1981 film.

The story has changed radically. All the events of the 1981 film placed in the hospital are presented as a dream of Laurie that lasts about 25 minutes. The rest of the film is a new story in the light of the changes made to the remake of the first *Halloween*, as the 2009 film is a sequel to it. We follow the lives of the three main characters of the first film, Laurie (Scout Taylor-Compton), Michael (Tyler Mane), and Dr. Loomis and how they manage to leave behind the events that took place in the first film. Laurie tries to leave behind all the injuries, physical and psychological; Michael, though considered dead, lives in a undisclosed area until he returns to Haddonfield;

Dr. Loomis has abused the glory and reputation of events and has made a lot of money.

The remake of 2009 is steeped in classical conventions of the genre, does not embrace sexual punishment, and goes one step further than the first film of 2007, keeping up with the conventions of the cycle it belongs to. The 2009 film puts even more political commentary and represents a battle of social classes in a corrupt society. The Normality of the film is based on the new franchise agenda, leaving behind the representation of gender and sexuality and exploring the representation of classes and social groups.

The 2007 *Halloween*, which is the prequel to this particular film, represents a battle between the two social classes, the middleclass and the working class. In *Halloween II* of 2009 we see a change in the social fabric of Normality. In Haddonfield we do not see any middle-class houses with clean and attentive interiors and exteriors. The entire spatial structure in which the action is placed resembles a working class setting. Even Laurie, who in the first film of 2007 was the main representative of the middle class, is now portrayed as a girl who works in a decadent shop for a living.

Within this setting, the representation of the forms of authority of Normality of the filmic text has changed. Characters representing social powers appear more corrupt, indifferent to the rest of the social fabric. Due to sociopolitical changes, citizens have lost their faith in the forms of power and the institutions of society, which have also been translated into the syntactic links of the Normality of this particular filmic text. This is evident almost from the beginning of the film, where two stretcher-bearers, while carrying Michael's corpse, talk about the corpse of a young teen in conjunction with necrophilic acts. But the biggest example of the filmic text for a corrupt form of power is Dr. Loomis.

In the first films, the character of Dr. Loomis appears as Michael's counterweight, trying to help the society without personal gain. In the 2009 film, he is portrayed as a corrupt man who exploited the pain of people for personal gain. He is the author of a book with the events that took place in the 2007 film, has made a lot of money and has become famous. Moreover, he gives television interviews and has an agent. Of course, if his success is based on the misery of others, the character is possessed of a negative connotation. An example of this is that he is attacked by the father of one of the victims at a promotion of his book.

If we look at Normality in the light of the social fabric of the film as a whole, there is the working class, several members of which derive from the destroyed middleclass, and a representative of the bourgeoisie, Dr. Loomis, who enriches through the misery of the lower strata. This representation does not differ much from the social fabric of the United States of America at the time.

The Final Survivor is a more distinctive three-dimensional character and not just based on her sexual identity. At the same manner is represented the Other too, who is removed from the stereotypical ritual of the "superhuman" and presented as a man among others. Both belong to the working class, which confronts them with the representatives of Normality. In the final sequence of the film, the police have encircled Michael, who holds Laurie captive. Dr. Loomis enters the dark wooden house where the two main characters are. Michael is trying to kill Dr. Loomis. Loomis and the police find the opportunity to shoot him several times and kill him. Dr. Loomis is stabbed down on the ground and we do not know whether he's dead or not. Laurie takes Michael's knife from his body and approaches Dr. Loomis in order to stab him. The police shoot her and Laurie falls dead.

In *Halloween II* of 2009, there is no open ending, a customary convention in the classical cycle, as the main characters are being murdered. The open ending was part of the subgenre in order to leave the feeling that evil is invincible and perpetuated in time. There is no need to do this in the specific text, because there are simply no distinct lines separating good from evil. All the protagonists can be considered as anti-heroes, containing many negative characteristics and placed in the environment of a corrupt Normality. Thus, without an open ending, the viewer remains with the feeling of pessimism and fear that evil, which has entered the foundations of the social fabric, can not be defeated.

Although one is considered a remake of the other, *Halloween II* is different not only in aesthetics but also in its story itself. They are, therefore, a good example of the significant differentiation of the subgenre from the classical cycle to the new millennium and the emergence of neoslashers. The first film of 1981 follows the concrete standard conventions of the classical Normality with sexual punishment being at the forefront of creating a conservative narrative community that promotes the "family values" of American society at the time, while the remake worsens the limits of good and bad based on the cause/effect pattern, creating syntactic links that allow for a controversial Normality.

The *Halloween* film series is considered to be one of the most important of the subgenre and is an excellent example of the shift of the slasher film by changing its syntax. Seeing the first two films and comparing them with their remakes analyzed in the chapter of the classical cycle, we can see the great differences with the neoslashers and how the norms of each cycle are structured. Although they belong to the same subgenre and narrate the same story, the changes made are enormous and are due to the evolution of the syntax.

Having studied a powerful example of the modulation of the syntactic links of Normality with the other semantic elements, the analysis will continue to an extreme expression and interaction of this semantic element through the post-apocalyptic society of *The Texas Chainsaw Massacre*, which will help in the further understanding of Normality.

Twenty-nine years after the first version of *The Texas Chainsaw Massacre*, its remake is coming to the theaters. The film is screened in October 2003, directed by Marcus Nispel and produced by Michael Bay. Of course, the creators of the original filmic text, Tobe Hooper and Kim Henkel, also play an important role as co-producers. The story follows the pattern of the remake rules, as it resembles the narrative of the original, with very few changes, some of which will be discussed below. Of course, as David Manning observes, the remake has better aesthetic and production values, and the image is based on a bloodthirsty tendency towards the gore's aesthetics.[3] Of course, that was the goal of the creators of the film, with Andrew Form, co-producer of Bay, saying that they wanted to go back to the old-fashioned horror, by creating a more stylized, dark and lively film.[4] Finally, the story is set back in the 1970s. Kevin Heffernan comments that the transfer of the story to 2003 with the extensive existence of mobile phones would make isolation between characters impossible.[5]

This particular text appeared in a period of conservatism in American society under the presidency of George W. Bush. The citizens had already experienced real terror through the 9/11 attacks and the war in Afghanistan was under way as part of the War on Terror. Douglas Kellner talks about a large increase in post-apocalyptic films under Bush's presidency because of their allegorical use as a representation of the fears of society, linking this fact to other events that occurred at times when the Republicans served two Presidential terms, such as Reagan's case.[6] The film is set at the beginning of the new millennium, when a wave of remakes of classic horror film and/or new films influenced by older horror films began, with the majority of them coming from the 1970s. Linnie Blake highlights:

> As Iraq becomes Bush's Vietnam and a new generation of civil rights campaigners emerge, a whole new generation of filmmakers have set out to pay homage to their 1970s predecessors in their exploration of the will to social and cultural heterogeneity currently demanded by the War on Terror, as it was earlier demanded by the Vietnam conflict.[7]

Blake refers to horror films such as *Cabin Fever* (2002), *Wrong Turn* (2003), *Wrong Turn 2: Dead End* (2007) and *The Hills Have Eyes* (2006), including the 2003 remake of *The Texas Chainsaw Massacre*.

Bush's presidency was a catalyst for the reappearance of both conservatism in American society and slasher films at the forefront of horror. In this franchise, however, we can identify a substantial difference. The classical version of the first film, as we have seen in the second chapter, does not consist of a narrative centered on the punishment of sexuality, but as it appeared four years before the standard conventions, it has the structure of a post-apocalyptic, capitalist society. This base is an appropriate ground for the third cycle of the subgenre.

The main cause of this recurrence can be considered the form of the Other. In 2003, as in 1974, there was a generalized view that the enemy of the United States had a national identity and was outside the borders (by making attacks inside the country, like 9/11), with these filmic texts calling for vigilance and re-examination of the interior enemy. In addition to this, there is also the view of Kevin Wetmore, who states that, according to a popular primordial representation, the form of people from the American South (rednecks and hillbillies) can be perceived as "city monsters" and as a substitute for terrorists.[8] Blake adds that for films after 9/11, the South was a symbolic analogy with the impersonal threat of Islamic anti-Americanism.[9] This is done, to a certain extent, through the different culture and the state's own treatment of the social classes and their place of residence. There is usually a peaceful invasion of urban people in working class cities, whose inhabitants are represented by the diversity of their Normality, attacking the middle class and killing them until they go into the counter-attack. As Wetmore mentions, there is a clash of cultures between the representations of these two classes,[10] meaning both the separation of the place of origin and the class division itself that pushes them into conflict.

Although the aesthetics of Nispel and Bay's video clips are evident in the film's image, the approach that the filmic text wants to rely on a true story still exists. The first and the last sequence are made as if they were amateurish and their placement, in conjunction with the narrator who analyzes the facts of the story, gives the feeling of a documentary. These two sequences, which give a form of circularity in narrative, are the only ones that come in line with the first text of the franchise. There, of course, the documentary aesthetics are present throughout the narrative and are even found in the aesthetic of the picture, like the 16mm film in which the film was shot.

The narrative retains the sense of a post-apocalyptic era with the cannibalism at its center. An important difference with regard to the first filmic text is that the act of cannibalism is implied and not represented here. Cannibalism exists through Leatherface's actions and the way it manages and behaves in human beings, without any scene representing him or a family member eating human flesh. This shift in the choice of indirect representation is logical, as the forced conservatism "impose" in the 2003 filmic text does not show any specific elements but, through their suspicion, increase the magnitude of the critique of the society in which it was made, creating an allegory between the real society and a post-apocalyptic Normality.

The conservatism of the period is generally reflected in the Normality of the narrative of the 2003 film, and through the representation, a fierce critique is created, with its main recipient being the society itself that sustains the capitalist model of the western world against the inhabitants of the isolated city. Normality is portrayed as the main perpetrator of the creation of the Other through negligence or, sometimes, its clear support. The family and every member of the city depicted in the narrative supports Leatherface to a certain extent and no one tries to prevent his actions. Indeed, these characters are represented by a stereotypical form resulting from their abandonment by society itself.

Even the supreme authority figure, the sheriff, not only does nothing to stop the violence against the middle class visitors to the city, but in his actions, which are part of the diversion and opposed to Normality, he often works as a substitute for the Other and pushes the victims to their punishment. Examples of his behavior are how he reacts to the innocent middle-class visitors, the shootings towards them while they are lying on the ground, and the suspicion of necrophilia, in the scene with the corpse of the girl who committed suicide. Of course, during the film the audience learns that the sheriff belongs to the family of Leatherface, so the representation of diversity and the non-integration into Normality is not surprising. But the choice of narrative to include the sheriff in a cannibalistic family is a harsh critique against the forms of power, and through the conservatism of the narrative comes a free criticism against the sociopolitical system of the time in which the film was produced.

Since the 1970s, the franchise has taken a fiery look at America's political life, driven by the Vietnam War and the Watergate scandal, through the allegory of a post-apocalyptic community influenced by a capitalist system that overcame. With this legacy, the franchise's first neoslasher evolves the post-apocalyptic representation, under the preserve of Bush's conservative presidency. The film is preserved by a conservatism and the promotion of certain character interaction models; however, the narration continues the franchise's tradition of caustic comments. The audience accepted the film, giving it a significant financial success, which led to the second neoslasher of the franchise, which came into theaters just three years later. After that, in 2013, a new neoslasher was added to the Texas Chainsaw franchise.

In the period between 2003 and 2013, there have been several sociopolitical developments both in the United States and abroad. The most significant change was that of the country's presidency, as after Bush's conservative approach, the country was in the hands of the Democrats under the leadership of Barack Obama. In 2009, Obama became the forty-fourth president of the United States and the first African American to hold the highest office of the country. The country seemed to leave behind a conservative period in which fear was an integral part of every citizen. Of course, after the initial optimistic climate, the financial crisis broke out, which began as a national crisis in 2008 culminating in the bankruptcy of Lehman Brothers, but it soon became global. The United States was going through its worst crisis since the Great Depression of the 1930s.[11]

Within this sociopolitical context, *Texas Chainsaw 3D* made its appearance. The film is a sequel to the original story, and the narrative begins exactly where the 1974 film has ended. In the first sequence, we see all the members of the family of Leatherface (Dan Yeager) being punished by the rest of the community, despite the willingness to deliver those responsible to the authorities. The rest of the community burns them alive in their own home while a man from the furious crowd steals a child of the family to raise it with his wife. Then, Heather (Alexandra Daddario), the infant who has grown up, inherits her grandmother's home and returns to the city in which the events of the first film took place together with her two friends and her boyfriend. Her arrival in the city reveals the secrets of her real family, one of which is the conflict with the whole community. This controversy is expressed through the rivalry with another major family of the town, whose representatives are Burt Hartman (Paul Rae), the mayor of the city, and his son, Carl (Scott Eastwood), the policeman of the community. Heather is starting to become familiar with the identity of her real family when she meets Leatherface after he has hunted her and killed her friends. The narrative evolves with the two characters joining forces against the community and the opposing family. The end of the film finds them as winners of the narrative, with Heather deciding to stay permanently there to look after Leatherface.

As its title suggests, the film is created in such a way that viewers see it in three dimensions. Three-dimensional is an increasing trend in recent years, especially in films designed to reach economic success, such as *Avatar* (2009). The three-dimensional technology, however, is quite widespread in the slasher subgenre, as various texts were filmed and/or screened in 3D (*My Bloody Valentine 3D* [2009] and *My Soul to Take* [2010]). An explanation of this trend is that the 3D technology serves better the slasher's essential goal, which is to scare the audience as much as possible. With the use of such technology, there are some partial changes to storytelling and filming aimed at fulfilling this goal. An example in *Texas Chainsaw* is the scene where Leatherface is in the amusement park and chases Heather. There, Carl tries to immobilize Leatherface, who, in order to escape, throws the chainsaw over him. This particular shot is filmed in such a way that the camera is in the same direction as Leatherface and the saw comes essentially to the viewer. If this was done in two-dimensional form, the result would be graphic and stereotypical, but with 3D technology, such aesthetic choice helps enough to increase the sense of fear and horror of viewers.

In addition to technological advancements, innovations in narration are equally important, as we see that this franchise has made important advances in the way in which semantic elements are expressed and/or merged, meaning the syntax of the narrative. In addition, the film is experimenting quite well with the structure of Normality and its expression in narrative, leading to a sophisticated expression model within the neoslasher cycle. While in the 1974 and 2003 films there was a post-apocalyptic society and cannibalism was at the heart of the family, in the film of 2013 this is not the case, since there is no suspicion of cannibalism at all. Through this act, the 2013 film makes an important step away from the trademark of the entire franchise, namely cannibalism, and the post-apocalyptic development of the capitalist system.

This is to a certain extent justified by the sociopolitical situation of the United States when these films were created. The texts of 1974 and 2003 appeared in a society where the main concern of the citizens as a whole was outside the borders of the U.S. (Vietnam in the first case, Afghanistan and Iraq in the second). Regarding the 2013 film, the main concerns were mainly transported inside the borders, with rising unemployment and poverty affecting specific social strata.

Thus, there is the creation of a different Normality with respect to the rest of the franchise and syntactic links that once again turn against the forms of power, promoting their negative representation. In the particular filmic text, we can distinguish three main forms of power that are negatively represented. The first form of power is Sheriff Hooper (Thom Barry), who is negatively represented by his neutrality. In the first sequence, it is he who neither prevents the brutal murder of the family of Leatherface, the Sawyers, nor punishes the culprits. In the last sequence, when Heather and Leatherface murder Mayor Burt, although Hooper is an eyewitness, he does not do anything to prevent it. Narratively, it may be considered to be Sawyers's vindication and the sheriff's redemption of past acts, but if you look at it from the point of view of the representation of a form of power, it once again violates its duties and hence the legal function of Normality, thus taking on a negative tone as a character.

The other two forms of authority are Mayor Burt and his son, Carl, who is a police officer. Unlike the sheriff, we are not talking about two characters who get a negative tone because of neutrality, but two characters that naturally contradict Normality and violate narrative rules. Burt is a member of the team that burned the Sawyer family alive and is the main representative of the counterweight family, those who want to exterminate the latest members of the Sawyer family. His son, even though a minor character, is actively involved in his father's plans, and he is the one who delivers Heather in his hands towards the end of the narrative.

Also worthy of analysis is the element of the Sawyer family that is part of Normality. The film starts with all the members being gathered at home and the majority of them are willing to obey the rules of Normality and hand over Leatherface to the competent authorities. Of course, instead of being "rewarded" for obedience to Normality, they are massively massacred by the community itself. In the rest of the film, the two remaining characters of the family, Heather and Leatherface, are portrayed in such a way that Heather is intended for the role of the Final Survivor and Leatherface for the role of the Other. But the next question is whether, in the end, these narrative aspirations are fulfilled. To answer this question, a third semantic element retains a key role: the victims.

The victims are murdered on the basis of the Normality represented in the narrative. The first victims of the film are the Sawyer family. Since the film itself links itself to the 1974 film, as the first scenes of the film are "borrowed" footage of it, it is a logical consequence of further linking narrative elements. Since in the first film the Sawyers were responsible for several murders, their mass murder requires the implementation of a code that "punishes" offenders of the well-known western civilization system in the event of murder. The same pattern is followed by Leatherface, with his first victim being Darryl (Shaun Sipos), a hitchhiker picked up by the youth group who tries to rob them. Syntactic links of Normality are defined in such a way as to punish those who violate ethical and legal rules of importance, such as murder and theft. However, murders are systematically committed from both sides throughout the narrative. One is Leatherface, the Other who contravenes the rules of Normality, and the other is the representatives of Normality itself, forms of power, such as the mayor and a police officer. In the first chapter, the dual nature of the Other regarding its relation to Normality was documented. Based on the approaches of Lacan and Kristeva, it was argued that there is a conflict but also an indirect expression of Normality in the Other. In this filmic text, although there is still an indirect projection of a collective Ego in the face of the Other, there are also direct expressers of Normality who, through various murders, try to keep it intact.

Summarizing, the following paradox is presented in this particular filmic text: the narrative divides the characters into two groups who, although both trying to enforce the rules of Normality, collide and try to survive by defeating the opposing team. In simple words, the narrative's syntax "breaks" the semantic elements into two groups and is structured in such a way that these groups are permanently in conflict. One group, under the umbrella of the representation of the Sawyer family, consists of two important semantic elements, the Other/Final Survivor binary. The second group is made by the representatives of Normality: Mayor Burt and his family. Thus, the final dipole created in this particular filmic text is that of the two families expressing the confrontation of the main semantic elements and proving that it can lead to significant conflicts and unthinkable social injustices.

Texas Chainsaw 3D has decided to renounce the trademark of its franchise that is cannibalism in a post-apocalyptic society and chose this syntactic structure by confronting its semantic elements. Thus, this film possesses an innovative narrative, both within the franchise itself and in the entire slasher subgenre. It gave up forms that have been tested in a series of similar films, and through its reconstruction and remodeling, created a new allegory of social representation and a peculiar neoslasher Normality. Moreover, the alliance of the Other with the Final Survivor against Normality proves this innovative approach. The representation of two social groups in conflict creates a strong critique of Normality and ultimately of the social system itself. Although the post-apocalyptic pattern is absent, the narrative manages with the new syntax to maintain the franchise's critical eye toward society itself.

The Texas Chainsaw Massacre is a milestone for the slasher film. Besides being the first film of the subgenre, it remains one of the most well-known and important franchises, as well as a remarkable source of inspiration and influence, while it contains a particularity in the representation of Normality, which is also influenced by the sociopolitical situation during the production period of each film.

Another of the most important neoslasher films, the analysis of which enlightens the functionality and interactions of Normality in narrative, is *The Cabin in the Woods*. It was noted that the self-referential cycle was defined by the *New Nightmare*, which gave its aesthetic choices and bases, and *Scream*, which made these bases known to the general public and gave the self-referential horror film the popularity it was looking for. The first one deals with the structure and the representation of terror in general, while the narrative of the latter deals in particular with the structures and classical conventions of slashers, which at that time began to change. *The Cabin in the Woods*, though belonging to the third cycle, has been influenced by the self-referential trend that came to the subgenre in the 1990s and follows New Nightmare's approach as it deals with themes that concern the entire cinematic genre of horror and not necessarily just the slasher film. As Joe Lipsett says, the film is a clear post-commentary on the horror genre.[12] Gerry Canavan talks about a metafictional parody of horror cinema, and of Hollywood more generally.[13] These features belong to the sphere of parody and pastiche, and the self-referentiality itself has also a leading role in the narrative.

The story of the film is as follows: a group of five young characters goes out to a cabin in the woods. At the same time, a mysterious company set up a whole plan for killing young people, which it observes through high-tech systems. Through the actions of the five youngsters, they choose the way they are murdered, which is by a zombie family. During the filmic text, we learn that the whole process is in the context of a sacrifice to the Ancient Ones, and that sacrifices in all other countries have failed in addition to that of the U.S. One after another, the characters are slaughtered, with Dana (Kristen Connolly) and Marty (Fran Kranz) staying alive. In the end, since the American sacrifice fails too, as the two characters survive, the filmic text has a teleological ending, with the old gods reacting and a giant hand coming out of the earth, which implies the destruction of the world.

The general context of the story does not differ much from the general context of the subgenre. Five seemingly stereotypical characters are hunted by some force and murdered one after another. The guys are the constant representations of the subgenre: Curt (Chris Hemsworth) is the alpha male, Jules (Anna Hutchison) the whore, Holden (Jesse Williams) the scholar/nerd, Marty the fool, and Dana the virgin. However, what adds authenticity to the filmic text and separates it from the stereotyped representation of old conventions is the mysterious company and how it affects the outcome of the story of the young people. The representation of Normality and its relation to the Other differs greatly from the rest of the subgenre, as the element of the incarnation of the Other in one or more characters is subtracted. The semantic element is covered by an ideology represented by an entire company.

The Cabin in the Woods begins with a sequence that does not reminisce at all with a slasher film: two high-ranking employees of a big company, Sitterson (Richard Jenkins) and Hadley (Bradley Whitford), are at work, and the audience is starting to learn more about this fictional company. It is based on a hierarchical structure with Sigourney Weaver as the director, and the main annual goal of the company is the completion of a human sacrifice in order to please the old gods and to continue life on the planet.

The Other has a close relationship with the mysterious company and what it represents. Although in the majority of slasher films there are one or more characters embodying the meaning of the Other, in the case of *The Cabin in the Woods* things are complicated. This semantic element is not found in a character, but is represented by a portion of cinematic narrative elements contributing to Normality, which are built around the multinational mysterious company specifications represented by both employees and the director. This component depicts the narrative mechanism of the subgenre and helps to make the dual character of the Other in the neoslashers more understandable. Since we do not have the incarnation of the Other by one or more characters, the concept of a collective Ego becomes part of the narrative, while Kristeva's notion of abject, one's reaction to a threatened collapse under the light of the loss of distinction between one's self and the Other, comes at the first level. A concept like the hierarchical work within the framework of a capitalist system functions at the same time as Normality because of the intimacy of the audience with it, while at the same time it functions as the Other trying to preserve the dominance of Normality through the indirect projection of a Collective Ego.

Of course, there is a risk of misinterpreting the concept of the Other and attributing it to the characters that make up the company, which would be wrong as they are the representatives of Normality. Sitterson and Hadley are simple employees who give no opinion and simply execute the instructions of a company that is represented as an impersonal entity of the narrative. There is a lack of personal and social consciousness and that is why we cannot characterize them as Others. For example, in the initial session, we are following a discussion amongst officials about the future murder of the protagonists of the film. Despite the seriousness of the issue, the discussion is presented in such a way and through a working routine that no one sees these employees as the rival of Normality.

The separation of employees from the actions of the company as a whole contributes also to the cynicism they possess, which is evidenced by the fact that before the five young people "choose" how and by whose hands they will die, the employees bet money. Another example of cynicism is the scene in which they organize parties to celebrate their supposed professional success, while in the depth of the room, through the screens, Dana seems to try to survive the attack of the zombie family.

At this point, it must be made clear that none of the cinematic monsters that appear will cover the position of the Other. These particular monsters, of which the zombie family covers most of the narration, are unconscious beings used as a way of enforcing the acts of the Other. We could compare the monsters with the weapons of the Other in other slasher films, on the grounds that their functionality in narrative is exactly the same. Like Freddy of *A Nightmare on Elm Street* has and uses his blades, so the Other in *The Cabin in the Woods* has these "monsters" as weapons.

We therefore realize that although the element of the Other exists and is preserved, it does not exist as a character, but as a concept coexisting with Normality. The concept of the Other continues to have the same functionality as the subgenre, enforcing the narrative rules through the projection of the collective Ego, while at the same time clashing with the Normality itself. The Other in *The Cabin in the Woods* could be defined as the union of the actions and objectives of the mysterious company, but without being specified and incarnated by characters and/or situations. Even the director of the company could not be classified as Other as its hierarchical position is placed within the proper functioning of the capitalist system and the actions and objectives of the company do not preclude personal gain or pleasure of the specific character.

Of course, the company/Normality, in an effort to keep its "pure" profile as long as possible, enforces its rules by choosing a monster from the long list of horror films over the decades that is the result of the free will of the five characters, but without the option of allowing them to escape. The five characters are forced to go down to the cellar of the cabin and find various objects, each of which is linked to a different "monster." The unconscious choice of an object also activates the release of a monster from the company's premises.

The list of monsters is enormous and forms part of the self-referential narrative experience, as it is a reference to other films of the genre. Michael Starr emphasizes that the film makes references to a myriad of horror films and tries to explore in depth already existing cinematic universes.[14] All of this mechanism adds a self-referential essence, as it unleashes the process of producing horror, while it also has references to the genre itself. Although the monster of the film is determined by the actions of the characters to be the Buckner family, or as referred to by the company, "Zombie Redneck Torture Family," viewers can see several other names and/or monsters in the company list. In the sequence where the Final Couple release the monsters that attack both those and the employees of the company, we observe ghosts, demons, unicorns, and even the clown from *It* (ABC, 1990).

So, the Other in *The Cabin in the Woods* consists of two main elements: the ideology of the company that is the core of Normality, and the actions of the monsters. Although the company is seemingly "pure" and acts in the best interests of the planet within a simple Normality, while the monster is what makes the job "dirty," it does not mean the monsters can be claimed to be the Others of the film. In simple terms, the Other forces situations and enforces the code of Normality through its indirect reflection and projection of the collective Ego, which is in full agreement with the more general theoretical framework that has been defined in the first chapter.

The Other of the Neoslasher Cycle

The expression, placement and interaction of the semantic element of the Other with the rest of the narrative is one of the key points of the syntax of the subgenre, whose evolution and differentiation has contributed drastically to the formation of neoslashers. On the one hand, the Other is now at the forefront of these narratives, creating a peculiar protagonist, while the entire narrative tries to identify the causes of the evil that are contained in the Other. Thus, in the third cycle of the subgenre, this semantic element influences the differentiation of these narratives more significantly compared to the two cycles that preceded it.

An early example of this great change of the syntax around the Other is *Freddy vs. Jason* (2003). The story relates to Freddy's attempt to manipulate Jason to raise fear in Springwood, which will give him back his power to chase and kill innocent victims. There are a lot of self-referential elements in the narrative, which is evidenced by the union of two franchises in a single filmic text, which is due to its influence from the second cycle of the subgenre that had come to an end a few years ago.

Freddy vs. Jason is the only film that merges two famous Others into one narrative. Of course, such a tactic is not a phenomenon for the whole horror genre, as there have been previously such films, like *Frankenstein meets the Wolf Man* (1943). Such a move by a big U.S. film studio is primarily aimed at making profit. Andy Klein in Variety says that it's more of a marketing concept than aesthetic, and problems inherent in both series are only multiplied.[15] The response to these criticisms comes from Russell Schwartz, who was in charge of promoting the film on behalf of the New Line Cinema distributor, who emphasizes that "[the film] worked because it's a brand new series. It's an original movie with name recognition."[16]

Irrespective of production incentives, we must recognize that *Freddy vs. Jason* is the first slasher to unite two emblematic forms of Others in a cinematic narrative and therefore needs analysis. The roots of the film are in two different franchises, so in two different Normalities. By combining two different Normalities, even if they have a common origin based on the classical cycle, the narrative places two different Others with the direct effect of both trying to prevail. So, we have two Others that do not work together and the evolution of the narrative confronts them in a battle that will judge which franchise (and by extension, which Normality) will prevail. The audience never learns the outcome of this battle, as when one seems to prevail, the story takes another turn. In the last shots, Jason (Ken Kirzinger) comes out of the lake with Freddy's head (Robert Englund), but just before the titles appear, Freddy turns to the camera and winks at the viewers, which certifies that he was not defeated.

Of course, besides this extreme example of the association of two famous Others in a filmic text, there are many other films that certify the radical influence of the Other in the syntax of the third cycle and how it was shaped.

A distinctive example of a neoslasher Other comes from the *Halloween* franchise. In the chapter on the classical cycle, there was an analysis of Michael in the filmic texts of the period. In the two films of the franchise in the third cycle, there is a significant change in the syntax that affects this semantic element; a change in the mode of representation of the Other's backstory, giving more ground to the causes of evil. Thus, powerful narrative structures are created that do not resemble anything similar to that of the classical cycle. In particular, in the 2007 film, in the first half of the story we are watching the factors that prompted Michael to become the infamous murderer we all know. Simply put, a shift is made to the realistic justification of the Other's actions, while narration is more closely related to the cause/effect structure.

The 2007 film begins by consolidating the family of the Other. His mother, Deborah (Sheri Moon Zombie), is a stripper, which indicates indirectly the poor financial situation of the whole family. The father figure is Michael's stepfather, Ronnie (William Forsythe), a drunken man who exploits and mistreats Deborah. Michael's sister, Judith (Hanna Hall), treats him rudely by mocking him. A new character, not shown in the first film, is the little baby (later Laurie), which expresses the only positive and innocent aspect of this family.

Within this context of indirect or direct violence, we see the birth of the Other. Michael first kills animals and then passes on to humans. However, every victim of the first half of the film is possessed of such a strong negative tone that the audience fails to empathize. For example, the first victim is a classmate of Michael, who was terrorizing him, mocking his family and practicing physical violence on him. Another element that contrasts with the first filmic text is the way of filming. While in the Halloween of 1978 there were long-lasting POV shots from the perspective of the murderer, a feature incorporated into all the classical cycle films, there are absolutely no POV shots of the Other at *Halloween* in 2007. It could be argued that the addition of a negative tone to the first victims fills the gap of the lack of POVs. With POV shots, the viewer is "forced" to identify with the killer, while in this particular film the narrative itself plays that role. As it was mentioned in the first chapter, POV shots are not a separate element of the narrative and are part of the way of expressing the semantic element of the Other. The different syntax of the 2007 film expresses the element of the Other with different means, removing POV shots and adding more time to the Other, so that the audience identifies with him.

Even the murders of the family members are covered by the aforementioned indirect identification convention. Ronnie is a negative parental model and his sister mocks him, beats him and does not keep the promise to accompany him to Halloween. In addition to them, Michael kills both his sister's boyfriend and a nurse at the institution where he is being hospitalized later. Despite the many murders, the Other is the only leading character up to the first half of the film and so the audience identifies with him.

Based on the realistic depiction, the narrative shows Michael as a child and then an adult of the next door. Therefore, although the mask is present in this film, we see his face for a long time. This removes the most important non-human element of the 1978 film in the first half of the 2007 film, where we are watching the process of evolving into an incarnation of absolute evil. The mask systematically appears when the narration begins to step away from Michael's point of view and is transferred to Laurie. This helps the audience to adapt to the changing point of view of the narrative, while at the same time it has been following all the causes that lead to this change.

Michael of the 2009 film too fulfills this convention. He is portrayed as a simple man and does not remind the character of the original filmic texts.

The beginning of Michael's realistic representation was set in *Halloween* 2007, but the sequel goes one step further. The mask appears minimally and its face is seen several times. The clothes he wears are casual, and we even watch him eat, which reminds us in the simplest way that he is a man and not a supernatural being. We see that in this film there is a shift from the emphasis on the elements of the Horror of the Demonic to the projection of a narrative that has the basis of the Horror of Personality. Finally, the element that differentiates him from the conventions of the classical cycle is that there is no rupture with the Final Survivor, because Normality itself, in the form of the police, defeats him and kills him. Although the Other applies the rules of Normality and thus maintains its structure, it still holds on to its autonomy by being a separate element that is not part of Normality. The narrative of 2009 demonstrates this fact, as these two autonomous elements are in conflict, with Normality to finally win.

This differentiation of the above films is not accidental and its explanation lies in the significant change that happened to the subgenre from the classical to the neoslasher cycle. During the third cycle of slasher films, there is a tendency to trace the causes of evil and to represent the gradual transformation of a person who could fit smoothly into society into an Other. At the same time, the syntax tries to elicit the empathy of viewers with regard to the Other. Consequently, the neoslasher of the 21st century represents corrupt societies, which are pushing people of the next door to transform into "monsters." This is also what the neoslashers' themes address, which helps the narrative to develop and shed light on the aspects of the appearance and spread of evil.

Other representative examples that emphasize the justification of creating evil in society and the birth of the Other as a symbolic form are *The Texas Chainsaw Massacre* (2003), *Friday the 13th* (2009), *A Nightmare on Elm Street* (2010) and *Texas Chainsaw 3D* (2013). Being part of a big and famous franchise of the subgenre, the Others of their narratives are known to the general public and thus, there is greater flexibility for the filmmakers to experiment in relation to their representation and the creation of a backstory, as the audience already knows their acts from previous films.

Another well-known example of modulation of the syntax around the Other is the prequel of *The Texas Chainsaw Massacre* of 2006, where the story is about what happened before the events of the original film. This film was directed by Jonathan Liebesman, who was familiar with the horror genre, having directed *Darkness Falls* (2003) three years before. The film's story is about Leatherface's past and the reasons that led him to murder and cannibalism. The film starts with the birth of Leatherface in an animal slaughterhouse in 1939, his subsequent adoption by the family and their evolution into cannibals, by transferring their knowledge of meat to humans. Then, we see the story of a group of youngsters in 1969: two brothers, Eric (Matt Bomer) and Dean (Taylor Handley), and their girlfriends. Eric is a soldier in the Vietnam War and tries to persuade Dean to follow him, which he is trying to avoid. The trip made by the group concerns the transfer of the boys to Vietnam, until of course Leatherface and his family arrive. The group of young people is murdered and in the end no one survives, a rare event for a slasher film.

By studying the story of the film, we realize the great change that occurs in the filmic text in relation to the classical cycle, as the narrative directs itself entirely to the Other, studying the causes of the evil itself and attempting to elicit the full empathy of the audience, as happened in *Halloween*. According to Andrew Patrick Nelson, this is no surprise to the subgenre (always speaking for the third cycle), as there has been a similar shift in other neoslasher films.[17] Of course, *The Texas Chainsaw Massacre* is an innovation because it puts the life and deeds of the Other at the forefront of film's narration. Such a move promotes the view of breaking the limits of good and evil, arguing that every act is created by the system of values of the society in question. In an America where enormous efforts have been made to curb public opinion by creating stereotypical features of evil and terrorists based on their place of origin and/or religion, such an approach, always under the veil of the post-apocalyptic society, is considered to be quite innovative in its implementation. The narrative of this film promotes a view that, regardless of origin, religion and social class, evil can only occur through the situations that excite a part of society to be cut off from Normality and through the diversity that will be created, the Other will be born.

A confirmation of the above argument is the way in which Leatherface came to the family of the cannibals and became the bloodthirsty killer we learned about from previous filmic texts. At the beginning of the film, we see a female working class member working in the slaughterhouse with an obnoxious boss, who does not respect the state of her advanced pregnancy. The woman prematurely spawns the infant, which will develop into Leatherface, but, due to its deformed appearance, the boss throws the infant in the trash. A woman finds it as she seeks food in the trash and takes it under her protection. Thirty years later, we see Leatherface working in the same slaughterhouse the last day before his final closure, with the same shameful boss.

In the twelfth minute we have the first victim of Leatherface, who is the boss. The narrative justifies the act of the Other with events that reach his birth. The first victim abused his biological mother, became the cause of him going to a foster family, and fired him with acts and expressions that hinted at his inferiority, exiling him to further poverty. Consequently, the audience does not identify with the pain and fear of the victim, but basically sympathizes with Leatherface, demonstrating once again the great importance of the concept of empathy, which assists in the emotional union with the Other.

Even the way the family ends up in cannibalism is justified similarly to the aforementioned example. A family of three adults decides to adopt an infant found in the trash. The slaughterhouse, a unique source of income for the family, but also an economic symbol for the entire city, is closing down, turning the family and the citizens of the region into poverty and misery. As a result, the family is forced into cannibalism for survival reasons. None of them have enough to eat and thus they practice their previous profession on human meat. Viewers, under normal circumstances, would be disgusted with such acts. The narrative, however, fully justifies the flow of the choices of the fictional family. And let us not forget, of course, that it is these same people who saved an innocent (at that moment) infant from a certain death, which gives a positive essence to their representation.

The Normality of this film is set on the foundations of diversity. The reasons for the creation of evil are mostly social and class, with the bourgeois class exhorting the workers into a post-apocalyptic reality, which even involves eating human beings. Normality is slowly being built on a diversity that is born under social injustices, such as poverty and high unemployment. Through justified creation of diversity, Normality acquires a hint of post-apocalyptic environment, which is not present from the beginning of the narrative. Of course, this condition also comes from the fact that the 2006 film is a prequel, and even its title, which contains the word "Beginning," predisposes it.

Thus, there is an affinity, both literally and metaphorically, between the Other and the Normality. The Other/Leatherface is part of the social fabric. He works (at least until his dismissal), meaning that he is a productive member of the community and a member of a family that faithfully obeys its rules, which is also the basis of the post-apocalyptic Normality of the text.

This neoslasher is another instance of trying to locate the roots of evil and the causes of its occurrence. Its narrative states indirectly that the culprit for the actions of the Other is not the individual person/character, but the rules of the community and by extension of Normality, which extorts the characters into criminal acts, recalling the projection of a collective Ego by the Other. This particular film deals with issues of injustice of characters belonging to low social strata, unreliability of forms of power, while creating a sense of impunity and the inability of the system to impose its own rules. Of course, all this happens again in a dystopian environment, which is born through a dysfunctional society in crisis, as is the case in *Halloween*.

Finally, an extreme around the syntax that influences the Other is *Scream 4*, the latest film of one of the most well-known franchises of the subgenre, which helped spread the self-referential element in the slasher film narratives. Each film of this franchise helped the subgenre to evolve into a variety of areas, which boosted its popularity and commerciality.

The story is about Sidney (Neve Campbell), the protagonist of the entire franchise, who is returning to her city as part of the promotion of her book and meets with her relatives and friends, among them her niece, Jill (Emma Roberts). There, a murderer with the familiar Ghostface mask repels and murders young members of the community. In the end, it is revealed that behind this is Jill, aiming to gain personal reputation and glory. The roles of the characters are completely distinct, with Sidney playing the role of Final Survivor and Jill of the Other. However, with a second look at the narrative structure, things are complicated enough and the semantic elements, with an emphasis on the Final Survivor, are not clearly separated.

The narrative begins and all the events suggest that Jill is destined for the role of the Final Survivor, having the stereotypical characteristics of the Final Girl of the classical cycle: a teenager that is possessed of virginal characteristics and is characterized by intense ingenuity. Of course, the "Other-y" Final Girl is helped by a minor character, acting as the catalyst of the Other, Charlie (Rory Culkin). This character helps to keep the identity of the Other as a secret up to the critical point of revelation in the narrative, by giving an alibi to the real Other. Finally, Jill manipulates Charlie through an erotic relationship, which contrasts with her virginal representation that preceded the narrative.

Finally, it is also noteworthy that there is a distinct character that covers the position of the Final Survivor and does not merge with the semantic element of the Other into one person. In *Scream 4* we have Jill as the Other, reminiscent of the stereotypical form of the Final Girl, but the Final Survivor of the narrative is Sidney, the constant survivor of the entire franchise. Sidney is the rival awe of the Other in the filmic text, thus keeping the narrative balances of the syntax of the subgenre.

Comparing Jill with Sidney (and especially on the first *Scream*), we see that the first is the alter ego of the second and/or a "new version" of her. Both are high school students, with several friends and a "bad" boyfriend, who contributes negatively to their lives. Their difference is in their representation. Sidney's first *Scream* had the role of the Final Survivor, while Jill played the role of the Other. In addition, Sidney had an aversion to publicity, while Jill even sacrifices human lives to become famous. As she says: "sick is the new sane." Sidney and Jill's contradictory views on publicity are summarized in Sidney's quote when Jill asks how she can manage such publicity: "I try not to think about me. I have people I care about. I focus on them." This is exactly the opposite of Jill's words, saying, "I don't need friends. I need fans. Don't you get it? … You had your 15 minutes, now I want mine!"

However, regardless of the substantial difference in the use of the two semantic elements in the narrative syntax, the use of this technique yields the same results as the above case studies. In *Scream 4*, the representation and positioning of the Other in the narrative serves the generalized effort of neoslashers to identify and outline the causes of the birth and spread of evil. Jill murders her friends one after another with the aim of fame. Her aim is to create all this traumatic scenery and to become the only survivor, hoping in this way to gain the reputation she seeks. The narrative has a predisposition to the 15 minutes of fame culture culminating in revealing the real Other, Jill, and confessing to Sidney her true purposes. Eventually, viewers follow an outline of the development of this culture, which is portrayed as the root of evil.

Scream 4 is an important example of the allegory made by the representation of the Other in the third cycle of the subgenre. Although it is an exception to the neoslashers syntactic rule, it helps to better understand the functional purpose of the particular semantic element, which is the effort to find the causes of evil.

The Final Survivors of the Neoslasher Cycle

The third cycle of the subgenre brought significant changes to the expression and positioning in the narrative of the semantic element of the Final Survivors. While in the classical cycle it was dominated by the Final Girl archetype, the self-referential cycle brought an increase in the number of survivors, to get to the neoslashers cycle, where we see a greater diversity of expression of this element. There are Final Girls, but with other features compared to classical films, Final Boys, or even Final Couples.

The diversity of expression of Final Survivors during the neoslasher period has two main aspects: the release from the stereotyped gender rules of the main characters, and the possibility of increasing the number of characters that will embody this semantic element in a narrative. From the analysis of the following examples we can see that there is a wide range of expression, but always under the rules set in the syntax of the third cycle.

There are several examples showing the change of Final Girls in the third cycle of the subgenre. One of these is Erin (Jessica Biel) from *The Texas Chainsaw Massacre* (2003), which falls into the theory of Clover with the only difference being not having virginal features. This is to some extent expected since the Normality of neoslashers is absent from sexual punishment. Erin does not smoke, she's against drugs, and she cares for the good of others, while her activeness promotes the progress of the narration. It is a sophisticated version of the Final Girl that goes hand in hand with the representations of the third wave of feminism, away from sexual and gender stereotypes and, on the other hand, obeys the new syntax of the third cycle.

In almost all cases, the Final Survivor is called to kill the Other with the ultimate goal of survival. In *The Texas Chainsaw Massacre* in 2003, this is not true as Erin is asked to kill twice but not Leatherface. The second murder committed by Erin concerns the sheriff. Erin saves a baby from the family—with the maternity instinct coming into the foreground by exaggerating the characteristics of the Final Girl—and then escaping with his car. Even though she can run away without killing him, she hits the sheriff with the car three times and then fades away. This seems normal to viewers because, although it is not the Other of the narrative, the sheriff did not agree with Normality and promoted a diversity that conflicts with western culture.

The first murder, however, has a greater narrative value, since it is one of the few times that in a slasher film a Final Survivor is called to kill a friend. Andy (Mike Vogel), being heavily injured by Leatherface, asks Erin to stop his pain, and Erin, though with difficulty, kills him. In all the aspects of the narrative, there is the post-apocalyptic reality of another society, which, although it looks so alien, is essentially an allegory of the period the film was produced.

The *Halloween* of 2007, too, features an advanced form of Final Girl covering the semantic element of the Final Survivor. The characters that survive are two, Laurie (Scout Taylor-Compton) and Annie (Danielle Harris). Taking into account that Annie is a secondary character, we can designate Laurie as the Final Survivor despite the fact that she is not the only one who survives.

Laurie lives in a middle-class environment, with her family being present and without any major problems. This part of Normality is disturbed by the Other. Laurie is not portrayed as the virgin among "sinful" teenagers. All the youngsters in the film are portrayed as socially acceptable without emphasizing extreme behaviors. Of course, there is a lot of goodness about Laurie, and that's when her friends in a scene call her "Mother Teresa." Finally, Laurie is not asexual and although she does not have a boyfriend, she seems to be interested in finding one.

Contrary to the original film, Laurie does not have masculine features and does not have activeness. Of course, the end of the film slightly changes this rationale, as the Laurie of the original film managed to stay alive with the help of a male character, while neoslasher Laurie is forced to act alone. In the 1978 film, Dr. Loomis saves Laurie and forces Michael to escape by shooting him. In 2007, the action continues after this incident as Michael injures Dr. Loomis and Laurie is left alone. The film ends with Laurie covered in blood, holding a gun over the unconscious Michael, aiming it at his head. Playing a peculiar type of Russian roulette, she continuously pulls the trigger until she finds a bullet and shoots him. The last scene ends with the Final Survivor shooting the Other in the head and then screaming and crying. Upon analysis of the Normality of the film, it is clear that the whole course of Laurie's character shows a sharp maturation by landing in another world, within the working class and in the light of the extreme contracts of horror films.

The neoslasher's originality in this franchise in its approach to the Final Survivor continues in the second remake, creating an even more extreme condition. In 2007 *Halloween* two girls survive, but in its sequel, *Halloween II* (2009), no character survives in the end. In the final sequence, Michael and Laurie are killed by the police's gunfire while they are trying to save the unconscious Dr. Loomis.

In any filmic text, it would be strange for the main characters to die. In the case of a slasher, it becomes even more bizarre, since such an act destroys the public's expectation regarding the Final Survivor of the narrative. Of course, this is because of the new syntax of the neoslashers. In the classical cycle, there was the structure "The Final Girl beats the Other"–"The Final Girl Survives." The *Halloween II* neoslasher does not adhere to this structure, as the police kill both characters, thus turning into a hostile Normality.

Halloween II is not the only neoslasher whose narration does not allow the Final Survivor to stay alive until the end of the film. Another is *The Texas Chainsaw Massacre: The Beginning* (2006). Along with the storyline of the cannibalistic family and how Leatherface became the Other we all know, there is the story of four young people who are moving toward the two boys' departure for the Vietnam War. The film keeps the pattern of a group of young people traveling across the country and getting confronted with terror, but there is a big difference in the cause of their journey. While in the previous filmic texts of the franchise, the trip of the young people was usually for leisure, in this film the opposite is true. There is a controversy between the two brothers about an external danger (the war outside the borders) and, without waiting, they fall into a larger threat inside the country.

When the two storylines merge and the cannibalistic family meets the group of young people, the narrative faithfully follows the rules of the subgenre with the victims being murdered one after another. What differentiates this particular text is that all young people are murdered and there are no Final Survivors. Though in the end, some elements create expectations for the audience that Chrissie (Jordana Brewster) will be the Final Girl as she enters a car and drives away, just minutes before the ending titles; these expectations dissolve unexpectedly as Leatherface appears suddenly in the back seat and kills the last member of the group of young people. In the last shot, there is Leatherface, the winner of the narrative walking on the street with the chainsaw in hand, returning home. This end breaks the expectations of one of the most well-known semantic elements of the subgenre and dissolves the dynamics of the Other/Final Survival. The film leaves the audience with the feeling that evil has roots that reach deep into the foundations of the social system and are often not punished.

In addition to the variation of the classical Final Girl and the removal of its basic feature of survival, there is also a third stream of representation that began with the self-referential cycle—that of the transformation into a Final Woman. One such example is Sidney from *Scream 4*, portrayed as an adult Final Girl, or a Final Woman, more bold and free from fear than ever before. It is one of the first times that we are watching a Final Girl become a Final Woman through the development of a franchise of the subgenre. Another example is Laurie who decides to face the killer in *Halloween H20: 20 Years Later* (1998) despite having the chance to leave. But four years later, Michael kills Laurie in *Halloween: Resurrection* (2002), punishing her for her past actions. Sidney is one of the finest Final Women of the subgenre who does not run away to survive, like the majority of the Final Survivors, but chases the killer herself at risk with her life to help her fellow friends. When Olivia (Marielle Jaffe) is murdered, Sidney is at home and sees the events from the window. Other Final Survivors (and especially Final Girls of the classical cycle) would have shouted and would try to call the police. Sidney, however, runs towards them and faces the murderer.

Typically, the only fixed element of a franchise of a slasher is the Other. Victims and Final Survivors are created for each individual filmic text, but the killer survives and continues to exist into the franchise. This is shattered in the *Scream* franchise, since the Final Survivor is the fixed element. Sidney is a character that we follow from adolescence to adult life, or, from Final Girl to Final Woman.

Through these representations, we observe that the female characters cover the semantic element of the Final Survivor in several narratives, with a significant differentiation from the classical cycle. While at the beginning of the subgenre Final Girls had virginal features to contrast with other sexually active characters, the syntax change allows narrative diversity—from eradication of gender stereotypes to downplaying survival expectations. Here, there is also the emergence of Final Boys in the neoslasher narratives, far from gender-standard agendas.

Removing from the narrative agenda the sexual punishment and thus the non-necessity of rewarding the virginal characteristics of the Final Survivor has also brought significant changes in the dynamics of the gender identity of that character. The syntax of narratives no longer requires the Final Survivor to be a female character, and filmic texts often do not maintain this classical convention. In the third cycle, a few narrations appeared with male characters in the role of the Final Survivor, creating a kind of Final Boy.

There are also few classical texts that have male characters that survive in the end, such as *Jason Lives: Friday the 13th Part VI* (1986) and *A Nightmare on Elm Street Part 2: Freddy's Revenge* (1985), but these are individual incidents during the saturation of the classical cycle, without systematic reproduction and with representations that have a stereotypical complexion based on the syntax of that period. Neoslashers, on the other hand, radically adapt the narratives to the requirements of the third cycle.

A basic example that worked as a turning point in the gender identity of the Final Survivors is *Final Destination* (2000), an early slasher of the third cycle, which, with its structure, removed the subgenre from the self-referential structure of the second cycle. The story is about Alex (Devon Sawa), a high school student who, while he is on an airplane to Paris during a school trip, has a vision that the plane will blow up in the air. Being in fear, he causes panic, which leads him and another six out of the flight. These seven characters are witnesses to the explosion of the plane and the death of all passengers. Then, the characters begin to die one after another, with Alex claiming that death has a plan to take them in the order they would have died on the plane. Thus, the narrative focuses on Alex's efforts to confront and defeat death.

It should be noted that this particular film belongs to the slasher film, although it follows a peculiar pattern. Even though the Other adapts a strange form and does not appear on the screen as it is not material, it chases unsuspecting victims who are trying to escape from it. Normality is based on the assumption that death has a pattern and you cannot fool him, so the community of the narrative is built, with the Other/Death, the group of victims (the seven characters that get off the plane in time), and the Final Survivor/ Alex.

In the last set, we see Alex, Clear (Ali Larter) and Carter (Kerr Smith) seemingly out of the danger of the Other. However, through one last narrative surprise, the Other "appears" again and jeopardizes the group of young people, with the last frames of the film indicating the death of Carter. The narrative has an open ending that leaves two characters alive. It is not, however, both Final Survivors, because only Alex is in conflict with the Other. Alex perceives the danger before it even appears, saving at the same time—even temporarily—the lives of the remaining six characters, decoding the pattern of "murders" and trying to change it and defeat the Other. Clear simply faithfully follows Alex and never comes into conflict with the Other.

Alex is one of the first complete Finals Boys whose representation has stepped away from the stereotypical and conventional norms. It is not the pure personification of good that used to be the classical Final Girls, as the narrative suspects that he may be responsible for the events. Two FBI agents are investigating the case of the airplane's explosion and the subsequent strange deaths of some of the victims, with Alex being the number one suspect. Naturally, viewers doubt the momentum of their intentions and motives, leaving the moral side of the Final Survivor untouched. Besides that, the film belongs to one of the very early stages of the neoslasher cycle, and the syntax is not fully crystallized around the shift towards a justification of the birth of evil and inconspicuous boundaries between good and evil.

Final Destination was followed by four other films, creating a powerful and influential franchise of the horror genre. In the slasher film genre it was considered innovative, not only for the extreme condition of death itself being the Other of the narrative, but also for deciding to break the convention of a female character that lived and to introduce a Final Boy that is not reminiscent of the previous, stereotypical attempts of the subgenre. This particular Final Boy is not consumed in gendered agendas, but through the paranormal complexion of the narrative, it is represented as a three-dimensional character. After Alex from *Final Destination* other male Final Survivors followed, enriching the range of the term and creating a remarkable second pole that contrasts with the Final Girl.

Some films combine the two archetypes and create a Final Couple. Final Couples usually consist of a Final Girl and a Final Boy and their relationship can range from siblings to erotic. Here are two examples of Final Couples to make their functionality clear: the remakes of *Friday the 13th* (2009) and *A Nightmare on Elm Street* (2010). Remakes of the well-known classical films adapt to the new millennium rules and follow the trends of the neoslasher cycle. Both adopt the Final Couple model, with significant effects on the syntax, as it breaks the Other/Final Survivor binary and creates new dynamic relationships between the characters and, by extension, the semantic elements.

In 2009, the first remake of *Friday the 13th* appears. The story is about the disappearance of Whitney (Amanda Righetti) and her search by her brother, Clay (Jared Padalecki). Whitney has been kidnapped by Jason (Derek Mears), following the mass murder of her friends and boyfriend. During the search, Clay is acquainted with a group of youngsters. In the end, the two brothers, as the only survivors, join forces and successfully face Jason. The last scene is a reference to the 1980 film, with Jason (an adult this time) fleeing from the waters of the lake and grabbing Whitney. The film, with a budget of $19 million, was a commercial success by making $42.2 million profit during the first weekend of screenings. As Justin Strawser points out, despite the fact that almost three decades have passed, the franchise has remained popular with the loyal audience of the subgenre.[18]

The remake was directed by Marcus Nispel and produced by Michael Bay. The duo is not unknown in the neoslasher cycle, as they collaborated in *The Texas Chainsaw Massacre* (2003), a film that laid the groundwork for several third-cycle film conventions. In his critique of *Friday the 13th*, Kent Wolgamott finds quite common elements between the two neoslashers that Nispel directed, such as gore images and nudity.[19] Bay was also the producer of *The Texas Chainsaw Massacre: The Beginning* (2006).

With a first comparison of the story with the classical 1980 film, we find that it is not completely faithful. In fact, although it was named and promoted as the remake of the first film, its narrative is a patchwork of stories from the first three films (1980, 1981 and 1982). The first sequence of the remake is the final part of the 1980 text, with Mrs. Voorhees (Nana Visitor) to be beheaded by the stereotypical Final Girl. Then, the story is divided into two parts; the first consists of Whitney's story, the murder of her friends and how she is a prisoner of Jason, and the second part consists of the story of Clay and the attempt to find his lost sister. In the first part, Jason first appears without the notorious mask, a convention borrowed from the second classical text of 1981. During the second part, he finds the hockey mask that is part of his appearance. The most important difference between the 1980 film and its remake is the change of the person embodying the Other. In the first film the Other was Mrs. Voorhees, while in the remake we have Jason. The choice was made for obvious reasons, as the franchise has been linked to Jason's appearance and could not become a new film without him.

Before moving on to the most important element of innovation in the 2009 film, namely the division of the semantic element of the Final Survivor and its two-character embodiment, an analysis of Normality and of the representation of society will first be made. Normality agrees with the bases of previous neoslashers, with the main feature of inhospitable society. Characters, such as the old woman who does not intend to help with Clay's research, the vendor who does not hang the disappearance brochure in the shop, but also the warehouse employee trying to sell weed to Clay, make up the mosaic of a society in a crisis of institutions and ethics, which is expressed through xenophobia and an inhospitable attitude towards non-members.

Within this Normality, the logical consequence is to change the representation of the forms of power, embodied in the face of Officer Bracke (Richard Burgi). While in the first film of the franchise, the police were represented as active but not able to stop the spread of evil in the community, in the 2009 remake they are almost non-existent. Bracke is the only one to represent the police and he only appears twice during the entire film. In his first appearance he is reluctant to help Clay in his investigations, while in the second he is almost murdered by Jason. Normality is formulated to give more insight into the negative characteristics, such as individualism, indifference and xenophobia, which prevail in this fictional society. The main representative of this decline is the Other, who persecutes and kills the victims of the narrative.

The representation of the Other differs from the classical cycle and comes into line with the way that previous neoslashers have handled this semantic element. As in *Halloween* and *The Texas Chainsaw Massacre*, in the case of *Friday the 13th* there is a tendency to justify the cause of the birth and progression of evil. More specifically, Jason is represented as a character trying to take revenge for his mother. Having watched the events that led Jason to become the current, bloodthirsty killer, a three-dimensional portrait is created. Taking into account Whitney's storyline of being kidnapped because she looks like his mother, the character also acquires a human side, a fact rare for a slasher film that does not belong to the third cycle.

The Other-Final Survivor binary breaks, as the film creates three poles: the Other, the Final Girl and the Final Boy. The two Final Survivors are siblings. If we also take into account Mrs. Voorhees, we conclude that the narrative maintains a harmony between evil and good. On the one hand, we have a family that promotes violence and, on the other, another family that tries to defuse and restrict it. Taking families as allegories of a society, we notice that the family that is a member of Normality embraces the principles of the dominant decay, as opposed to the Final Couple, which is a family coming from a different, "civilized" community.

The Final Couple consists of two characters, Whitney and Clay. If studied separately, it will be found that they share quite a lot in common regarding their character, but also their social behavior. Whitney is structured on the stereotypical characteristics of the Final Girl. Although she has a boyfriend, she does not express her sexual urges; she is modest and cares for her family and her sick mother. These attributes are also associated with the fact that Jason likens her to his mother and therefore does not murder her. Whitney is the embodiment of the Final Girl theory, as it is portrayed as a virginal and maternal figure. But the element that is very much different from the characters of the 1980 film is that Whitney is mainly passive and she does not help in the narrative development. Clover's theory asserts a female character who, through her activeness, will be able to defeat the Other, which is not the case in *Friday the 13th*.

The character who has the active role of the narrative is Clay, the other half of the Final Couple. If we exclude his gender, Clay is closer to Clover's theory, because he is the one who is chasing the Other, and also possesses the features mentioned above, such as family affection, because he is trying to find his lost sister, and has no sexual impulses, although he is given the opportunity with Jenna (Danielle Panabaker). The narrative gives Clay features that have been combined with a representation of female characters and have been incorporated into Clover's theory. If we look at the two characters as one semantic element, we find that they are the ideal Final Survivor, which helps in the progression of the narrative and at the same time is the opposite awe of the Other, as well as the rest of the victims. Finally, the characters of the Final Couple are in harmony with the general representation, resulting a three-dimensional and not stereotypical appearance.

As the end of the film is approaching, Whitney takes on a more active role without, however, negating her passiveness. Although Clay inactivates the Other, Whitney is the one who murders him through a peculiar vindication of her character. However, this is temporary, because the film leaves an open ending where Jason returns and attacks.

Friday the 13th of 2009 is a dynamic restart of the franchise through the conventions of neoslashers. It follows the new trends, such as the presentation of evil from birth to the evolution and spread of it, but it puts two characters in place of the semantic element of the Final Survivor. The main feature of the Final Couple's expression is the emphasis on family ties, but also the effort to differentiate it from the other characters. The narrative achieves its goals, by creating a peculiar triangle of three poles consisting of the characters of the Final Couple and the Other. Of course, the choice of the family as the ultimate means of expressing the Final Couple is not the only option and an example that is differentiated is the neoslasher version of *A Nightmare on Elm Street*.

After a break of about seven years, the paranormal franchise of the slasher film comes back with a remake of the first classical film, directed by Samuel Bayer. This remake follows to a certain extent the events of the classical filmic text, with some scenes resembling those of 1984, while there are several storylines that are original elements of the new narrative. Thus, the 2010 filmic text succeeds in distinguishing and conciliating with many innovative elements. One year after the remake of *Friday the 13th*, *A Nightmare on Elm Street*'s narrative follows the model of the Final Couple, yet removing the family background and adding an erotic tone to the interpersonal relationship of the two characters.

The narrative of the film, like the remake of *Friday the 13th*, follows the motif established in the third cycle. There are scenes of violence with the gore component dominating and the main element of Normality is the decay and decline of its members in their behavior towards social structures. The main example is the parents' abusive behavior towards Freddy. Moreover, in this remake, the representation of police and social forms of power is almost non-existent.

The position of the Other belongs again to Freddy Krueger (Jackie Earle Haley). Its features, however, have been modeled to fit smoothly into the new Normality. There is, therefore, a strong gore element in his behavior, but also in the way he kills the victims. While in the first film of the franchise, Freddy was quite talkative, making fun and "playing" with his victims, in the 2010 film, his behavior has become darker. This becomes known to the viewers from the first murder, in which we see Dean's neck (Kellan Lutz) being massacred in a violent way in front of the customers of a diner. Another example is when Freddy kills Jesse (Thomas Dekker) and hangs him from his legs, saying, "Did you know that after the heart stops beating, the brain can function for well over seven minutes? We got six more minutes to play." Such a phrase proves that the Other does not just kill and proceed to the next victim, something common in the classical and self-referential cycles, but possesses sadistic feelings that they express through the torture of the victims, even if they are virtually dead.

Finally, in this neoslasher film too there is a tendency to justify evil and add a human side to the Other, but to a much lesser extent than the rest of the films of the third cycle. We see Freddy before his biological death, which is unprecedented for the whole franchise, while in some scenes he is presented as a victim of the parents. In the end, of course, the narrative is in favor of the new generation and the Final Couple, and the Other is guilty and punished by his own victims.

The Final Couple, like the one on *Friday the 13th*, is made by the Final Girl, Nancy (Rooney Mara) and the Final Boy, Quentin (Kyle Gallner). In this case, there is sexual and erotic attraction among them, evident from the first scene of the film. Nancy works as a waitress at the diner where the first murder occurs. There, Quentin is a customer. The dialog suggests that Quentin goes there every time Nancy works, while the obvious embarrassment of both implies erotic feelings.

Apart from the difference between *Friday the 13th* and *A Nightmare on Elm Street* regarding the Final Couple relationship, another one is the fact that in the first filmic text the main representative of the couple is the Final Boy, while in the second it is the Final Girl. Nancy is the one who helps in the progression of the narrative and appears from the very first scene as a simple, working girl. She is an unconventional Final Girl, with many features contradicting the usual, classical representation of the past. There are indications of a lack of faith towards God, which contrasts with the classical form of the character, since in 1984 the cross was considered a way of protection for the Final Girl.

Nancy stands out with her activeness and the influence she exerts on the narrative, with the Final Boy following and executing her commandments. She is not afraid when she first confronts the Other. This encounter is more like a sexual harassment, with Freddy verbally harassing her. However, Nancy's dynamics and her decision not to run and confront him puts her in the not so conventional role of an energetic female character. On the other hand, the first time the Other and the Final Boy are meeting the exact opposite occurs, with Quentin being frightened. The narrative of this particular neoslasher puts a couple in the role of the Final Survivor and reverses the classical forms of gender representation: the fearless girl moves the action and the passive boy follows the girl. Based on classical feminist theory, this contrasts with the general rule of classical, cinematic storytelling, where the woman is part of the spectacle that slows the narrative's progression, which often translated into turning the character into an erotic object for the male characters, but also for the viewers.[20]

In the triangle created by these three poles, there is an erotic essence between the Final Girl and the Final Boy, but the Other cuts off this dynamic through the ejection of sick sexual desires. This structure between the relationship of the two most important semantic elements of the subgenre reminds one of Bruce F. Kawin's view, which is based on classical horror films of the 1920s, 1930s, and 1940s and claims that in these films there is an unfulfilled love triangle between the boy, The girl and the "monster," with the boy and the monster representing the two faces of female sexual desire.[21] Of course, the sexual connotation, due to the presence of pedophilia by the Other, has taken a form of caustic sociopolitical comment that is not reminiscent of anything in the classical cycle regarding the punishment of sexual desire.

The filmic text leaves an open ending, faithful to the franchise traditions. Nancy's mother is violently murdered by Freddy, who comes from a mirror and the film ends with her daughter's screams. Although the film remains faithful to the narrative elements of the franchise, through its influence from other neoslashers it stands out and is a good example of shaping and presenting a Final Couple through an erotic relationship without re-establishing obsolete conventions of the classical cycle.

The Victims of the Neoslasher Cycle

The general principle that has been translated into the representation of the victims and their relation to Normality is the support of the cause/effect structure. At this point, we must emphasize the arbitrary link between victims and Others during the classical cycle. Even if the theoretical approach of classical filmic texts speaks of penalizing sexually activeness, this is a conclusion that derives from an academic approach. The Other of the classical narration does not say that it will kill characters because of sexual choices, but the selection is being made through loose narrative connections. The narrative itself does not provide a justification for the murders of the victims, but the murders are covered within a more general context of arbitrary connections.

The neoslashers tried to put an end to it and the murders began to be justified through narrative links. A new trend emerged in which victims began to be portrayed as relatives of the Other and/or people in their close environment, while their murders were justified by their interpersonal relationship established in the narrative. This important transformation of the representation of the semantic element of the victims lies in the change of the syntax of the third cycle. Although the victims as a semantic element are present throughout the life of the subgenre, the syntax has changed in such a way that the element is influenced by a more justified choice of characters in relation to Normality. An example of this is *Halloween*. While, as we saw in the second chapter, in the 1978 film there is the concept of punishing the "naughty" children who have sex through the bogeyman himself, in the neoslasher version of 2007 there is justification of the acts of the Other, while to a certain extent there is an identification of the audience with him instead of the victims. If we exclude Michael's sister and her boyfriend, the first (unnecessary) adolescent murder occurs around the seventieth minute, shortly after the middle of the film. Before that, there have been several murders that were exclusively adult and justified on the basis of the story. Even the subsequent murders of teenagers are few in number and justified to some extent. For example, the first victims went to Michael's abandoned house to make love while he was there. It could be said that he did not hunt them himself, but the victims bothered him in his own space. The passage to realism, coupled with the extensive justification for the choice of victims, are part of the third cycle's syntax, in which the neoslashers have realistic narratives, structured on the basis of the caused/effect binary. Another example is *Friday the 13th* of 2009, where there is a reason to justify the actions of the Other through the promise of revenge for the death of his mother.

The same goes for *A Nightmare on Elm Street* (2010), extending further the convention. The film divides the characters into two generations, with the new generation being punished for the acts of the old one, which tried to put an end to a possible crime, though its members did not know for sure if it really occurred. Through a trauma, a social group (young people) acquires a common "nightmare," which can be understood as an allegory that finds expression in many aspects of the western world. Of course, as Adam Lowenstein points out, the percentage of family and community presence in narrative has been drastically reduced compared to the classical filmic text.[22] Dennis Harvey adds that choosing to change the Other into a pedophile changes the victims too, by being represented in a process of recovery from repressed memories of a trauma.[23]

Of course, although the majority of the victims fall into the above category, there are also victims who simply were in the wrong place at the wrong time. This practice continues to some extent the arbitrary link of the classical cycle, but its academic approach is radically different, as these victims do not stand out because of their sexual and/or gender identity. This representation is closely linked to the sociopolitical developments of the period, as futile death is a collective fear of society stemming from the rise of terrorism.

Finally, the third cycle broke the convention about teenage victims.

Although the majority are teenagers, the stereotyped attachment stops and adult characters are incorporated into that semantic element. However, this chapter will mainly deal with adolescent victims for two reasons: firstly, because adolescents constitute the majority of the characters, and secondly because the comparison with the classical and self-referential representation will be more substantial. The following analysis will help to deepen and understand the expression of the victims, according to the syntax of the subgenre established in the neoslasher cycle.

Scream 4 was created 15 years after the first film and had to fill the gap between the two generations represented in its narrative and also to adapt to the new conventions of the subgenre. As Valerie Wee observes, after challenging and undermining the rules that made the first film, new rules had to be established to make *Scream 4* attractive to the teenage generation of the 2010s.[24] Craven explains, "you're addressing a generation of young fans, but also the generation that has gone with you for three, as well as a decade worth of other films. You have to be as good, or better, than all these films."[25] He also adds "we had to do something distinctive and unique to its time, not just do a repeat of something we've done before with *Scream* ... keeping that freshness called for a lot of work. I think what we have is original and wonderful."[26] Indirectly but clearly, the director himself admits the differentiation of the subgenre and the need to replace the conventions of the films.

The main characters of *Scream 4* are divided into two broad categories, the old and the new generation. The main characters of the old generation–Sidney, Gale and Dewey—come from previous films, while the victims and the Other belong to the new generation and are new characters.[27] Due to the 15-year distance between the two films, there are many differences in the structure of the story. The most important is the huge evolution of technology due to the digital age. Technology has become an integral part of everyone's everyday life. Craven observes:

> The growth of social networking, smartphones, video cameras and recorders has a tremendous presence in every nook and cranny of our life, and we're very much in that world. I can't imagine doing a film set in today's world without those things being important to plot and character.[28]

In the first *Scream* it was rare for a teenager to have a cell phone. In fact, Billy was accused of murder because he was close to attacking Sidney with having a cell phone on him. On the other hand, in *Scream 4* every teen has their own smartphone and uses it during the narrative plot. A typical example is the scene where a school class learns about the first murders. While the teacher delivers the lesson, all students' phones begin to ring and the tragic news is spread in a very short time.

Another important function brought by the new technology is that it allows young people to operate lot of parallel activities, or in other words, multitasking. *Scream 4* incorporates this feature in its narrative and the opening sequence is indicative of that: three fairly similar scenes, succeeding one another and each one with female victims and at least one killer. The first scene is considered to be part of *Stab 6*, which is followed by the girls from the second scene. The second scene is part of *Stab 7*, where the viewers are the girls of the third scene, who are also the first "real" characters of *Scream 4*. The *Stab* films are part of a fictional film franchise inside the *Scream* franchise and are supposed to be a cinematic adaptation of the events from the first *Scream* films. So, the first 10 minutes of the film are based on the combination of pastiche and multitasking.

Many of the deaths of the victims are based on multitasking, with the murder of Olivia being an example of this. Olivia is Jill's girlfriend and stays across from her house. Jill is in her room with Kirby and they are watching a movie. Olivia appears to be returning to her home while talking on the phone with the two girls. The killer calls and threatens Jill and Kirby, but there is a misunderstanding of where he is. Finally, the viewers and the two female characters see the murderer killing Olivia in her room.

Jill, the Other of the narrative, does everything to succeed. She turns into a murderer, and all because her motives are purely self-centered. Among the victims are her friends and her mother, whom she sacrifices for her personal success. The representation of Jill is purely negative, as she appears to be able to kill almost all of her close friends with the ultimate goal of becoming the recipient of glory and success. Jill is an extreme example of this tendency toward perseverance for glory, which can be justified by the fact that she holds the role of the Other of the narrative. Yet, other young characters of the film who are in the role of victims support similar views. Two examples are Charlie, who helps Jill in her plan until she kills him, and Robbie, who has a small camera installed on his head and is relaying his life on the internet.

In contrast to the negative representation of young people through the Other and the victims, the old generation of the franchise is represented as selfless and willing to offer help to the community. Sidney, Gale and Dewey are trying to solve the mystery surrounding the murders by risking their lives, while victims appear to be indifferent, since they are not interested in whether the killer will be arrested or not. An example of their apathy is when, despite recent killings, Stabathon takes place, creating a lack of respect for the human lives that have been lost and the tragedy experienced by the city. Here, there is a shift and at the same time a contrast in the way of representing the generations in relation to the classical cycle. In classical slasher films, the oldest generation was always the one with the apathy, and it did not help to solve the problem at all, while the young generation was the one who was victimized and had to find the solution on its own. In *Scream 4* the opposite happens; the younger generation is possessed of apathy, and the older ones are trying to end the murders. Of course, the victims continue to be part of the new generation, which makes it even more interesting, because while they are the ones who are affected, they do not do anything to change the facts.

Through the *Scream* franchise we see a great variation in the expression of the semantic element of the victims, which is due to the change of the subgenre's syntax. In the context of the effort of the third cycle to find and represent the causes of evil, the Other acquired a positive complexion such that, through the empathy discussed above, the audience identifies to a certain extent with him/her. Correspondingly, the victims narratively acquire a negative tone in their representation that further enhances the development of the empathy of the audience towards the Other that kills them. More specifically, in *Scream 4* there is a narrative impulse of the audience to identify with the Other, while the young generation that is also the victim of narration is represented negatively. This entire tendency is essentially another aspect of the turn of the subgenre in an attempt to explore the causes of the birth of evil. This tendency to represent the victims in such a way has prevailed in neoslashers, but there are other examples of the specific expression of the semantic element in the third cycle.

Another example that sheds light on the representation of the victims in neoslashers is *The Cabin in the Woods*. As mentioned, the main characters of the victims and the Final Survivors of narration are structured around archetypal stereotypes of the subgenre. Marty and Dana, who are the Final Couple of the narrative, are portrayed as the fool and the virgin, while the main victims are Curt, who is represented as the alpha male, Jules as the whore, and Holden as the scholar. The victims are murdered by the peculiar company that covers the position of the Other. As the filmic text goes on, the audience is informed that the goal of the company, which is part of a global chain, is to make at least one human sacrifice in honor of the old gods. This sacrifice is part of a representation of a form of teleology, and as Erin Giannini says, it concerns stereotypical (and even archetypal) adolescents, who are sacrificed in order not to destroy the world.[29]

The film is about the effort of the American side, but the story tells us about other countries too, knowing from the beginning that only the United States and Japan have not failed. The example of Japan is present all the time, and it is the only one for which the narrative gives us further information until the audience is informed that it has failed, which pushes the U.S. side to want to succeed. The mission of Japan is set in a classroom full of little girls (the victims of the narrative) and the assault is done by a female ghost. The ghost is not an unknown figure for fans of horror films, since it is a widespread form of Other in the Asian culture (water ghost), widely known in the western world through *The Ring* (2002), an American remake of the Japanese film *Ringu* (1998). Through self-referentiality, there is evidence from other horror subgenres in a parallel and peculiar story that is independent of the main narrative and manages terror as a global phenomenon where each country, based on its own needs, has created its own version.

The missions of each country act as an allegory of the representation of their national cinema regarding the horror genre. On the one hand, we have the Japanese side that, although it is not represented extensively, can easily be likened to an autonomous Japanese horror film. On the other hand, the entire narrative deals with the contracts of a predominantly American, cinematic subgenre that have marked the revival of horror over the last decades in the United States. L. Andrew Cooper underlines: "one by one, other countries fail, but the Americans remain confident that their movie formulae will succeed, just as American films have long dominated global box offices."[30]

The position of the horror film viewer is also added to the narrative. A typical scene is the one where employees of the company are watching in the monitor Curt and Jules preparing to have sex in the forest shortly before the young man's murder. The actions of the victims very much resemble the classical cycle of the subgenre: the alpha male and the whore are preparing to have sexual intercourse, but one of the two characters (or both) is slaughtered by the Other. Of course, in this neoslasher, this scene escapes from the stereotypical structure. High-ranking officials try to achieve the sexual encounter of the two young people and the appearance of the girl's breasts on the grounds that they are not the only ones who are watching and that they have to keep customers happy. The specific words of the employee are not accidental, as the sexual intercourse of the victims and the appearance of naked women's bodies just before their killing is a contract of the genre. Thus, this scene is self-referential, as there is a clear reference and parody of the conventions of the subgenre. When the employee refers to the satisfaction of customers who watch the two characters, the viewer is automatically placed in the customer's position. The creators of *The Cabin in the Woods* construct a mise-en-scène, according to which the viewing experience is an allegory of seeing the film itself. Rick McDonald adds that "*The Cabin in the Woods* does an excellent job of forcing the audience to consider its own responsibility for instigating the violence of horror."[31]

This "appearance" of the viewer in the narrative is linked to the commentary of national horror films. In the case of the main focus of the narrative, the American effort through the mysterious company, there is an attempt to recreate a slasher film, a popular American subgenre, in order for the viewers to be satisfied by the murders of stereotypical victims. Kristopher Woofter and Jasie Stokes argue that *The Cabin in the Woods* is like a survival reality

TV show, in which players are not aware they are involved and the script is written by the mysterious company.[32] The particular filmic text examines the relationships between the horror filmmakers, the studios that produce and distribute them, and their consumers.[33] The narrative treats horror like an available commodity, which, depending on domestic production and demand, is created and put to "sale" with the help of the Other who shares it in the community.

Hence, and through this example, the shift of the third cycle's syntax to the identification of the audience with the other is confirmed, while the victims act as a mechanism to further achieve this connection. In this film, through the study of the interaction of the film industry, the production mechanism, the narration, and the viewers, we see the narrative effort of developing the audience's involvement in the murders, with a generally simplified allegory focusing on the desire to see these films and hence the desire for murder. While in the classical cycle the victims functioned as a means of intimidating the audience through the common cultural identity based on conservative practices of sexual behavior, the neoslashers create an indirect viewer's desire for victims to be killed.

This is also confirmed by the story of the narrative and its efforts to find the reasons for the birth of evil. Several neoslashers focus on the development of the Other and the conversion of the next door man into a serial killer, thus causing several victims to be represented negatively to enhance the identification of the audience (for example, *Scream 4*). So, in this case too, the audience agrees (or even wishes) indirectly the murder of the victims.

An Epilog on the Neoslasher Cycle

The third cycle of the subgenre began in 2000, the year in which the self-referential cycle ended, and lasted until 2013 with 24 films in its entirety. Having preceded the transitional second cycle with basic elements of self-referentiality, intertextuality and parody, the syntax of the third cycle was completely differentiated from the classical but also the self-referential cycle, creating new connections, interactions and expressions of the semantic elements of the subgenre that brought to the fore the concerns that prevailed over the period in the United States of America.

A key element of the third cycle's syntax is the fact that the Other and its backstory come to the fore and the search for the causes of the birth of evil become the basic narrative structure. Having as the main protagonist the Other, the creation of evil is more justified and thus creates powerful narrative links that contradict the loose connections of the classical cycle. While in the classical films we had loose narrative connections between the Other and the Final Survivor making him the second protagonist of the narrative, and in the self-referential cycle we had a whodunit structure that left the identity and backstory of the Other in the dark until the last scenes of the film, in the neoslasher cycle there is a great shift of the syntax that brings to the forefront the Other and its backstory, which comes in complete contrast to the syntaxes of the first two cycles. Finally, gender representations are now considered to be in the past and their position is taken by representations of social classes and the atypical fights between them.

The neoslasher cycle has ended after 2013, as in the years 2014, 2015 and 2016 no slasher film has been able to get into the top–100 of the U.S. box office. The end of the third cycle is due to both the change in the production and distribution procedure of such films, as it is common for independent horror films to have direct distribution via video-on-demand platforms, as well as the transfer of the subgenre into the television landscape. The subgenre still dominates the pop culture, but has been channeled into other forms of audiovisual entertainment, such as television and the internet. However, a new production of slasher films is already starting to expand well-known franchises, such as the new *Halloween* movie that is expected in 2018 and the remake of *A Nightmare on Elm Street* that has not yet received a distribution date. Based on the present study, the subgenre functions as an organization adapted to the needs of each period, so there will most likely be an emergence of a new cycle of slasher films in the immediate future.

Conclusions

The horror genre, and more specifically, the slasher film, is an important part of the film industry of the United States and influences pop culture of the western world in general. The subgenre counts hundreds of films over four decades of life, having conquered other mediums, such as television, video games, comics and games. Also, the influence of the subgenre on the horror genre in general is enormous, with conventions being transferred to other subgenres over the decades, enhancing and evolving cinematic horror as a whole.

Several studies have been made around slasher films and valuable scholars have tried to create theoretical tools for their analysis. Two of the most renowned scholars that dealt with slasher films are Carol J. Clover and Vera Dika. Clover analyzed gender and sexuality representations of the main characters in these narratives, introducing the concept of the Final Girl, a term used to describe the female character that usually lives in the end of these films. On the other hand, Dika took a structuralist approach in analyzing these film narratives. Although the two theories are important for the theoretical background of the subgenre, their problem lies in the fact that they both refer to a certain number of films that do not extend beyond the 1980s. The subgenre exists even today, but no study tried to analyze slasher films as a whole and study the evolution of their narratives over the years.

Although the production of these films has been around for almost four decades, most of the theoretical studies were consumed over limited periods of time or specific narrative features. The theoretical studies of Clover and Dika have limited use due to the study of limited filmic samples; however, they are usually the basis of every academic text written for these films, and thus because they have limited use as they refer to a short period of time, they can not draw conclusions about the great evolution of the subgenre itself. This lack of a systematized analysis covering all slasher films has tried to be covered by the current theoretical and historical approach to the subgenre.

Through this book, an attempt was made to approach the subgenre as an organism that evolves and is subjected to changes based on influences, both by the interaction of narrative elements themselves and by elements of the evolution of society that can affect the narratives. The present theory aims to fill the void of the theoretical community dealing with this subgenre trying to approach the slasher film as a whole, taking into account its own internal evolution.

This book studied the evolution of the subgenre in the four decades of its life, beginning in 1974 and reaching to this day. The study was based on a semantic/syntactic approach, isolating key narrative elements and proving that the subgenre has evolved considerably, which can divide it into three film cycles. A useful tool in this analysis was Rick Altman's theory of a semantic/syntactic approach. The semantic/syntactic approach of slasher films helps to illuminate several aspects of the narrative structure and essence of specific filmic texts, creating a tool for a more systematic study of them. Through this theory and by defining the list of the main narrative elements of the films, we realize that the syntax of the subgenre did not remain stable throughout its history.

More specifically, the semantic elements are the Normality, the Others, the Final Survivors, and the Victims, while based on the data obtained from the study of the analyzed film corpus, the syntax is divided into three major categories: The backstory of the Other, the connection of the Other with the Final Survivors, and the relationship of Normality with the other three semantic elements. As we have seen in the case studies, the main categories, both semantic and syntactic, are based on umbrella terms that cover other sub-elements. Through these groupings, the approach was improved, creating a more usable theory for the present study.

Through the identification and study of the four semantic elements and the analysis of the syntax of these narratives, it was proven that the slasher films could be divided into three cycles. The main reason for this separation is the change of the syntax of the filmic texts and the redefinition of semantic elements through interactions and influences between them. In particular, the first cycle of slasher films, being largely conservative, was based on a link between the elements under the punishment of sexual acts and the general divergent behavior in a context of social conservatism and "family values." In the mid–1990s, the syntax of the slasher films was radically influenced by the self-referentiality that was diffused in pop culture in general, thus creating the second cycle that embraced whodunit elements in its self-referential narratives. At the beginning of the new millennium, the syntax of the subgenre changed again, creating the neoslasher cycle, where the justification of the violence and the transfer of the narrative focus to the Other came to light.

After the theoretical framework that was established, case studies were carried out aiming at an in-depth understanding of the separation of the subgenre into cycles. Through the analyses of Normality, the Other, the Final

Survivor and the victims, as well as the syntax per cycle, the major changes suffered by the subgenre itself were influenced by the changes in the conditions of each period. More specifically, each chapter dealt with the analysis of a cycle and the study of examples that strengthen the theory established in the first chapter.

The classic cycle concerns the films from 1974 to 1993. This cycle has the longest duration and the most films compared to the other two, while during this period, the subgenre stabilized its structure of narratives around stereotypical and conservative representations. Through film analysis, it was found that the syntax was structured around conservative norms with an emphasis on the stereotyped representation of gender and sexuality. Also, there was a systematic loose connection between the Other's backstory with the narrative present events and the victims he chooses to murder. The relationship of the Other with the victims or even with the Final Survivor is not strong, and many times it is non-existent. Thus, the classical cycle places more emphasis on its stereotypical structure than on strengthening the links of its narratives. By the end of the cycle, however, there was a saturation of the conservative structure and the classical syntax, with many films trying to move away from the punishment of sexual acts, while the number of slasher films dropped noticeably in relation to earlier years. This fact led to the birth of the second cycle in the mid-1990s.

The self-referential cycle lasted from 1994 to 2000. The basic formulation of the syntax during the self-referential cycle brought to the fore the self-referentiality and the intertextuality under the veil of parody and/or pastiche. Of course, self-referential narratives kept some basic structures of the classical cycle, but brought a tone of mockery to them. Finally, the new form of the syntax created whodunit narratives, keeping whole structure of the films around the question of what the real identity of the murderer is. While in classical filmic texts we have seen that the identity and the backstory of the Other is revealed in the first scenes of films, the self-referential cycle conceals the identity of the Other and its motives until the last scene of the film. Although the second cycle lasted for a shorter time than that of the classical and the neoslasher, it constituted a groundbreaking movement of the subgenre by making a transition to the complete release of classical norms during the third cycle. Thus, the second cycle is considered to be a transitional cycle between classical films and neoslashers. The self-referential cycle lasted until 2000, a landmark year for the third cycle as well, as *Final Destination*, the first neoslasher, was released.

The neoslasher cycle took place between 2000 and 2013. The new syntax completely removed the whodunit structure of the self-referential cycle and brought to the foreground the true identity of the Other and its backstory. Through the case studies, the argument that the syntax of the neoslashers is structured with strong narrative links between the backstory of the Other, the Other and the victims, was strengthened, while the Other came to the fore and forced the story of narration into a quest to find the causes of creation of evil. Within this narrative setting, the gender representations have completely disappeared from the subgenre and instead there are the representations of social classes and the fights between them. At the end of the third cycle, it is once again noticed that the subgenre has come to a decline, as in the years 2014, 2015 and 2016 no filmic text was able to enter the top-100 of the American box office.

Through this theoretical and historical approach of the slasher film, the functionality of the narrations of these films and their ability to adapt according to the evolution of the audience, the film industry, and society itself was observed. Each cycle redefined its syntax with the main objective of surviving the subgenre in the conditions of each period. Through the constant list of the semantic elements, their adaptation and differentiation in the interactions between them occurred, creating new syntactic links and pushing to create or end a film cycle.

Thus, the present study has consolidated a theoretical tool that forms the basis of an overall approach to the slasher film, covering the theoretical gap, and can also act as a model for approaching other film genres and/or subgenres. Finally, with the present semantic and syntactic approach to the slasher film, the future of the subgenre can be studied, as new cycles will probably emerge in the coming years. Having established the argument that each genre/subgenre functions as a living entity that evolves and adapts to the circumstances, it is expected that the slasher film will continue to exist in the future through new cycles of films that will format their own syntax based on future requirements, always using the list of the fixed semantic elements of their narratives.

Appendix A: Films Referenced

The Texas Chain Saw Massacre—Bryanston Pictures (1974); *Director:* Tobe Hooper; *Screenwriters:* Kim Henkel, Tobe Hooper; *Cast:* Marilyn Burns, Edwin Neal, Allen Danziger; *Box Office:* $30,860,000

Black Christmas—Warner Bros. (1974); *Director:* Bob Clark; *Screenwriter:* Roy Moore; *Cast:* Olivia Hussey, Keir Dullea, Margot Kidder; *Box Office:* $4,053,000

The Hills Have Eyes—Vanguard (1977); *Director:* Wes Craven; *Screenwriter:* Wes Craven; *Cast:* Suze Lanier-Bramlett, Robert Houston, John Steadman; *Box Office:* $25,000,000 (WW)

Halloween—Compass (1978); *Director:* John Carpenter; *Screenwriters:* John Carpenter, Debra Hill; *Cast:* Jamie Lee Curtis, Donald Pleasence, Tony Moran, Nancy Kyes; *Box Office:* $47.000,000

When a Stranger Calls—Columbia (1979); *Director:* Fred Walton; *Screenwriters:* Steve Feke, Fred Walton; *Cast:* Carol Kane, Charles Durning, Rutanya Alda; *Box Office:* $21,411,158

Friday the 13th—Paramount (1980); *Director:* Sean S. Cunningham; *Screenwriters:* Victor Miller, Sean S. Cunningham, Ron Kurz; *Cast:* Betsy Palmer, Adrienne King, Jeannine Taylor; *Box Office:* $39,754,601

Prom Night—Embassy (1980); *Director:* Paul Lynch; *Screenwriters:* William Gray, Robert Guza, Jr.; *Cast:* Leslie Nielsen, Jamie Lee Curtis, Casey Stevens; *Box Office:* $14,796,236

He Knows You're Alone—MGM (1980); *Director:* Armand Mastroianni; *Screenwriter:* Scott Parker; *Cast:* Don Scardino, Caitlin O'Heaney, Elizabeth Kemp; *Box Office:* $4,875,436

Halloween II—Universal (1981); *Director:* Rick Rosenthal; *Screenwriters:* John Carpenter, Debra Hill; *Cast:* Jamie Lee Curtis, Donald Pleasence, Charles Cyphers; *Box Office:* $25,533,818

Friday the 13th Part 2—Paramount (1981); *Director:* Steve Miner; *Screenwriters:* Ron Kurz, Victor Miller; *Cast:* Betsy Palmer, Amy Steel, John Furey; *Box Office:* $21,722,776

The Fun House—Universal (1981); *Director:* Tobe Hooper; *Screenwriter:* Lawrence Block; *Cast:* Elizabeth Berridge, Shawn Carson, Jeanne Austin; *Box Office:* $7,886,857

My Bloody Valentine—Paramount (1981); *Director:* George Mihalka; *Screenwriters:* Stephen A. Miller, John Beaird; *Cast:* Paul Kelman, Lori Hallier, Neil Affleck; *Box Office:* $5,672,031

Night School—Paramount (1981); *Director:* Ken Hughes; *Screenwriter:* Ruth Avergon; *Cast:* Leonard Mann, Rachel Ward, Drew Snyder; *Box Office:* $1,169,875

Friday the 13th Part III—Paramount (1982); *Director:* Steve Miner; *Screenwriters:* Martin Kitrosser, Carol Watson; *Cast:* Dana Kimmell, Tracie Savage, Richard Brooker; *Box Office:* $34,581,519

Visiting Hours—Fox (1982); *Director:* Jean-Claude Lord; *Screenwriter:* Brian Taggert; *Cast:* Michael Ironside, Lee Grant, Linda Purl; *Box Office:* $13,258,670

The House on Sorority Row—Film Ventures Intl (1983); *Director:* Mark Rosman; *Screenwriter:* Mark Rosman; *Cast:* Kate McNeil, Eileen Davidson, Janis Ward; *Box Office:* $10,604,986

Friday the 13th: Final Chapter—Paramount (1984); *Director:* Joseph Zito; *Screenwriter:* Barney Cohen; *Cast:* Erich Anderson, Judie Aronson, Peter Barton; *Box Office:* $32,980,880

A Nightmare on Elm Street—New Line (1984); *Director:* Wes Craven; *Screenwriter:* Wes Craven; *Cast:* Heather Langenkamp, Johnny Depp, Robert Englund; *Box Office:* $25,504,513

A Nightmare on Elm Street 2: Freddy's Revenge—New Line (1985); *Director:* Jack Sholder; *Screenwriters:* David Chaskin, Wes Craven (characters); *Cast:* Robert Englund, Mark Patton, Kim Myers; *Box Office:* $29,999,213

Friday the 13th–Part V—Paramount (1985); *Director:* Danny Steinmann; *Screenwriters:* Martin Kitrosser, David Cohen, Danny Steinmann; *Cast:* Melanie Kinnaman, John Shepherd, Anthony Barrile; *Box Office:* $21,930,418

Friday the 13th Part VI—Paramount (1986); *Director:* Tom McLoughlin; *Screenwriter:* Tom McLoughlin; *Cast:* Thom Mathews, Jennifer Cooke, David Kagen; *Box Office:* $19,472,057

April Fool's Day—Paramount (1986); *Director:* Fred Walton; *Screenwriter:* Danilo Bach; *Cast:* Deborah Foreman, Griffin O'Neal, Clayton Rohner; *Box Office:* $12,947,763

The Texas Chainsaw Massacre 2—Cannon Films (1986); *Director:* Tobe Hooper; *Screenwriters:* L.M. Kit Carson, Tobe Hooper; *Cast:* Dennis Hopper, Caroline Williams, Jim Siedow; *Box Office:* $8,025,872

A Nightmare on Elm Street 3: Dream Warriors—New Line (1987); *Director:* Chuck Russell; *Screenwriters:* Wes Craven, Bruce Wagner, Frank Darabont, Chuck Russell; *Cast:* Heather Langenkamp, Robert Englund, Craig Wasson; *Box Office:* $44,793,222

A Nightmare on Elm Street 4: The Dream Master—New Line (1988); *Director:* Renny Harlin; *Screenwriters:* Brian Helgeland, Jim Wheat, Ken Wheat; *Cast:* Robert Englund, Rodney Eastman, John Beckman; *Box Office:* $49,369,899

Child's Play—United Artists (1988); *Director:* Tom Holland; *Screenwriters:* Don Mancini, John Lafia, Tom Holland; *Cast:* Catherine Hicks, Chris Sarandon, Alex Vincent; *Box Office:* $33,244,684

Friday the 13th Part VII—Paramount (1988); *Director:* John Carl Buechler; *Screenwriters:* Daryl Haney, Manuel Fidello; *Cast:* Jennifer Banko, John Otrin, Susan Blu; *Box Office:* $19,170,001

Halloween 4: The Return of Michael Myers—Galaxy International (1988); *Director:* Dwight H. Little; *Screenwriter:* Alan B. McElroy; *Cast:* Donald Pleasence, Ellie Cornell, Danielle Harris; *Box Office:* $17,768,757

Bad Dreams—Fox (1988); *Director:* Andrew Fleming; *Screenwriters:* Andrew Fleming, Steven E. de Souza; *Cast:* Jennifer Rubin, Bruce Abbott, Richard Lynch; *Box Office:* $9,797,098

A Nightmare on Elm Street 5: The Dream Child—New Line (1989); *Director:* Stephen Hopkins; *Screenwriter:* Leslie Bohem; *Cast:* Robert Englund, Lisa Wilcox, Kelly Jo Minter; *Box Office:* $22,168,359

Shocker—Universal (1989); *Director:* Wes Craven; *Screenwriter:* Wes Craven; *Cast:* Michael Murphy, Mitch Pileggi, John Tesh; *Box Office:* $16,554,699

Friday the 13th Part VIII—Paramount (1989); *Director:* Rob Hedden; *Screenwriters:* Rob Hedden, Victor Miller (characters); *Cast:* Jensen Daggett, Kane Hodder, Todd Caldecott; *Box Office:* $14,343,976

Halloween 5—Galaxy International (1989); *Director:* Dominique Othenin-Girard; *Screenwriters:* Michael Jacobs, Dominique Othenin-Girard, Shem Bitterman; *Cast:* Donald Pleasence, Danielle Harris, Ellie Cornell; *Box Office:* $11,642,254

Child's Play 2—Universal (1990); *Director:* John Lafia; *Screenwriter:* Don Mancini; *Cast:* Alex Vincent, Jenny Agutter, Gerrit Graham; *Box Office:* $28,501,605

Freddy's Dead: The Final Nightmare—New Line (1991); *Director:* Rachel Talalay; *Screenwriter:* Michael De Luca; *Cast:* Robert Englund, Lisa Zane, Shon Greenblatt; *Box Office:* $34,872,033

Child's Play 3—Universal (1991); *Director:* Jack Bender; *Screenwriter:* Don Mancini; *Cast:* Justin Whalin, Perrey Reeves, Jeremy Sylvers; *Box Office:* $14,960,255

Candyman—TriStar (1992); *Director:* Bernard Rose; *Screenwriter:* Bernard Rose; *Cast:* Virginia Madsen, Xander Berkeley, Tony Todd; *Box Office:* $25,792,310

Jason Goes to Hell: The Final Friday—New Line (1993); *Director:* Adam Marcus; *Screenwriters:* Dean Lorey, Jay Huguely; *Cast:* John D. LeMay, Kari Keegan, Kane Hodder; *Box Office:* $15,935,068

New Nightmare—New Line (1994); *Director:* Wes Craven; *Screenwriter:* Wes Craven; *Cast:* Heather Langenkamp, Robert Englund, Jeff Davis; *Box Office:* $18,090,181

Halloween: The Curse of Michael Myers—Dimension Films (1995); *Director:* Joe Chappelle; *Screenwriter:* Daniel Farrands; *Cast:* Donald Pleasence, Paul Rudd, Marianne Hagan; *Box Office:* $15,116,634

Candyman: Farewell to the Flesh—Gramercy (1995); *Director:* Bill Condon; *Screenwriters:* Rand Ravich, Mark Kruger; *Cast:* Tony Todd, Kelly Rowan, William O'Leary; *Box Office:* $13,940,383

Scream—Dimension Films (1996); *Director:* Wes Craven; *Screenwriter:* Kevin Williamson; *Cast:* Neve Campbell, Courteney Cox, David Arquette; *Box Office:* $103,046,663

Scream 2—Dimension Films (1997); *Director:* Wes Craven; *Screenwriter:* Kevin Williamson; *Cast:* Neve Campbell, Courteney Cox, David Arquette; *Box Office:* $101,363,301

I Know What You Did Last Summer—Sony/Columbia (1997); *Director:* Jim Gillespie; *Screenwriter:* Kevin Williamson; *Cast:* Jennifer Love Hewitt, Sarah Michelle Gellar, Anne Heche; *Box Office:* $72,586,134

Halloween: H20—Dimension Films (1998); *Director:* Steve Miner; *Screenwriters:* Robert Zappia, Matt Greenberg; *Cast:* Jamie Lee Curtis, Josh Hartnett, Adam Arkin; *Box Office:* $55,041,738

I Still Know What You Did Last Summer—Sony/Columbia (1998); *Director:* Danny Cannon; *Screenwriters:* Lois Duncan (characters), Trey Callaway; *Cast:* Jennifer Love Hewitt, Freddie Prinze, Jr., Brandy Norwood; *Box Office:* $40,002,112

Urban Legend—Sony/Columbia (1998); *Director:* Jamie Blanks; *Screenwriter:* Silvio Horta; *Cast:* Jared Leto, Alicia Witt, Rebecca Gayheart; *Box Office:* $38,072,438

Bride of Chucky—Universal (1998); *Director:* Ronny Yu; *Screenwriters:* Don Mancini (characters), Don Mancini; *Cast:* Jennifer Tilly, Brad Dourif, Katherine Heigl; *Box Office:* $32,383,850

1990—No Slasher Films

Scream 3—Dimension Films (2000); *Director:* Wes Craven; *Screenwriters:* Kevin Williamson (characters), Ehren Kruger; *Cast:* David Arquette, Neve Campbell, Courteney Cox; *Box Office:* $89,143,175

Final Destination—New Line (2000); *Director:* James Wong; *Screenwriters:* Glen Morgan, James Wong, Jeffrey Reddick; *Cast:* Devon Sawa, Ali Larter, Kerr Smith; *Box Office:* $53,331,147

Urban Legends: Final Cut—Sony/Columbia (2000); *Director:* John Ottman; *Screenwriters:* Paul Harris Boardman, Scott Derrickson; *Cast:* Jennifer Morrison, Matthew Davis, Hart Bochner; *Box Office:* $21,468,807

Jeepers Creepers—United Artists (2001); *Director:* Victor Salva; *Screenwriter:* Victor Salva; *Cast:* Gina Philips, Justin Long, Jonathan Breck; *Box Office:* $37,904,175

Valentine—Warner Bros. (2001); *Director:* Jamie Blanks; Donna Powers, Wayne Powers, Gretchen J. Berg, Aaron Harberts; *Cast:* Denise Richards, David Boreanaz, Marley Shelton; *Box Office:* $20,384,136

Halloween: Resurrection—Dimension Films (2002); *Director:* Rick Rosenthal; *Screenwriters:* Larry Brand, Sean Hood; *Cast:* Jamie Lee Curtis, Busta Rhymes, Brad Loree; *Box Office:* $30,354,442

Freddy Vs. Jason—New Line (2003); *Director:* Ronny Yu; *Screenwriters:* Damian Shannon, Mark Swift; *Cast:* Robert Englund, Ken Kirzinger, Kelly Rowland; *Box Office:* $82,622,655

The Texas Chainsaw Massacre—New Line (2003); *Director:* Marcus Nispel; *Screenwriter:* Scott Kosar; *Cast:* Jessica Biel, Jonathan Tucker, Andrew Bryniarski; *Box Office:* $80,571,655

Final Destination 2—New Line (2003); *Director:* David R. Ellis; J. Mackye Gruber, Eric Bress; *Cast:* A.J. Cook, Ali Larter, Tony Todd; *Box Office:* $46,961,214

Jeepers Creepers 2—United Artists (2003); *Director:* Victor Salva; *Screenwriter:* Victor Salva; *Cast:* Jonathan Breck, Ray Wise, Nicki Aycox; *Box Office:* $35,667,218

2004—No Slasher Films

House of Wax—Warner Bros. (2005); *Director:* Jaume Collet-Serra; *Screenwriters:* Chad Hayes, Carey Hayes; *Cast:* Chad Michael Murray, Paris Hilton, Elisha Cuthbert; *Box Office:* $32,064,800

Final Destination 3—New Line (2006); *Director:* James Wong; *Screenwriters:* Glen Morgan, James Wong; *Cast:* Mary Elizabeth Winstead, Ryan Merriman, Kris Lemche; *Box Office:* $54,098,051

When a Stranger Calls—Sony/Screen Gems (2006); *Director:* Simon West; *Screenwriter:* Jake Wade Wall; *Cast:* Camilla Belle, Tommy Flanagan, Katie Cassidy; *Box Office:* $47,860,214

The Hills Have Eyes—Fox Searchlight (2006); *Director:* Alexandre Aja; *Screenwriters:* Alexandre Aja, Grégory Levasseur; *Cast:* Ted Levine, Kathleen Quinlan, Dan Byrd; *Box Office:* $41,778,863

The Texas Chainsaw Massacre: The Beginning—New Line (2006); *Director:* Jonathan Liebesman; *Screenwriter:* Sheldon Turner; *Cast:* Jordana Brewster, Matt Bomer, Diora Baird; *Box Office:* $39,517,763

Halloween—MGM (Weinstein) (2007); *Director:* Rob Zombie; *Screenwriter:* Rob Zombie; *Cast:* Scout Taylor-Compton, Malcolm McDowell, Tyler Mane; *Box Office:* $58,272,029

Prom Night—Sony/Screen Gems (2008); *Director:* Nelson McCormick; *Screenwriter:* J.S. Cardone; *Cast:* Brittany Snow, Scott Porter, Jessica Stroup; *Box Office:* $43,869,350

The Final Destination—Warner Bros. (New Line) (2009); *Director:* David R. Ellis; *Screenwriters:* Eric Bress, Jeffrey Reddick (characters); *Cast:* Nick Zano, Krista Allen, Andrew Fiscella; *Box Office:* $66,477,700

Friday the 13th—Warner Bros. (New Line) (2009); *Director:* Marcus Nispel; *Screenwriters:* Damian Shannon, Mark Swift; *Cast:* Jared Padalecki, Amanda Righetti, Derek Mears; *Box Office:* $65,002,019

My Bloody Valentine 3-D—Lionsgate (2009); *Director:* Patrick Lussier; *Screenwriters:* Todd Farmer, Zane Smith; *Cast:* Jensen Ackles, Jaime King, Kerr Smith; *Box Office:* $51,545,952

Halloween II—Weinstein/Dimension (2009); *Director:* Rob Zombie; *Screenwriter:* Rob Zombie; *Cast:* Scout Taylor-Compton, Tyler Mane, Malcolm McDowell; *Box Office:* $33,392,973

A Nightmare on Elm Street—Warner Bros. (New Line) (2010); *Director:* Samuel Bayer; *Screenwriters:* Wesley Strick, Eric Heisserer; *Cast:* Jackie Earle Haley, Rooney Mara, Kyle Gallner; *Box Office:* $63,075,011

Final Destination 5—Warner Bros. (New Line) (2011); *Director:* Steven Quale; *Screenwriters:* Eric Heisserer, Jeffrey Reddick (characters); *Cast:* Nicholas D'Agosto, Emma Bell, Arlen Escarpeta; *Box Office:* $42,587,643

Scream 4—Weinstein/Dimension (2011); *Director:* Wes Craven; *Screenwriter:* Kevin Williamson; *Cast:* Neve Campbell, Courteney Cox, David Arquette; *Box Office:* $38,180,928

The Cabin in the Woods—Lionsgate (2012); *Director:* Drew Goddard; *Screenwriters:* Joss Whedon, Drew Goddard; *Cast:* Kristen Connolly, Chris Hemsworth, Anna Hutchison; *Box Office:* $42,073,277

Texas Chainsaw 3D—Lionsgate (2013); *Director:* John Luessenhop; *Screenwriters:* Adam Marcus, Debra Sullivan, Kirsten McCallion; *Cast:* Alexandra Daddario, Tania Raymonde, Scott Eastwood; *Box Office:* $34,341,945

2014—No Slasher Films

2015—No Slasher Films

2016—No Slasher Films

Appendix B: Semantic Elements

CLASSICAL CYCLE

Title	Other	Final Survivor(s)	Victims
The Texas Chain Saw Massacre (1974)	Male	Final Girl	Teens
Black Christmas (1974)	Male	Final Girl	Teens
The Hills Have Eyes (1977)	Male	3 Final Survivors	Adults
Halloween (1978)	Male	Final Girl	Teens
When a Stranger Calls (1979)	Male	Final Girl	Teens
Friday the 13th (1980)	Female	Final Girl	Teens
Prom Night (1980)	Male	Final Girl	Teens
He Knows You're Alone (1980)	Male	Final Girl	Teens
Halloween II (1981)	Male	Final Girl	Teens
Friday the 13th Part 2 (1981)	Male	Final Girl	Teens
The Fun House (1981)	Male	Final Girl	Teens
My Bloody Valentine (1981)	Male	Final Girl	Teens and Adults
Night School (1981)	Female	Final Man	Teens
Friday the 13th Part III (1982)	Male	Final Girl	Teens
Visiting Hours (1982)	Male	Final Girl	Teens and Adults
The House on Sorority Row (1983)	Male	Final Girl	Teens
Friday the 13th: Final Chapter (1984)	Male	Final Girl	Teens
A Nightmare on Elm Street (1984)	Male	Final Girl	Teens
A Nightmare on Elm Street 2: Freddy's Revenge (1985)	Male	Final Girl + Boy	Teens
Friday the 13th Part V (1985)	Male	Final Girl + Boy	Teens
Friday the 13th Part VI (1986)	Male	Final Girl + Boy	Teens
April Fool's Day (1986)	No One (Joke)	No One (Joke)	Teens
The Texas Chainsaw Massacre 2 (1986)	Male	Final Girl	Teens and Adults
A Nightmare on Elm Street 3: Dream Warriors (1987)	Male	Final Girl	Teens
A Nightmare on Elm Street 4: The Dream Master (1988)	Male	Final Girl + Boy	Teens
Child's Play (1988)	Male	Final Girl + Boy	Adults

Title	Other	Final Survivor(s)	Victims
Friday the 13th Part VII (1988)	Male	Final Girl	Teens
Halloween 4: The Return of Michael Myers (1988)	Male	2 Final Girls	Teens and Adults
Bad Dreams (1988)	Male	Final Girl + Male	Teens and Adults
A Nightmare on Elm Street 5: The Dream Child (1989)	Male	Final Girl	Teens
Shocker (1989)	Male	Final Boy	Teens and Adults
Friday the 13th Part VIII (1989)	Male	Final Girl + Boy	Teens
Halloween 5 (1989)	Male	Final Girl	Teens and Adults
Child's Play 2 (1990)	Male	Final Girl + Boy	Teens and Adults
Freddy's Dead: The Final Nightmare (1991)	Male	Final Girl	Teens
Child's Play 3 (1991)	Male	Final Boy	Teens and Adults
Candyman (1992)	Male	Final Girl Dies	Adults
Jason Goes to Hell: The Final Friday (1993)	Male	Final Girl + Boy	Teens and Adults

SELF-REFERENTIAL CYCLE

Title	Other	Final Survivor(s)	Victims
New Nightmare (1994)	Male	Final Woman	Adults
Halloween: The Curse of Michael Myers (1995)	Male	Final Couple	Teens and Adults
Candyman: Farewell to the Flesh (1995)	Male	Final Woman	Teens and Adults
Scream (1996)	2 Males	3 Final Survivors	Teens
Scream 2 (1997)	Male and Female	3 Final Survivors	Teens and Adults
I Know What You Did Last Summer (1997)	Male	Final Couple	Teens
Halloween: H20 (1998)	Male	Final Woman	Teens and Adults
I Still Know What You Did Last Summer (1998)	2 Males	Final Couple	Teens and Adults
Urban Legend (1998)	Female	Final Couple	Teens
Bride of Chucky (1998)	Male and Female	Final Couple	Adults
Scream 3 (2000)	Male	3 Final Survivors	Adults
Urban Legends: Final Cut (2000)	Male	5 Final Survivors	Teens

NEOSLASHER CYCLE

Title	Other	Final Survivor(s)	Victims
Final Destination (2000)	Paranormal	3 Final Survivors	Teens and Adults
Jeepers Creepers (2001)	Paranormal	Final Girl	Teens and Adults
Valentine (2001)	Male	Final Girl	Teens and Adults
Halloween: Resurrection (2002)	Male	Final Couple	Teens and Adults
Freddy Vs. Jason (2003)	2 Males	Final Couple	Teens and Adults

Appendix B

Title	Other	Final Survivor(s)	Victims
The Texas Chainsaw Massacre (2003)	Male	Final Girl	Teens
Final Destination 2 (2003)	Paranormal	Final Couple	Teens and Adults
Jeepers Creepers 2 (2003)	Paranormal	7 Final Survivors	Teens
House of Wax (2005)	2 Males	Final Couple	Teens and Adults
Final Destination 3 (2006)	Paranormal	3 Final Survivors (Die)	Teens and Adults
When a Stranger Calls (2006)	Male	Final Girl	Teens and Adults
The Hills Have Eyes (2006)	Mutants	3 Final Survivors	Teens and Adults
The Texas Chainsaw Massacre: The Beginning (2006)	Male	Final Girl (Dies)	Teens and Adults
Halloween (2007)	Male	Final Girl	Teens and Adults
Prom Night (2008)	Male	Final Girl	Teens
The Final Destination (2009)	Paranormal	3 Final Survivors (Die)	Teens and Adults
Friday the 13th (2009)	Male	Final Couple	Teens and Adults
My Bloody Valentine 3-D (2009)	Male	Final Couple (the Boy is the Other)	Teens and Adults
Halloween II (2009)	Male	Final Girl (Dies)	Teens and Adults
A Nightmare on Elm Street (2010)	Male	Final Couple	Teens and Adults
Final Destination 5 (2011)	Paranormal	Final Couple (Die)	Teens and Adults
Scream 4 (2011)	Male and Female	Final Woman	Teens and Adults
The Cabin in the Woods (2012)	Corporation	Final Couple	Teens
Texas Chainsaw 3D (2013)	Male	Final Girl	Teens and Adults

Chapter Notes

Introduction

1. For more, see Carroll, Noel. *The Philosophy of Horror, or Paradoxes of the Heart*. New York: Routledge, 1990, p. 162.

2. Kendrick, James. "Slasher Films and Gore in the 1980s." In *A Companion to the Horror Film*, edited by Harry M. Benshoff. Hoboken, NJ: Wiley-Blackwell, 2014, p. 316.

3. The term "neoslashers" has been used sporadically by some theorists to describe the films from the mid–1990s and onwards. Such examples are Kerner, Aaron Michael. *Torture Porn in the Wake of 9/11: Horror, Exploitation, and the Cinema of Sensation*. New Brunswick, NJ: Rutgers University Press, 2015; and Nelson, Andrew Patrick. "Franchise Legacy and Neo-slasher Conventions in Halloween H20." In *Style and Form in the Hollywood Slasher Film*, edited by Wickham Clayton. New York: Palgrave Macmillan, 2015. In the present book, the term neoslashers will be systematically used as a stand-alone for the films of the new millennium only, defining the films of the 1990s as self-referential. This separation in the generalized use of the term by some scholars will be supported later in the book with arguments that differentiate self-referential slashers from neoslashers.

Chapter 1

1. Kerswell, J.A. *The Slasher Movie Book*. Chicago: Chicago Review Press, 2012, pp. 18–19.

2. Among those who consider *Halloween* to be the first filmic text of the subgenre are two important scholars of the specific films—Vera Dika and Adam Rockoff. For more information, see Dika, Vera. "The Stalker Film, 1978–1981." In *American Horrors: Essays on the Modern American Horror Film*, edited by Gregory A. Waller. Champaign: University of Illinois Press, 1987, and Rockoff, Adam. *Going to Pieces: The Rise and Fall of the Slasher Film, 1978–1986*. Jefferson, NC: McFarland, 2002. Another texts that support this view are Schoell, William. *Stay out of the Shower: 25 Years of Shocker Films Beginning with "Psycho."* New York: Dembner Books, 1985, and Jones, Alan. *The Rough Guide to Horror Movies*. London: Rough Guides, 2005.

3. Lakoff, George. *Women, Fire, and Dangerous Things: What Categories Reveal About the Mind*. Chicago: University of Chicago Press, 1987, p. 12.

4. Grindon, Leger. "Cycles and Clusters: The Shape of Film Genre History." In *Film Genre Reader IV*, edited by Barry Keith Grant. Austin: University of Texas Press, 2012, p. 44.

5. Altman, Rick. *Film/Genre*. London: BFI Publishing, 2006, p. 61.

6. See Tudor, Andrew. "Genre." In *Film Genre Reader IV*, edited by Barry Keith Grant. Austin: University of Texas Press, 2012.

7. The method that was followed for the creation of the corpus is mostly based on the method Betty Kaklamanidou followed in order to define and examine the political films as a genre. For more, see Kaklamanidou, Betty. *The "Disguised" Political Film in Contemporary Hollywood: A Genre's Construction*. New York: Bloomsbury, 2016.

8. Gledhill, Christine. "Rethinking Genre." In *Reinventing Film Studies*, edited by Christine Gledhill and Linda Williams. London: Arnold, 2000, p. 221.
9. See Tudor, Andrew. *Theories of Film*. New York: Viking Press, 1973.
10. Staiger, Janet. "Hybrid or Inbred: The Purity Hypothesis and Hollywood Genre History." In *Film Genre Reader III*, edited by Barry Keith Grant. Austin: University of Texas Press, 2003, p. 187.
11. See Wittgenstein, Ludwig. *Philosophical investigations*, translated by and G. E. Anscombe. Oxford, UK: Blackwell, 1997.
12. Grindon, "Cycles and Clusters," p. 44.
13. *Ibid.*, p. 42.
14. Neale, Steve. "Questions of Genre." In *Film Genre Reader III*, edited by Barry Keith Grant. Austin: University of Texas Press, 2003, p. 171.
15. *Ibid.*, p. 171.
16. See Cohen, Ralph. "History and Genre." *New Literary History* 17, No. 2 (Winter 1986): p. 205–206; Jauss, Hans Robert. *Towards an Aesthetic of Reception*. Brighton, UK: Harvester Press, 1982, p. 80; and Neale, Steve. *Genre*. London: BFI, 1980, p. 19.
17. See Carroll, Noel. *The Philosophy of Horror, or Paradoxes of the Heart*. New York: Routledge, 1990.
18. Clover, J. Carol. *Men, Women and Chain Saws: Gender in the Modern Horror Film*. Princeton: Princeton University Press, 1992, p. 21.
19. These elements are thoroughly analyzed at Clover's book, *Ibid.*, pp. 26–42.
20. *Ibid.*, p. 30.
21. *Ibid.*, p. 31.
22. *Ibid.*, p. 33.
23. *Ibid.*, pp. 34–35.
24. *Ibid.*, p. 35.
25. Creed, Barbara. "Horror and the Monstrous-Feminine. An Imaginary Abjection." In *Horror, The Film Reader*, edited by Mark Jancovich. London: Routledge, 2002, p. 74.
26. Clover, *Men, Women and Chain Saws*, p. 35.
27. *Ibid.*, p. 39.
28. *Ibid.*, p. 47.
29. *Ibid.*, p. 48.
30. Williams, Linda. "When the Woman Looks." In *Horror: The Film Reader*, edited by Mark Jancovich. London: Routledge, 2002, p. 64.
31. In Tarratt, Margaret. "Monsters from the Id." In *Film Genre Reader III*, edited by Barry Keith Grant. Austin: University of Texas Press, 2003, p. 346.
32. Clover, *Men, Women and Chain Saws*, pp. 49–50.
33. Evans, Walter. "Monster Movies: A Sexual Theory." In *Planks of Reason: Essays on the Horror Film*, edited by Barry Keith Grant. Lanham, MD: Scarecrow Press, 1984, pp. 55–56.
34. Dika, "The Stalker Film, 1978–1981," p. 86.
35. *Ibid.*, pp. 93–94.
36. *Ibid.*, p. 94.
37. *Ibid.*, p. 88.
38. *Ibid.*, p. 91.
39. Rockoff, *Going to Pieces*, pp. 5–15.
40. Altman, Rick. "A Semantic/Syntactic Approach to Film Genre." In *Film Genre Reader III*, edited by Barry Keith Grant. Austin: University of Texas Press, 2003, p. 29.
41. *Ibid.*, p. 31.
42. Altman, Rick. *The American Film Musical*. Bloomington: Indiana University Press, 1987, p. 107.
43. Altman, "A Semantic/Syntactic Approach to Film Genre," pp. 32–33.
44. See Altman, *Film/Genre*, pp. 207–215.
45. Wood, Robin. *Hollywood from Vietnam to Reagan…and Beyond*. New York: Columbia University Press, 2003, pp. 65–66.

46. Freud, Sophie. "The Social Construction of Normality." *Families in Society*, 80:4 (1999): p. 335.
47. For more information, see Pinedo, Isabel Cristina. *Recreational Terror: Women and the Pleasures of Horror Film Viewing*. Albany: SUNY Press, 1997, and Benshoff, Harry. *Monsters in the Closet: Homosexuality and the Horror Film*. Manchester: Manchester University Press, 1997.
48. Creed, Barbara. "Film and Psychoanalysis." In *The Oxford Guide to Film Studies*, edited by Hill, John, and Church Gibson, Pamela. Oxford: Oxford University Press, 1998, p. 83.
49. Both Clover and Rockoff include the location in their list of the subgenre's elements naming it 'terrible place' and 'setting' respectively. For more information, see Clover, J. Carol. *Men, Women and Chain Saws. Gender in the Modern Horror Film*. Princeton, NJ: Princeton University Press, 1992, pp. 30–31, and Rockoff, Adam. *Going to Pieces: The Rise and Fall of the Slasher Film, 1978–1986*. Jefferson, NC: McFarland, 2002, pp. 10–12.
50. Truffaut, François. *Hitchcock* (Greek translation by G. Ioannidis). Athens: Ipsilon, 1986, p. 216.
51. Gomery, Douglas. *The History of Cinema* (Greek translation by M. Talantopoulou). Athens: Ellin, 1998, p. 331.
52. Worland, Rick. *The Horror Film: An Introduction*. Hoboken, NJ: Wiley-Blackwell, 2007, p. 87.
53. For more information, see Freud, Sigmund. *The Uncanny*, translated by David McLintock. London: Penguin Books, 2003.
54. Israeli, Noam. "Reflections on Freud's The Uncanny." *Journal of the Society for Existential Analysis* 16, 2 (2005): p. 379.
55. Derry, Charles. *Dark Dreams 2.0.: A Psychological History of the Modern Horror Film from the 1950s to the 21st Century*. Jefferson, NC: McFarland, 2009, pp. 21–106.
56. Worland, *The Horror Film*, p. 87.
57. Thomas, Kevin. "The Other." *Peace Review* 14, 3 (2002): p. 331.
58. For more information, see Williams, Robert R. *Recognition: Fichte and Hegel on the Other*. New York: SUNY Press, 1992.
59. See Sartre, Jean-Paul. *Being and Nothingness: An Essay on Phenomenological Ontology*, translated by Hazel E. Barnes. London: Routledge, 2003.
60. See Beauvoir, Simone de. *The Second Sex*, translated by H. M. Parshley. New York: Vintage, 1989.
61. See Levinas, Emmanuel. *Totality and Infinity: An Essay on Exteriority*, translated by Alfonso Lingis. Netherlands: Kluwer Academic Publishers, 1991.
62. See Kristeva, Julia. *Powers of Horror: An Essay on Abjection*, translated by Leon S. Roudiez. New York: Columbia University Press, 1982; and Kristeva, Julia. *Strangers to Ourselves*. New York: Columbia University Press, 1991.
63. See Lacan, Jacques. *Écrits: The First Complete Edition in English*, translated by Bruce Fink. New York: W. W. Norton & Co., 2006.
64. See Kristeva, Julia, *Powers of Horror*.
65. Wood, *Hollywood from Vietnam to Reagan*, p. 65.
66. For more information regarding the Other, see Lacan, Jacques. *The Seminar of Jacques Lacan, Book II: The Ego in Freud's Theory and in the Technique of Psychoanalysis, 1954–1955*, translated by Sylvana Tomaselli. New York: W. W. Norton & Co., 1991, pp. 235–247.
67. Evans, Dylan. *An Introductory Dictionary of Lacanian Psychoanalysis*. London: Routledge, 1996, pp. 135–136.
68. Žižek, Slavoj. *How to Read Lacan*. New York: W. W. Norton & Co., 2006, p. 8.
69. *Ibid.*, p. 11.
70. Morrison, Cary. "Creature Conflict: Man, Monster and the Metaphor of Intractable Social Conflict." In *Monsters and the Monstrous. Myths & Metaphors of Enduring Evil*, edited by Paul L. Yoder and Peter Mario Kreuter. Oxford, UK: Inter-Disciplinary Press, 2004, p. 172.

71. Sharrett, Christopher. "The Horror Film as Social Allegory (And How it Comes Undone)." In *A Companion to the Horror Film*, edited by Harry M. Benshoff. Hoboken, NJ: Wiley-Blackwell, 2014, p. 69.

72. Rockoff, *Going to Pieces*, p. 15.

73. For more information, see Metz, Christian. *Psychoanalysis and Cinema: The Imaginary Signifier*. Bloomington: Indiana University Press, 1982; Baudry, Jean-Louis. "Ideological Effects of the Basic Cinematographic Apparatus." In *Narrative, Apparatus, Ideology*, edited by P. Rosen. New York: Columbia University Press, 1986; and Baudry, Jean-Louis. "The Apparatus: Metaphysical Approaches to Ideology." In *Narrative, Apparatus, Ideology*, edited by P. Rosen. New York: Columbia University Press, 1986.

74. Lacan argued that there are three orders in human life: the real, the imaginary, and the symbolic. The mirror stage, which takes place at the imaginary order, happens in infancy when the child faces himself in the mirror. Until then, the infant is incomplete and has physical ambitions that exceed its ability to move. But looking in the mirror, it perceives itself as a whole, a perfect image as the adults around him. Thus, recognition is overwhelmed by a non-recognition. When the infant looks at the mirror, it recognizes itself, but at the same time it creates an idealized self by neglecting his imperfections. In this way, preparations are made for future identification with others. For more information, see Evans, *An Introductory Dictionary of Lacanian Psychoanalysis*.

75. Jemmer, Patrick. "The O(the)r (O)the(r)..." In *Engage Newcastle Volume 1—Café Philosophique: A Season of "the Other,"* edited by Patrick Jemmer. Newcastle, UK: Newcastle Philosophy Society, 2010, p. 9.

76. Marriott, James. *Horror Films*. London: Virgin, 2007, p. 214.

77. If we take into account the fact that a male character has virginal characteristics, we can understand that the subgenre has stepped away from the stereotyped gender representation and sexuality.

78. Wetmore, Kevin J. *Post-9/11 Horror in American Cinema*. New York: Continuum, 2012, p. 195.

79. Greven, David. *Representations of Femininity in American Genre Cinema: The Woman's Film, Film Noir, and Modern Horror*. New York: Palgrave Macmillan, 2011, p 146.

80. See Hogan, Joseph. *The Reagan Years: The Record in Presidential Leadership*. Manchester: Manchester University Press, 1990.

81. Altman, *The American Film Musical*, pp. 116–117.

82. Altman. *Film/Genre*, p. 195.

83. Nowell, Richard. *Blood Money: A History of the First Teen Slasher Film Cycle*. New York: Continuum, 2011, p. 18.

84. Palmer, William J. *The Films of the Eighties: A Social History*. Carbondale: Southern Illinois University Press, 1993, p. ix.

85. *Ibid.*, p. x.

86. Benshoff, Harry and Sean Griffin. *America on Film: Representing Race, Class, Gender and Sexuality at the Movies*. Oxford, UK: Blackwell Publishing, 2004, p. 323.

87. *Ibid.*, p. 323.

88. *Ibid.*, pp. 325–326.

89. Parker, Richard. "Sexuality, Culture, and Power in HIV/AIDS Research." *Annual Review of Anthropology* 30 (2001):p. 164.

90. Benshoff and Griffin, *America on Film*, p. 326.

91. *Ibid.*, p. 322.

92. Rockoff, *Going to Pieces*, p. 177.

93. Altman, *Film/Genre*, p. 195.

94. Stam, Robert. *An Introduction to Film Theory* (Greek translation by K. Kaklamani). Athens: Pataki, 2006, p. 198.

95. Jameson, Frederic. *Postmodernism or the Cultural Logic of Late Capitalism*. Durham: Duke University Press, 1991, p. 16–17.

96. Phillips, *Projected Fears*, p. 170.

97. Hutcheon, Linda. *A Poetics of Postmodernism: History, Theory, Fiction.* London: Routledge, 1988, p. 11.
98. Stam, *An Introduction to Film Theory*, p. 383.
99. Carroll, Noel. "The Future of Allusion: Hollywood in the Seventies (And beyond)." *October*, 20 (1982): p. 52.
100. Derry, Charles. *The Suspense Thriller: Films in the Shadow of Alfred Hitchcock.* Jefferson, NC: McFarland, 2001, p. 59.
101. Wee, Valerie. "The Scream Trilogy, 'Hyperpostmodernism,' and the Late-Nineties Teen Slasher Film." *Journal of Film and Video*, 57:3 (2005): p. 49.
102. All financial data are coming from the website *Box Office Mojo*.
103. Wyrick, Laura. "Horror at Century's End: Where Have All the Slashers Gone?" *Pacific Coast Philology*, Vol. 33, No. 2 (1998): p. 123.
104. Trencansky, Sarah. "Final Girls and Terrible Youth: Transgression in 1980s Slasher Horror." *Journal of Popular Film & Television*, 29, 2 (2001): p. 71.
105. Rockoff, *Going to Pieces*, p. 193.
106. Michotte, Albert. "The Emotional Involvement of the Spectator in the Action Represented in a Film: Toward a Theory." In *Michotte's Experimental Phenomenology of Perception*, edited by G. Thines, A. Costall, G. Butterworth. Hillsdale, NJ: Lawrence Erlbaum, 1991, p. 209.
107. Jarrett, Murphy. "Reagan & Bush, Father & Son." *CBS News*, December 5, 2007. http://www.cbsnews.com/2100-500345_162-622031.html.
108. Holloway, David. *9/11 and The War on Terror.* Edinburgh, UK: Edinburgh University Press, 2008, p. 1.
109. Smith, Kathy. "Reframing Fantasy: September 11 and the Global Audience." In *The Spectacle of the Real: From Hollywood to Reality TV and Beyond*, edited by Geoff King. Bristol, UK: Intellect, 2005, p. 62.
110. Žižek, Slavoj. *Welcome to the Desert of the Real! Five Essays on September 11 and Other Relevant Dates* (Greek translation by Vicky Iakovou). Athens: Scripta, 2003, p. 21.
111. Briefel, Aviva and Miller, Sam J. "Introduction." In *Horror After 9/11. World of Fear, Cinema of Terror*, edited by Aviva Briefel and Sam J. Miller. Austin: University of Texas Press, 2011, p. 1.
112. Miller, Sam J. "Assimilation and the Queer Monster." In *Horror After 9/11. World of Fear, Cinema of Terror*, edited by Aviva Briefel and Sam J. Miller. Austin: University of Texas Press, 2011, p. 225.
113. Hand, Richard and Jay McRoy. *Monstrous Adaptations: Generic and Thematic Mutations in Horror Film.* Manchester, UK: Manchester University Press, 2007, p. 1.
114. Wetmore, *Post-9/11 Horror in American Cinema*, p. 196.
115. In Breznican, Anthony. "Texas Chainsaw Massacre Passes Old Saw to New Generation." *Whitehorse Star*, October 15, 2003, p. 28.
116. Asma, Stephen T. "Monsters on the Brain: An Evolutionary Epistemology of Horror." *Social Research* 82:4 (2014): p. 958.
117. For more information, see Asma, Stephen T. *On Monsters: An Unnatural History of Our Worst Fears.* New York: Oxford University Press, 2009.

Chapter 2

1. *Halloween* (1978), *Halloween II* (1981), *Halloween III: Season of the Witch* (1982), *Halloween 4: The Return of Michael Myers* (1988), *Halloween 5* (1989), *Halloween: The Curse of Michael Myers* (1995), *Halloween H20: 20 Years Later* (1998), *Halloween: Resurrection* (2002), *Halloween* (2007) and *Halloween II* (2009).
2. Sleepers are called films that have earned many profits, although their economic success has not been predicted. For more, see Berra, John. *Declarations of Independence: American Cinema and the Partiality of Independent Production.* Bristol, UK: Intellect Books, 2008, p. 68.

3. For more, see Kaklamanidou, Despoina. *Introduction to Hollywood Romantic Comedy: Cinema Genre and Gender Representation (in Greek)*. Athens: Aigokeros, 2007, p. 120.

4. Benshoff, Harry, and Sean Griffin. *America on Film: Representing Race, Class, Gender and Sexuality at the Movies*. Oxford, UK: Blackwell Publishing, 2004, pp. 320–321.

5. Phillips, Kendall R. *Projected Fears, Horror Films and American Culture*. Westport, CT: Praeger, 2005, p. 131.

6. Phillips, *Projected Fears*, p. 138.

7. For more about the importance of Halloween in the horror genre, see Hutchings, Peter. *The A to Z of Horror Cinema*. Lanham, MD: Scarecrow Press, 2009, p. 52 and p. 116.

8. The films of the franchise are: *The Texas Chain Saw Massacre* (1974), *The Texas Chainsaw Massacre 2* (1986), *Leatherface: Texas Chainsaw Massacre III* (1990), The *Return of the Texas Chainsaw Massacre* (1994), *The Texas Chainsaw Massacre* (2003), *The Texas Chainsaw Massacre: The Beginning* (2006) and *Texas Chainsaw 3D* (2013).

9. Indicatively, I mention the neoslasher films from the three most famous franchises of the subgenre: From *Halloween* there are two films, *Halloween* (2007) and *Halloween II* (2009); from *Friday the 13th* there is only the film of 2009 and from *A Nightmare on Elm Street* only the 2010 film. The aforementioned films are remakes of classical films, while the *Texas Chainsaw Massacre* franchise has a remake, a prequel and a sequel.

10. Of course, the premiere of the first took place in the United States while the second in Canada. *Black Christmas* premiered in the U.S. on December 20, 1974. The source of the above information is from the site IMDb, www.imdb.com.

11. Phillips, *Projected Fears*, p. 107.

12. Melanson, Richard A. *American Foreign Policy since the Vietnam War: The Search for Consensus from Richard Nixon to George W. Bush, Fourth Edition*. New York: M.E. Sharpe Inc., 2005, p. 45.

13. Simon, David R. "Watergate and the Nixon Presidency: A Comparative Ideological Analysis." In *Watergate and Afterward: The Legacy of Richard M. Nixon*, edited by Leon Friedman and William F. Levantrosser. Westport, CT: Greenwood Publishing Group Inc., 1992, p. 5.

14. For more, see Green, Robert. *Richard M. Nixon*. Minneapolis: Compass Point Books, 2003, pp. 44–48.

15. Robertson, David Brian. *Loss of Confidence: Politics and Policy in the 1970s*. University Park, PA: Penn State University Press, 1998, p. 1.

16. Macor, Alison. *Chainsaws, Slackers, and Spy Kids: Thirty Years of Filmmaking in Austin, Texas*. Austin: University of Texas Press, 2010, p. 19.

17. Farley, Ellen, and William K. Knoedelseder, Jr. "The Real Texas Chainsaw Massacre." *Los Angeles Times Calendar*, September 5, 1982.

18. Platts, Todd K. "The New Horror Movie." In *Baby Boomers and Popular Culture: An Inquiry into America's Most Powerful Generation*, edited by Brian Cogan and Thom Gencarelli. Westport, CT: Praeger, 2015, p. 153.

19. Merritt, Naomi. "Cannibalistic Capitalism and other American Delicacies: A Bataillean Taste of The Texas Chain Saw Massacre." *Film-Philosophy*, 14:1 (2010): p. 202.

20. Wood, Robin. "An Introduction to the American Horror Film." In *Planks of Reason: Essays on the Horror Film*, edited by Barry Keith Grant. Lanham, MD: Scarecrow Press, 1984, p. 174.

21. Becker, Matt. "A Point of Little Hope: Hippie Horror Films and the Politics of Ambivalence." *Velvet Light Trap*, 57 (2006): p. 43.

22. Sharrett, Christopher. "The Idea of Apocalypse in The Texas Chainsaw Massacre." In *Planks of Reason: Essays on the Horror Film*, edited by Barry Keith Grant. Lanham, MD: Scarecrow Press, 1984, p. 262.

23. Marriott, James. *Horror Films*. London: Virgin, 2007, p. 183.

Tallon, Philip. "Through a Mirror, Darkly: Art-Horror as a Medium for Moral Reflection." In *The Philosophy of Horror*, edited by Thomas Fahy. Lexington: University Press of Kentucky, 2010, p. 35.

24. Wood, Robin. "An Introduction to the American Horror Film," p. 189.
25. Clover, J. Carol. *Men, Women and Chain Saws. Gender in the Modern Horror Film*. Princeton, NJ: Princeton University Press, 1992, p. 130.
26. Phillips, *Projected Fears*, p. 114.
27. In Jones, Alan. *The Rough Guide to Horror Movies*, p. 158.
28. Simpson, Philip L. "Whither the Serial Killer Movie?" In *American Horror Film: The Genre at the Turn of the Millennium*, edited by Steffen Hantke. Jackson: University Press of Mississippi, 2010, p. 136.
29. Bulkeley, Kelly. "Touring the Dream Factory: The Dream-Film Connection in *The Wizard of Oz* and *A Nightmare on Elm Street*." *Dreaming*, 9:1 (1999): p. 104.
30. Kendrick, James. "Razors in the Dreamscape: Revisiting *A Nightmare on Elm Street* and the Slasher Film." *Film Criticism*, 33:3 (2009): p. 20.
31. Heba, Gary. "Everyday Nightmares: The Rhetoric of Social Horror in the Nightmare on Elm Street Series." *Journal of Popular Film and Television*, 23:3 (1995): p. 112.
32. MacGregor Johnston, David. "Kitsch and Camp and Things That Go Bump in the Night; or, Sontag and Adorno at the (Horror) Movies." In *The Philosophy of Horror*, edited by Thomas Fahy. Lexington: University Press of Kentucky, 2010, p. 234.
33. This term is used for films that appeared in the United States in the 1970s and had as main representation African-American characters. For more information, see Lawrence, Novotny. *Blaxploitation Films of the 1970s: Blackness and Genre*. London: Routledge, 2008.
34. In Rockoff, Adam. *Going to Pieces. The Rise and Fall of the Slasher Film, 1978–1986*. Jefferson, NC: McFarland, 2002, p. 57.
35. *Ibid.*, p. 54.
36. Telotte, J. P. "Faith and Idolatry in the Horror Film." In *Planks of Reason. Essays on the Horror Film*, edited by Barry Keith Grant. Lanham, MD: Scarecrow Press, 1984, p. 26.
37. Connelly, Kelly. "From Final Girl to Final Woman: Defeating the Male Monster in Halloween and Halloween H20." *Journal of Popular Film & Television*, Vol. 35 Issue 1 (2007): p. 15.
38. For more information regarding feminism, see Beasley, Chris. *What Is Feminism?: An Introduction to Feminist Theory*. Thousand Oaks, CA: Sage, 1999.
39. For more, see Krolokke, Charlotte and Anne Scott Sorensen. "Three Waves of Feminism: From Suffragettes to Grrls." In *Gender Communication Theories & Analyses: From Silence to Performance*. Thousand Oaks, CA: Sage, 2006, pp. 1–23.
40. Neale, Steve. "Halloween: Suspense, Aggression and the Look." In *Planks of Reason. Essays on the Horror Film*, edited by Barry Keith Grant. Lanham, MD: Scarecrow Press, 1984, p. 332.
41. Cherry, Brigid. *Routledge Film Guidebooks: Horror*. London: Routledge, 2009, p. 138.
42. The filmic texts are: *Friday the 13th* (1980), *Friday the 13th Part 2* (1981), *Friday the 13th Part III* (1982), *Friday the 13th: The Final Chapter* (1984), *Friday the 13th: A New Beginning* (1985), *Jason Lives: Friday the 13th Part VI* (1986), *Friday the 13th Part VII: The New Blood* (1988), *Friday the 13th Part VIII: Jason Takes Manhattan* (1989), *Jason Goes to Hell: The Final Friday* (1993), *Jason X* (2001), *Freddy vs. Jason* (2003) and *Friday the 13th* (2009).
43. The filmic texts are: *A Nightmare on Elm Street* (1984), *A Nightmare on Elm Street Part 2: Freddy's Revenge* (1985), *A Nightmare on Elm Street 3: Dream Warriors* (1987), *A Nightmare on Elm Street 4: The Dream Master* (1988), *A Nightmare on Elm Street: The Dream Child* (1989), *Freddy's Dead: The Final Nightmare* (1991), *New Nightmare* (1994), *Freddy vs. Jason* (2003) and *A Nightmare on Elm Street* (2010).
44. Hills, Matt and Steven Jay Schneider. "'The Devil Made Me Do It!': Representing Evil and Disarticulating Mind/Body in the Supernatural Serial Killer Film." In *The Changing Face of Evil in Film and Television*, edited by Martin F. Norden. Amsterdam, The Netherlands: Rodopi, 2007, p. 74.
45. In Grove, David. *Making Friday the 13th: The Legend of Camp Blood*. Godalming, UK: FAB Press, 2005, p. 15.

46. Nowell, Richard. "The Ambitions of Most Independent Filmmakers: Indie Production, the Majors, and *Friday the 13th* (1980)." *Journal of Film and Video*, 63:2 (2011): p. 37.
47. Borges, Andre. "Friday the 13th: One of the First 'True' Slasher Films." *DNA: Daily News and Analysis*, 14 September, 2013.
48. In Sharrett, Christopher. "Fairy Tales for the Apocalypse: Wes Craven on the Horror Film." *Literature/Film Quarterly*, 13:3 (1985): p. 144.
49. Markovitz, Jonathan. "Female Paranoia as Survival Skill: Reason or Pathology in *A Nightmare on Elm Street*?" *Quarterly Review of Film and Video*, 17:3 (2000): p. 218.
50. Modleski, Tania. "The Terror of Pleasure: The Contemporary Horror Film and Postmodern Theory." In *The Horror Reader*, edited by Ken Gelder. London: Routledge, 2000, p. 290.
51. Phillips, *Projected Fears*, p. 134.

Chapter 3

1. Kvaran, Kara M. "'You're All Doomed!' A Socioeconomic Analysis of Slasher Films." *Journal of American Studies* 50:4 (2016): p. 964.
2. Kahn, Paul W. *Finding Ourselves at the Movies: Philosophy for a New Generation*. New York: Columbia University Press, 2013, p. 169.
3. Jackson, Kimberly. *Technology, Monstrosity, and Reproduction in Twenty-first Century Horror*. New York: Palgrave MacMillan, 2013, p. 12.
4. Wee, Valerie. "Resurrecting and Updating the Teen Slasher: The Case of Scream." *Journal of Popular Film and Television* 34:2 (2006): p.54.
5. Pheasant-Kelly, Fran. "Reframing Parody and Intertextuality in Scream: Formal and Theoretical Approaches to the 'Postmodern' Slasher." In *Style and Form in the Hollywood Slasher Film*, edited by Wickham Clayton. New York: Palgrave Macmillan, 2015, p. 160.
6. Tietchen, Todd F. "Samplers and Copycats: The Cultural Implications of the Postmodern Slasher in Contemporary American Film." *Journal of Popular Film and Television* 26:3 (1998): p. 103.
7. Syder, Andrew. "Knowing the Rules. Postmodernism and the Horror Film." *Special Issue of Spectator* 22: 2 (Fall 2002): p. 87.
8. See Baudrillard, Jean. *Simulations*, translated by Paul Foss, Paul Patton, and Philip Beitchman. New York: Semiotext(e), 1983.
9. Baudrillard, Jean. "The Precession of the Simulacra." In *Cultural Theory and Popular Culture: A Reader*, edited by J. Storey. New Jersey: Prentice Hall, 1998, p. 351.
10. See Baudrillard, Jean. *The Gulf War Did Not Take Place*, translated by Paul Patton. Bloomington: Indiana University Press, 1995.
11. Shary, Timothy. *Teen Movies: American Youth on Screen*. New York and Chichester, New York: Columbia University Press, 2005, p. 101.
12. Stephens, John. "'I'll Never Be the Same After That Summer': From Abjection to Subjective Agency in Teen Films." In *Youth Cultures: Texts, Images, and Identities*, edited by Kerry Mallan and Sharyn Pearce. Westport, CT: Praeger, 2003, p. 123.
13. Worland, Rick. *The Horror Film: An Introduction*. Oxford, UK: Blackwell Publishing, 2007, p. 113.
14. Hutchings, Peter. *The Horror Film*. London: Routledge, 2013, p. 214.
15. Francis, James, Jr. *Remaking Horror: Hollywood's New Reliance on Scares of Old*. Jefferson, NC: McFarland, 2013, p. 66.
16. Perren, Alisa. *Indie, Inc.: Miramax and the Transformation of Hollywood in the 1990s*. Austin: University of Texas Press, 2012, p. 128.
17. Muir, John Kenneth. *Wes Craven: The Art of Horror*. Jefferson, NC: McFarland, 1998, p. 32.
18. Dixon, Wheeler Winston. "'Fighting and Violence and Everything, That's Always Cool': Teen Films in the 1990s." In *Film Genre 2000: New Critical Essays*, edited by Wheeler Winston Dixon. New York: SUNY Press, 2000, p. 125.

19. Perkins, Claire. "The Scre4m Trilogy." In *Film Trilogies: New Critical Approaches*, edited by Claire Perkins and Constantine Verevis. New York: Palgrave MacMillan, 2012, pp. 100–101.

Chapter 4

1. Tompkins, Joe. "Re-imagining the Canon: Examining the Discourse of Contemporary Horror Film Reboots." *New Review of Film and Television Studies* 12:4 (2014): p. 382.
2. In "Fright Exclusive Interview: Rob Zombie." *Icons of Fright*, 2007. Accessed November 07, 2015.
3. Manning, David. "A Great Legacy Slashed to Bits." *The Nelson Mail*, February 10, 2004, p. 15.
4. In Spong, John. "Oh, the Horror!" *Texas Monthly*, October 2002.
5. Heffernan, Kevin. "Risen from the Vaults: Recent Horror Film Remakes and the American Film Industry." In *Merchants of Menace: The Business of Horror Cinema*, edited by Richard Nowell. New York: Bloomsbury, 2014, p. 67.
6. Kellner, Douglas. *Cinema Wars: Hollywood Film and Politics in the Bush-Cheney Era*. Hoboken, NJ: Wiley-Blackwell, 2010, p. 91.
7. Blake, Linnie. "I Am the Devil and I'm Here to Do the Devil's Work: Rob Zombie, George W. Bush, and the Limits of American Freedom." In *Horror After 9/11. World of Fear, Cinema of Terror*, edited by Aviva Briefel and Sam J. Miller. Austin: University of Texas Press, 2011, p. 190.
8. Wetmore, Kevin J. *Post-9/11 Horror in American Cinema*. New York: Continuum, 2012, p. 45.
9. Blake, Linnie. *The Wounds of Nations: Horror Cinema, Historical Trauma and National Identity*. Manchester, UK: Manchester University Press, 2008, p. 143.
10. Wetmore, *Post-9/11 Horror in American Cinema*, p. 45.
11. Moseley, Fred. "The U.S. economic crisis." *International Socialist Review*, Issue 64 (March 2009). http://isreview.org/issue/64/us-economic-crisis.
12. Lipsett, Joe. "'One for the Horror Fans' vs. 'An Insult to the Horror Genre': Negotiating Reading Strategies in IMDb Reviews of *The Cabin in the Woods*." *Slayage* 10:2/11:1 (Fall 2013/Winter 2014): paragraph 7.
13. Canavan, Gerry. "'Something Nightmares Are From': Metacommentary in Joss Whedon's *The Cabin in the Woods*." *Slayage* 10:2/11:1 (Fall 2013/Winter 2014): paragraph 2.
14. Starr, Michael. "Whedon's Great Glass Elevator: Space, Liminality, and Intertext in *The Cabin in the Woods*." *Slayage* 10:2/11:1 (Fall 2013/Winter 2014): paragraph 2.
15. Klein, Andy. "Freddy vs. Jason" *Variety*, 391:12, 11–17 August, 2003, p. 20.
16. "Freddy vs. Jason Slashes Competition." *North Bay Nugget*, August 18, 2003.
17. Nelson, Andrew Patrick. "Traumatic Childhood Now Included. Todorov's Fantastic and the Uncanny Slasher Remake." In *American Horror Film: The Genre at the Turn of the Millennium*, edited by Steffen Hantke. Jackson: University Press of Mississippi, 2010, p. 113.
18. Strawser, Justin. "*Friday the 13th* Franchise Resurrected for New Generation of Slasher Film Devotees." *The News-Item*, February 14, 2009.
19. Wolgamott, Kent L. "Bloody Friday." *Lincoln Journal Star*, February 13, 2009.
20. For more information, see Mulvey, Laura. *Visual and Other Pleasures*. London: MacMillan, 1989.
21. Kawin, Bruce F. "Children of the Light." In *Film Genre Reader III*, edited by Barry Keith Grant. Austin: University of Texas Press, 2003, p. 327–328.
22. Lowenstein, Adam. "Alone on Elm Street." *Film Quarterly*, 64:1 (2010): p. 19.
23. Harvey, Dennis. "A Nightmare on Elm Street." *Variety*, 418:3 (May 3–May 9, 2010): p. 21.
24. Wee, Valerie. "New Decade, New Rules. Rebooting the Scream Franchise in the Digital Age." In *Merchants of Menace: The Business of Horror Cinema*, edited by Richard Nowell. New York: Bloomsbury, 2014, p. 153.

25. In Portman, Jamie. "The debate over *Scream 4*; Revolting slasher film or classical theatre for a modern age? The argument continues." *The Ottawa Citizen*, April 14, 2011.

26. In Johnson, Kevin C. "Craven promises new twist for horror film *Scream 4*." *McClatchy—Tribune Business News*, April 10, 2011.

27. There is an extensive analysis of the two generations of *Scream 4* in Petridis, Sotiris. "The Scream of a Generation: "Generation Me" in Scream 4." In *The Millennials on Film and Television: Essays on the Politics of Popular Culture*, edited by Betty Kaklamanidou and Margaret Tally. Jefferson, NC: McFarland, 2014.

28. In Johnson, "Craven Promises New Twist."

29. Giannini, Erin. "'Charybdis Tested Well with Teens': *The Cabin in the Woods* as Metafictional Critique of Corporate Media Producers and Audiences." *Slayage* 10:2/11:1 (Fall 2013/Winter 2014): paragraph 7.

30. Cooper, L. Andrew. "*The Cabin in the Woods* and the End of American Exceptionalism." *Slayage* 10:2/11:1 (Fall 2013/Winter 2014): paragraph 4.

31. McDonald, Rick. "Sacred Violence and *The Cabin in the Woods*." *Slayage* 10:2/11:1 (Fall 2013/Winter 2014): paragraph 14.

32. Woofter, Kristopher and Jasie Stokes. "Once More into the Woods: An Introduction and Provocation." *Slayage* 10:2/11:1 (Fall 2013/Winter 2014): paragraph 3.

33. Renner, Karen J. "Generational Conflict, Twenty-First-Century Horror Films and *The Cabin in the Woods*." In *The Millennials on Film and Television: Essays on the Politics of Popular Culture*, edited by Betty Kaklamanidou and Margaret Tally. Jefferson, NC: McFarland, 2014, p. 118.

Filmography

April Fool's Day (Walton, 1986)
Avatar (Cameron, 2009)
Bad Dreams (Fleming, 1988)
The Bad Seed (LeRoy, 1956)
Batman Begins (Nolan, 2005)
Berserk (O'Connolly, 1967)
Black Christmas (Clark, 1974)
The Blair Witch Project (Myrick and Sánchez, 1999)
Bride of Chucky (Yu, 1998)
Cabin Fever (Roth, 2002)
The Cabin in the Woods (Goddard, 2012)
Candyman (Rose, 1992)
Candyman: Farewell to the Flesh (Condon, 1995)
Child's Play (Holland, 1988)
Child's Play 2 (Lafia, 1990)
Child's Play 3 (Bender, 1991)
Cover Girl Killer (Bishop, 1959)
Darkness Falls (Liebesman, 2003)
The Final Destination (Ellis, 2009)
Final Destination (Wong, 2000)
Final Destination 2 (Ellis, 2003)
Final Destination 3 (Wong, 2006)
Final Destination 5 (Quale, 2011)
Frankenstein (Whale, 1931)
Frankenstein meets the Wolf Man (Neill, 1943)
Freddy vs. Jason (Yu, 2003)
Freddy's Dead: The Final Nightmare (Talalay, 1991)
Freddy's Nightmares (Syndication, 1988–1990)
Friday the 13th (Cunningham, 1980)
Friday the 13th (Nispel, 2009)
Friday the 13th (Syndication, 1987–1990)
Friday the 13th Part 2 (Miner, 1981)
Friday the 13th Part III (Miner, 1982)
Friday the 13th Part VII: The New Blood (Buechler, 1988)
Friday the 13th Part VIII: Jason Takes Manhattan (Hedden, 1989)

Friday the 13th: A New Beginning (Steinmann, 1985)
Friday the 13th: The Final Chapter (Zito, 1984)
The Fun House (Hooper, 1981)
Grease (Kleiser, 1978)
Halloween (Carpenter, 1978)
Halloween (Zombie, 2007)
Halloween 4: The Return of Michael Myers (Little, 1988)
Halloween 5 (Othenin-Girard, 1989)
Halloween H20: 20 Years Later (Miner, 1998)
Halloween II (Rosenthal, 1981)
Halloween II (Zombie, 2009)
Halloween III: Season of the Witch (Wallace, 1982)
Halloween: Resurrection (Rosenthal, 2002)
Halloween: The Curse of Michael Myers (Chappelle, 1995)
Happy Days (ABC, 1974–1984)
He Knows You're Alone (Mastroianni, 1980)
The Hills Have Eyes (Craven, 1977)
The Hills Have Eyes (Aja, 2006)
House of Wax (Collet-Serra, 2005)
The House on Sorority Row (Rosman, 1983)
I Know What You Did Last Summer (Gillespie, 1997)
I Still Know What You Did Last Summer (Cannon, 1998)
It (ABC, 1990)
Jason Goes to Hell: The Final Friday (Marcus, 1993)
Jason Lives: Friday the 13th Part VI (McLoughlin, 1986)
Jason X (Isaac, 2001)
Jeepers Creepers (Salva, 2001)
Jeepers Creepers 2 (Salva, 2003)
The Last House on the Left (Craven, 1972)
Laverne and Shirley (ABC, 1976–1983)
Leatherface: Texas Chainsaw Massacre III (Burr, 1990)
The Leopard Man (Tourneur, 1943)
My Bloody Valentine (Mihalka, 1981)
My Bloody Valentine (Lussier, 2009)
My Soul to Take (Craven, 2010)
The Mysteries of Paris (Gandéra, 1935)
New Nightmare (Craven, 1994)
Night School (Hughes, 1981)
A Nightmare on Elm Street (Bayer, 2010)
A Nightmare on Elm Street (Craven, 1984)
A Nightmare on Elm Street 3: Dream Warriors (Russell, 1987)
A Nightmare on Elm Street 4: The Dream Master (Harlin, 1988)
A Nightmare on Elm Street Part 2: Freddy's Revenge (Sholder, 1985)
A Nightmare on Elm Street: The Dream Child (Hopkins, 1989)
The Omen (Moore, 2006)
Peeping Tom (Powell, 1960)
Prom Night (Lynch, 1980)

Prom Night (McCormick, 2008)
Psycho (Hitchcock, 1960)
The *Return of the Texas Chainsaw Massacre* (Henkel, 1994)
The Ring (Verbinski, 2002)
Ringu (Nakata, 1998)
Scream (Craven, 1996)
Scream 2 (Craven, 1997)
Scream 3 (Craven, 2000)
Scream 4 (Craven, 2011)
Scream Queens (Fox, 2015–2016)
Scream: The TV Series (MTV, 2015-Today)
Shocker (Craven, 1989)
The Silence of The Lambs (Demme, 1991)
The Sixth Sense (Shyamalan, 1999)
Strait-Jacket (Castle, 1964)
The Texas Chain Saw Massacre (Hooper, 1974)
The Texas Chainsaw Massacre (Nispel, 2003)
The Texas Chainsaw Massacre 2 (Hooper, 1986)
The Texas Chainsaw Massacre: The Beginning (Liebesman, 2006)
Texas Chainsaw 3D (Luessenhop, 2013)
Thirteen Women (Archainbaud, 1932)
Urban Legend (Blanks, 1998)
Urban Legends: Final Cut (Ottman, 2000)
Valentine (Blanks, 2001)
Visiting Hours (Lord, 1982)
When a Stranger Calls (Walton, 1979)
When a Stranger Calls (West, 2006)
Without Warning (Laven, 1952)
The Wolfman (Johnston, 2010)
Wrong Turn (Schmidt, 2003)
Wrong Turn 2: Dead End (Lynch, 2007)

Bibliography

Altman, Rick. *The American Film Musical.* Bloomington: Indiana University Press, 1987.
Altman, Rick. *Film/Genre.* London: BFI Publishing, 2006.
Altman, Rick. "A Semantic/Syntactic Approach to Film Genre." In *Film Genre Reader III,* edited by Barry Keith Grant. Austin: University of Texas Press, 2003.
Asma, Stephen T. "Monsters on the Brain: An Evolutionary Epistemology of Horror." *Social Research* 82:4 (2014): pp. 941–968.
Asma, Stephen T. *On Monsters: An Unnatural History of Our Worst Fears.* New York: Oxford University Press, 2009.
Baudrillard, Jean. *The Gulf War Did Not Take Place,* translated by Paul Patton. Bloomington: Indiana University Press, 1995.
Baudrillard, Jean. "The Precession of the Simulacra." In *Cultural Theory and Popular Culture: A Reader,* edited by J. Storey. Upper Saddle River, NJ: Prentice Hall, 1998.
Baudrillard, Jean. *Simulations,* translated by Paul Foss, Paul Patton, and Philip Beitchman. New York: Semiotext(e), 1983.
Baudry, Jean-Louis. "The Apparatus: Metaphysical Approaches to Ideology." In *Narrative, Apparatus, Ideology,* edited by P. Rosen. New York: Columbia University Press, 1986.
Baudry, Jean-Louis. "Ideological Effects of the Basic Cinematographic Apparatus." In *Narrative, Apparatus, Ideology,* edited by P. Rosen. New York: Columbia University Press, 1986.
Beasley, Chris. *What Is Feminism?: An Introduction to Feminist Theory.* Thousand Oaks, CA: Sage, 1999.
Beauvoir, Simone de. *The Second Sex,* translated by H. M. Parshley. New York: Vintage, 1989.
Becker, Matt. "A Point of Little Hope: Hippie Horror Films and the Politics of Ambivalence." *Velvet Light Trap,* 57 (2006): pp. 42–59.
Benshoff, Harry. *Monsters in the Closet: Homosexuality and the Horror Film.* Manchester, UK: Manchester University Press, 1997.
Benshoff, Harry and Sean Griffin. *America on Film: Representing Race, Class, Gender and Sexuality at the Movies.* Oxford, UK: Blackwell Publishing, 2004.
Berra, John. *Declarations of Independence: American Cinema and the Partiality of Independent Production.* Bristol: Intellect Books, 2008.
Blake, Linnie. "I Am the Devil and I'm Here to Do the Devil's Work: Rob Zombie, George W. Bush, and the Limits of American Freedom." In *Horror After 9/11: World of Fear, Cinema of Terror,* edited by Aviva Briefel and Sam J. Miller. Austin: University of Texas Press, 2011.
Blake, Linnie. *The Wounds of Nations: Horror Cinema, Historical Trauma and National Identity.* Manchester, UK: Manchester University Press, 2008.
Borges, Andre. "Friday the 13th: One of the First 'True' Slasher Films." *DNA: Daily News and Analysis,* September 14, 2013.
Box Office Mojo. http://www.boxofficemojo.com.
Breznican, Anthony. "Texas Chainsaw Massacre Passes Old Saw to New Generation." *Whitehorse Star,* October 15, 2003.

Briefel, Aviva, and Sam J. Miller. "Introduction." In *Horror After 9/11: World of Fear, Cinema of Terror*, edited by Aviva Briefel and Sam J. Miller. Austin: University of Texas Press, 2011.

Bulkeley, Kelly. "Touring the Dream Factory: The Dream-Film Connection in the *Wizard of Oz* and a *Nightmare on Elm Street*." *Dreaming*, 9:1 (1999): pp. 101–109.

Canavan, Gerry. "'Something Nightmares Are From': Metacommentary in Joss Whedon's the *Cabin in the Woods*." *Slayage* 10:2/11:1 (Fall 2013/Winter 2014).

Carroll, Noel. "The Future of Allusion: Hollywood in the Seventies (And Beyond)." *October*, 20 (1982): pp. 51–81.

Carroll, Noel. *The Philosophy of Horror, or Paradoxes of the Heart*. New York: Routledge, 1990.

Cherry, Brigid. *Routledge Film Guidebooks: Horror*. New York: Routledge, 2009.

Clover, J. Carol. *Men, Women and Chain Saws. Gender in the Modern Horror Film*. Princeton: Princeton University Press, 1992.

Cohen, Ralph. "History and Genre." *New Literary History* 17, No.2 (Winter 1986).

Connelly, Kelly. "From Final Girl to Final Woman: Defeating the Male Monster in Halloween and Halloween H20." *Journal of Popular Film & Television*, Vol. 35 Issue 1 (2007): pp. 12–21.

Conrich, Ian. "Seducing the Subject: Freddy Krueger, Popular Culture and the Nightmare on Elm Street Films." In *Trash Aesthetics: Popular Culture and Its Audience*, edited by Deborah Cartmell, Heidi Kaye, Imelda Whelehan and I. Q. Hunter. London: Pluto Press, 1997.

Cooper, L. Andrew. "*The Cabin in the Woods* and the End of American Exceptionalism." *Slayage* 10:2/11:1 (Fall 2013/Winter 2014).

Creed, Barbara. "Film and Psychoanalysis." In *The Oxford Guide to Film Studies*, edited by John Hill and Pamela Church Gibson. Oxford: Oxford University Press, 1998.

Creed, Barbara. "Horror and the Monstrous-Feminine. an Imaginary Abjection." In *Horror, the Film Reader*, edited by Mark Jancovich. London: Routledge, 2002.

Creed, Barbara. *The Monstrous-Feminine: Film, Feminism and Psychoanalysis*. New York: Routledge, 1993.

Derry, Charles. *Dark Dreams 2.0.: A Psychological History of the Modern Horror Film from the 1950s to the 21st Century*. Jefferson, NC: McFarland, 2009.

Derry, Charles. *The Suspense Thriller: Films in the Shadow of Alfred Hitchcock*. Jefferson, NC: McFarland, 2001.

Dika, Vera. "The Stalker Film, 1978–1981." In *American Horrors: Essays on the Modern American Horror Film*, edited by Gregory A. Waller. Champaign: University of Illinois Press, 1987.

Dixon, Wheeler Winston. "'Fighting and Violence and Everything, That's Always Cool': Teen Films in the 1990s." In *Film Genre 2000: New Critical Essays*, edited by Wheeler Winston Dixon. New York: SUNY Press, 2000.

Evans, Dylan. *An Introductory Dictionary of Lacanian Psychoanalysis*. New York: Routledge, 1996.

Evans, Walter. "Monster Movies: A Sexual Theory." In *Planks of Reason: Essays on the Horror Film*, edited by Barry Keith Grant. Lanham, MD: Scarecrow Press, 1984.

Farley, Ellen, and William K. Knoedelseder, Jr. "The Real Texas Chainsaw Massacre." *Los Angeles Times Calendar*, September 5, 1982, pp. 2–7.

Francis, James, Jr. *Remaking Horror: Hollywood's New Reliance on Scares of Old*. Jefferson, NC: McFarland, 2013.

"Freddy Vs. Jason Slashes Competition." *North Bay Nugget*, August 18, 2003.

Freud, Sigmund. *The Uncanny*, translated by David McLintock. London: Penguin Books, 2003.

Freud, Sophie. "The Social Construction of Normality." *Families in Society*, 80:4 (1999): pp. 333–339.

"Fright Exclusive Interview: Rob Zombie." *Icons of Fright*, 2007. Accessed November 7, 2015.

Giannini, Erin. "'Charybdis Tested Well with Teens': The *Cabin in the Woods* as Metafictional

Critique of Corporate Media Producers and Audiences." *Slayage* 10:2/11:1 (Fall 2013/Winter 2014).
Gledhill, Christine. "Rethinking Genre." In *Reinventing Film Studies*, edited by Christine Gledhill and Linda Williams. London: Arnold, 2000.
Gomery, Douglas. *The History of Cinema* (Greek translation by M. Talantopoulou). Athens: Ellin, 1998.
Green, Robert. *Richard M. Nixon*. Minneapolis: Compass Point Books, 2003.
Greven, David. *Representations of Femininity in American Genre Cinema: The Woman's Film, Film Noir, and Modern Horror*. New York: Palgrave Macmillan, 2011.
Grindon, Leger. "Cycles and Clusters: The Shape of Film Genre History." In *Film Genre Reader IV*, edited by Barry Keith Grant. Austin: University of Texas Press, 2012.
Grove, David. *Making Friday the 13th: The Legend of Camp Blood*. Godalming, UK: FAB Press, 2005.
Hand, Richard, and Jay McRoy. *Monstrous Adaptations: Generic and Thematic Mutations in Horror Film*. Manchester, UK: Manchester University Press, 2007.
Harvey, Dennis. "A Nightmare on Elm Street." *Variety*, 418:3 (May 3—May 9, 2010): p. 21.
Heba, Gary. "Everyday Nightmares: The Rhetoric of Social Horror in the Nightmare on Elm Street Series." *Journal of Popular Film and Television*, 23:3 (1995): pp. 106–115.
Heffernan, Kevin. "Risen from the Vaults: Recent Horror Film Remakes and the American Film Industry." In *Merchants of Menace: The Business of Horror Cinema*, edited by Richard Nowell. New York: Bloomsbury, 2014.
Hills, Matt and Steven Jay Schneider. "'The Devil Made Me Do It!': Representing Evil and Disarticulating Mind/Body in the Supernatural Serial Killer Film." In *The Changing Face of Evil in Film and Television*, edited by Martin F. Norden. Amsterdam, The Netherlands: Rodopi, 2007.
Hogan, Joseph. *The Reagan Years: The Record in Presidential Leadership*. Manchester, UK: Manchester University Press, 1990.
Holloway, David. *9/11 and the War on Terror*. Edinburgh, UK: Edinburgh University Press, 2008.
Hutcheon, Linda. *A Poetics of Postmodernism: History, Theory, Fiction*. London: Routledge, 1988.
Hutchings, Peter. *The A to Z of Horror Cinema*. Lanham, MD: Scarecrow Press, 2009.
Hutchings, Peter. *The Horror Film*. London: Routledge, 2013.
IMDb, www.imdb.com.
Israeli, Noam. "Reflections on Freud's the Uncanny." *Journal of the Society for Existential Analysis* 16, 2 (2005): pp. 378–389.
Jackson, Kimberly. *Technology, Monstrosity, and Reproduction in Twenty-First Century Horror*. New York: Palgrave MacMillan, 2013.
Jameson, Frederic. *Postmodernism or the Cultural Logic of Late Capitalism*. Durham, NC: Duke University Press, 1991.
Jarrett, Murphy. "Reagan & Bush, Father & Son." *CBS News*, December 5, 2007. http://www.cbsnews.com/2100-500345_162-622031.html.
Jauss, Hans Robert. *Towards an Aesthetic of Reception*. Brighton, UK: Harvester Press, 1982.
Jemmer, Patrick. "The O(The)R (O)The(R)…" In *Engage Newcastle Volume 1—Café Philosophique: A Season of "The Other,"* edited by Patrick Jemmer. Newcastle, UK: Newcastle Philosophy Society, 2010.
Johnson, Kevin C. "Craven Promises New Twist for Horror Film *Scream 4*." *McClatchy—Tribune Business News*, April 10, 2011.
Jones, Alan. *The Rough Guide to Horror Movies*. London: Rough Guides, 2005.
Kahn, Paul W. *Finding Ourselves at the Movies: Philosophy for a New Generation*. New York: Columbia University Press, 2013.
Kaklamanidou, Betty. *The "Disguised" Political Film in Contemporary Hollywood: A Genre's Construction*. New York: Bloomsbury, 2016.
Kaklamanidou, Despoina. *Introduction to Hollywood Romantic Comedy: Cinema Genre and Gender Representation (In Greek)*. Athens: Aigokeros, 2007.

Kawin, Bruce F. "Children of the Light." In *Film Genre Reader III*, edited by Barry Keith Grant. Austin: University of Texas Press, 2003.

Kellner, Douglas. *Cinema Wars: Hollywood Film and Politics in the Bush-Cheney Era*. Hoboken, NJ: Wiley-Blackwell, 2010.

Kendrick, James. "Razors in the Dreamscape: Revisiting a *Nightmare on Elm Street* and the Slasher Film." *Film Criticism*, 33:3 (2009): pp. 17–33.

Kendrick, James. "Slasher Films and Gore in the 1980s." In *A Companion to the Horror Film*, edited by Harry M. Benshoff. Hoboken, NJ: Wiley-Blackwell, 2014.

Kerner, Aaron Michael. *Torture Porn in the Wake of 9/11: Horror, Exploitation, and the Cinema of Sensation*. New Brunswick, NJ: Rutgers University Press, 2015.

Kerswell, J.A. *The Slasher Movie Book*. Chicago: Chicago Review Press, 2012.

Klein, Andy. "Freddy Vs. Jason" *Variety*, 391:12, 11–17 August 2003, p. 20.

Kristeva, Julia. *Powers of Horror: An Essay on Abjection*, translated by Leon S. Roudiez. New York: Columbia University Press, 1982.

Kristeva, Julia. *Strangers to Ourselves*. New York: Columbia University Press, 1991.

Krolokke, Charlotte, and Anne Scott Sorensen. "Three Waves of Feminism: From Suffragettes to Grrls." In *Gender Communication Theories & Analyses: From Silence to Performance*. Thousand Oaks, CA: Sage, 2006.

Kvaran, Kara M. "'You're All Doomed!': A Socioeconomic Analysis of Slasher Films." *Journal of American Studies* 50:4 (2016): pp. 953–970.

Lacan, Jacques. *Écrits: The First Complete Edition in English*, translated by Bruce Fink. New York: W. W. Norton & Co., 2006.

Lacan, Jacques. *The Seminar of Jacques Lacan, Book II: The Ego in Freud's Theory and in the Technique of Psychoanalysis, 1954–1955*, translated by Sylvana Tomaselli. New York: W. W. Norton & Co., 1991.

Lakoff, George. *Women, Fire, and Dangerous Things: What Categories Reveal About the Mind*. Chicago: University of Chicago Press, 1987.

Lawrence, Novotny. *Blaxploitation Films of the 1970s: Blackness and Genre*. New York: Routledge, 2008.

Levinas, Emmanuel. *Totality and Infinity: An Essay on Exteriority*, translated by Alfonso Lingis. Netherlands: Kluwer Academic Publishers, 1991.

Lipsett, Joe. "'One for the Horror Fans' Vs. 'An Insult to the Horror Genre': Negotiating Reading Strategies in IMDb Reviews of the *Cabin in the Woods*." *Slayage* 10:2/11:1 (Fall 2013/Winter 2014).

Lowenstein, Adam. "Alone on Elm Street." *Film Quarterly*, 64:1 (2010): pp. 18–22.

Lurie, Susan. "The Construction of the Castrated Woman in Psychoanalysis and Cinema." *Discourse* 4 (1981): 52–74.

MacGregor Johnston, David. "Kitsch and Camp and Things That Go Bump in the Night; Or, Sontag and Adorno at the (Horror) Movies." In *The Philosophy of Horror*, edited by Thomas Fahy. Lexington: University Press of Kentucky, 2010.

Macor, Alison. *Chainsaws, Slackers, and Spy Kids: Thirty Years of Filmmaking in Austin, Texas*. Austin: University of Texas Press, 2010.

Manning, David. "A Great Legacy Slashed to Bits." *The Nelson Mail*, February 10, 2004.

Markovitz, Jonathan. "Female Paranoia as Survival Skill: Reason or Pathology in a *Nightmare on Elm Street*?" *Quarterly Review of Film and Video*, 17:3 (2000): pp. 211–220.

Marriott, James. *Horror Films*. London: Virgin, 2007.

McDonald, Rick. "Sacred Violence and the *Cabin in the Woods*." *Slayage* 10:2/11:1 (Fall 2013/Winter 2014).

Melanson, Richard A. *American Foreign Policy Since the Vietnam War: The Search for Consensus from Richard Nixon to George W. Bush, Fourth Edition*. New York: M.E. Sharpe, 2005.

Merritt, Naomi. "Cannibalistic Capitalism and Other American Delicacies: A Bataillean Taste of the Texas Chain Saw Massacre." *Film-Philosophy*, 14:1 (2010): pp. 202–231.

Metz, Christian. *Psychoanalysis and Cinema: The Imaginary Signifier*. Bloomington: Indiana University Press, 1982.

Michotte, Albert. "The Emotional Involvement of the Spectator in the Action Represented in a Film: Toward a Theory." In *Michotte's Experimental Phenomenology of Perception*, edited by G. Thines, A. Costall, G. Butterworth. Hillsdale, NJ: Lawrence Erlbaum, 1991, pp. 209–217.

Miller, Sam J. "Assimilation and the Queer Monster." In *Horror After 9/11: World of Fear, Cinema of Terror*, edited by Aviva Briefel and Sam J. Miller. Austin: University of Texas Press, 2011.

Modleski, Tania. "The Terror of Pleasure: The Contemporary Horror Film and Postmodern Theory." In *The Horror Reader*, edited by Ken Gelder. London: Routledge, 2000.

Morrison, Cary. "Creature Conflict: Man, Monster and the Metaphor of Intractable Social Conflict." In *Monsters and the Monstrous: Myths & Metaphors of Enduring Evil*, edited by Paul L. Yoder and Peter Mario Kreuter. Oxford: Inter-Disciplinary Press, 2004.

Moseley, Fred. "The U.S. Economic Crisis." *International Socialist Review*, Issue 64 (March 2009). http://isreview.org/issue/64/us-economic-crisis.

Muir, John Kenneth. *Wes Craven: The Art of Horror*. Jefferson, NC: McFarland, 1998.

Mulvey, Laura. *Visual and Other Pleasures*. London: Macmillan, 1989.

Neale, Steve. *Genre*. London: BFI, 1980.

Neale, Steve. "Halloween: Suspense, Aggression and the Look." In *Planks of Reason: Essays on the Horror Film*, edited by Barry Keith Grant. Lanham, MD: Scarecrow Press, 1984.

Neale, Steve. "Questions of Genre." In *Film Genre Reader III*, edited by Barry Keith Grant. Austin: University of Texas Press, 2003.

Nelson, Andrew Patrick. "Franchise Legacy and Neo-Slasher Conventions in Halloween H20." In *Style and Form in the Hollywood Slasher Film*, edited by Wickham Clayton. New York: Palgrave Macmillan, 2015.

Nelson, Andrew Patrick. "Traumatic Childhood Now Included. Todorov's Fantastic and the Uncanny Slasher Remake." In *American Horror Film: The Genre at the Turn of the Millennium*, edited by Steffen Hantke. Jackson: University Press of Mississippi, 2010.

Newman, Kim. "Freddy Vs. Jason" *Sight and Sound*, 13:11 (November 2003), pp. 44, 46, 3.

Nowell, Richard. "The Ambitions of Most Independent Filmmakers: Indie Production, the Majors, and *Friday the 13th* (1980)." *Journal of Film and Video*, 63:2 (2011): pp. 28–44.

Nowell, Richard. *Blood Money: A History of the First Teen Slasher Film Cycle*. New York: Continuum, 2011.

Palmer, William J. *The Films of the Eighties: A Social History*. Carbondale: Southern Illinois University Press, 1993.

Parker, Richard. "Sexuality, Culture, and Power in HIV/AIDS Research." *Annual Review of Anthropology* 30 (2001): pp. 163–179.

Perkins, Claire. "The Scre4m Trilogy." In *Film Trilogies: New Critical Approaches*, edited by Claire Perkins and Constantine Verevis. New York: Palgrave MacMillan, 2012.

Perren, Alisa. *Indie, Inc.: Miramax and the Transformation of Hollywood in the 1990s*. Austin: University of Texas Press, 2012.

Petridis, Sotiris. "The Scream of a Generation: 'Generation Me' in Scream 4." In *The Millennials on Film and Television: Essays on the Politics of Popular Culture*, edited by Betty Kaklamanidou and Margaret Tally. Jefferson, NC: McFarland, 2014.

Pheasant-Kelly, Fran. "Reframing Parody and Intertextuality in Scream: Formal and Theoretical Approaches to the 'Postmodern' Slasher." In *Style and Form in the Hollywood Slasher Film*, edited by Wickham Clayton. New York: Palgrave Macmillan, 2015.

Phillips, Kendall R. *Projected Fears, Horror Films and American Culture*. Westport, CT: Praeger, 2005.

Pinedo, Isabel Cristina. *Recreational Terror: Women and the Pleasures of Horror Film Viewing*. Albany: SUNY Press, 1997.

Pinel, Vincent. *Ecoles, Genres Et Mouvements Au Cinéma* (Greek translation by Mrilena Karra). Athens: Metaixmio, 2006.

Platts, Todd K. "The New Horror Movie." In *Baby Boomers and Popular Culture: An Inquiry into America's Most Powerful Generation*, edited by Brian Cogan and Thom Gencarelli. Westport, CT: Praeger, 2015.

Portman, Jamie. "The Debate Over *Scream 4*; Revolting Slasher Film or Classical Theatre for a Modern Age? The Argument Continues." *The Ottawa Citizen*, April 14, 2011.

Renner, Karen J. "Generational Conflict, Twenty-First-Century Horror Films and the *Cabin in the Woods*." In *The Millennials on Film and Television: Essays on the Politics of Popular Culture*, edited by Betty Kaklamanidou and Margaret Tally. Jefferson, NC: McFarland, 2014.

Robertson, David Brian. *Loss of Confidence: Politics and Policy in the 1970s*. University Park: Penn State University Press, 1998.

Rockoff, Adam. *Going to Pieces: The Rise and Fall of the Slasher Film, 1978–1986*. Jefferson, NC: McFarland, 2002.

Sartre, Jean-Paul. *Being and Nothingness: An Essay on Phenomenological Ontology*, translated by Hazel E. Barnes. London: Routledge, 2003.

Schoell, William. *Stay Out of the Shower: 25 Years of Shocker Films Beginning with "Psycho."* New York: Dembner Books, 1985.

Sharrett, Christopher. "Fairy Tales for the Apocalypse: Wes Craven on the Horror Film." *Literature/Film Quarterly*, 13:3 (1985): pp. 139–147.

Sharrett, Christopher. "The Horror Film as Social Allegory (And How It Comes Undone)." In *A Companion to the Horror Film*, edited by Harry M. Benshoff. Hoboken, NJ: Wiley-Blackwell, 2014.

Sharrett, Christopher. "The Idea of Apocalypse in the Texas Chainsaw Massacre." In *Planks of Reason: Essays on the Horror Film*, edited by Barry Keith Grant. Lanham, MD: Scarecrow Press, 1984.

Shary, Timothy. *Teen Movies: American Youth on Screen*. New York: Columbia University Press, 2005.

Simon, David R. "Watergate and the Nixon Presidency: A Comparative Ideological Analysis." In *Watergate and Afterward: The Legacy of Richard M. Nixon*, edited by Leon Friedman and William F. Levantrosser. Westport, CT: Greenwood Publishing Group Inc., 1992.

Simpson, Philip L. "Whither the Serial Killer Movie?" In *American Horror Film: The Genre at the Turn of the Millennium*, edited by Steffen Hantke. Jackson: University Press of Mississippi, 2010.

Smith, Kathy. "Reframing Fantasy: September 11 and the Global Audience." In *The Spectacle of the Real: From Hollywood to Reality TV and Beyond*, edited by Geoff King. Bristol, UK: Intellect, 2005.

Spong, John. "Oh, the Horror!" *Texas Monthly*, October 2002.

Staiger, Janet. "Hybrid or Inbred: The Purity Hypothesis and Hollywood Genre History." In *Film Genre Reader III*, edited by Barry Keith Grant. Austin: University of Texas Press, 2003.

Stam, Robert. *An Introduction to Film Theory* (Greek translation by K. Kaklamani). Athens: Pataki, 2006.

Starr, Michael. "Whedon's Great Glass Elevator: Space, Liminality, and Intertext in the *Cabin in the Woods*." *Slayage* 10:2/11:1 (Fall 2013/Winter 2014).

Stephens, John. "'I'll Never Be the Same After That Summer': From Abjection to Subjective Agency in Teen Films." In *Youth Cultures: Texts, Images, and Identities*, edited by Kerry Mallan and Sharyn Pearce. Westport, CT: Praeger, 2003.

Strawser, Justin. "*Friday the 13th* Franchise Resurrected for New Generation of Slasher Film Devotees." *The News-Item*, February 14, 2009.

Syder, Andrew. "Knowing the Rules. Postmodernism and the Horror Film." *Special Issue of Spectator* 22: 2 (Fall 2002): pp. 78–88.

Tallon, Philip. "Through a Mirror, Darkly: Art-Horror as a Medium for Moral Reflection." In *The Philosophy of Horror*, edited by Thomas Fahy. Kentucky: The University Press of Kentucky, 2010.

Tarratt, Margaret. "Monsters from the Id." In *Film Genre Reader III*, edited by Barry Keith Grant. Austin: University of Texas Press, 2003.

Telotte, J. P. "Faith and Idolatry in the Horror Film." In *Planks of Reason: Essays on the Horror Film*, edited by Barry Keith Grant. Lanham, MD: Scarecrow Press, 1984.

Thomas, Kevin. "The Other." *Peace Review* 14, 3 (2002): pp. 331–336.
Tietchen, Todd F. "Samplers and Copycats: The Cultural Implications of the Postmodern Slasher in Contemporary American Film." *Journal of Popular Film and Television* 26:3 (1998): pp. 98–107.
Tincknell, Estella. "Feminine Boundaries. Adolescence, Witchcraft, and the Supernatural in Gothic Cinema and Television." In *Horror Zone: The Cultural Experience of Contemporary Horror Cinema*, edited by Ian Conrich. London: I.B. Tauris & Co Ltd., 2010.
Tompkins, Joe. "Re-Imagining the Canon: Examining the Discourse of Contemporary Horror Film Reboots." *New Review of Film and Television Studies* 12:4 (2014): pp. 380–399.
Trencansky, Sarah. "Final Girls and Terrible Youth: Transgression in 1980s Slasher Horror." *Journal of Popular Film & Television*, 29, 2 (2001): pp. 63–73.
Truffaut, François. *Hitchcock* (Greek translation by G. Ioannidis). Athens: Ipsilon, 1986.
Tudor, Andrew. "Genre." In *Film Genre Reader IV*, edited by Barry Keith Grant. Austin: University of Texas Press, 2012.
Tudor, Andrew. *Theories of Film*. New York: Viking Press, 1973.
Wee, Valerie. "New Decade, New Rules. Rebooting the Scream Franchise in the Digital Age." In *Merchants of Menace: The Business of Horror Cinema*, edited by Richard Nowell. New York: Bloomsbury, 2014.
Wee, Valerie. "Resurrecting and Updating the Teen Slasher: The Case of Scream." *Journal of Popular Film and Television* 34:2 (2006): pp. 50–61.
Wee, Valerie. "The Scream Trilogy, 'Hyperpostmodernism,' and the Late-Nineties Teen Slasher Film." *Journal of Film and Video*, 57:3 (2005): pp. 44–61.
Wetmore, Kevin J. *Post-9/11 Horror in American Cinema*. New York: Continuum, 2012.
Williams, Linda. "When the Woman Looks." In *Horror: The Film Reader*, edited by Mark Jancovich. London: Routledge, 2002.
Williams, Robert R. *Recognition: Fichte and Hegel on the Other*. New York: SUNY Press, 1992.
Wittgenstein, Ludwig. *Philosophical Investigations*, translated by and G. E. Anscombe. Oxford, UK: Blackwell, 1997.
Wolgamott, Kent L. "Bloody Friday." *Lincoln Journal Star*, February 13, 2009.
Wood, Robin. *Hollywood from Vietnam to Reagan…and Beyond*. New York: Columbia University Press, 2003.
Wood, Robin. "An Introduction to the American Horror Film." In *Planks of Reason: Essays on the Horror Film*, edited by Barry Keith Grant. Lanham, MD: Scarecrow Press, 1984.
Woofter, Kristopher, and Jasie Stokes. "Once More into the Woods: An Introduction and Provocation." *Slayage* 10:2/11:1 (Fall 2013/Winter 2014).
Worland, Rick. *The Horror Film: An Introduction*. Hoboken, NJ: Wiley-Blackwell, 2007.
Wyrick, Laura. "Horror at Century's End: Where Have All the Slashers Gone?" *Pacific Coast Philology*, Vol. 33, No. 2 (1998): pp. 122–126.
Žižek, Slavoj. *How to Read Lacan*. New York: W. W. Norton & Co., 2006.
Žižek, Slavoj. *Welcome to the Desert of the Real! Five Essays on September 11 and Other Relevant Dates* (Greek translation by Vicky Iakovou). Athens: Scripta, 2003.

Index

a priori method 7
abject 22, 23, 24, 103
adult(s) 13–16, 20, 28, 31, 41, 48–51, 54, 60, 70, 79, 80–84, 86, 90, 93, 107, 110, 115, 117, 123, 124, 141–143, 148
Afghanistan 96, 100
AIDS 36, 42
alcohol 13, 20, 30, 50, 64, 70, 81
allegory 12, 54, 97, 102, 112, 113, 123, 127, 128
allusion 38
Altman, Rick 6, 16–18, 30, 33, 37, 45, 131
April Fool's Day (1986) 136, 141
Avatar (2009) 99

backstory 2, 3, 32, 22, 25, 28, 41, 48, 56, 58–60, 64–66, 68, 71, 74–79, 87–89, 106, 108, 128, 129, 131–133
Bad Dreams (1988) 137, 142
The Bad Seed (1956) 6
Bates, Norman (character) 6, 12, 55
Batman Begins (2005) 91
Baudrillard, Jean 72
Baudry, Jean-Louis 26, 60
Bay, Michael 96, 97, 117, 118
Beauvoir, Simone de 22
Becker, Matt 53
Benshoff, Harry 36
Berserk (1967) 6
Black Christmas (1974) 6, 49, 52, 57, 58, 135, 141
The Blair Witch Project (1999) 40, 71
Blake, Linnie 96, 97
Borges, Andre 62
bourgeoisie 92, 94
box office 2, 7, 9, 37, 40, 66, 68, 88, 90, 127, 129, 133, 135–140
Box Office Mojo (website) 7, 149
Bride of Chucky (1998) 78, 84, 138, 142
Buffalo Bill (character) 55
Bulkeley, Kelly 57
Bush, George W. 42, 90, 96, 98

Cabin Fever (2002) 96
The Cabin in the Woods (2012) 25, 28, 40, 44, 90 102–105, 126, 127, 140, 143

Candyman (1992) 137, 142
Candyman: Farewell to the Flesh (1995) 40, 79, 137, 142
cannibalism 54, 55, 97, 100, 101, 110
Carpenter, John 49, 57, 59, 73
Carroll, Noel 11, 38
cause/effect 30, 35, 42, 74, 78, 89, 91–93, 95, 106, 122, 123
Child's Play (1988) 137, 141
Child's Play 2 (1990) 137, 142
Child's Play 3 (1991) 137, 142
Clover, Carol J. 11–16, 25, 27, 29, 32, 35, 36, 44, 45, 47, 54, 72, 79, 81, 112, 119, 130, 147
comedy 8
Connelly, Kelly 59
conservatism 34, 42, 47–49, 52, 56, 66, 68, 69, 87, 88, 90, 96–98, 131
Cooper, Andrew 127
Corpus 2, 7, 8, 10, 11, 14, 15, 17, 18, 32, 34, 43, 44, 47, 67, 77, 79, 131, 145
Cover Girl Killer (1959) 6
Crane, Marion (character) 13, 70
Craven, Wes 39, 40, 63, 124
Creed, Barbara 13
Cunningham, Sean S. 62

Darkness Falls (2003) 108
dead teenager (subgenre) 1
Derry, Charles 21
Dika, Vera 11, 15, 16, 29, 32, 45, 47, 130, 145
Dixon, Wheeler 84
Dracula (character) 22
drugs 13, 30, 50, 64, 72, 112

empathy 16, 41, 107–110, 126
empiricist dilemma 7
empiricist method 7
Evans, Walter 14

The Faculty (1998) 8
family values 30, 36, 42, 51, 58, 66, 90, 95, 131
feminism 60, 61, 63, 113, 151
Fichte, Johann Gottlieb 22
Final Boy 27, 28, 45, 79, 112, 115–117, 119, 121, 122, 141, 142

Index

Final Couple 28, 45, 76–79, 82, 83, 105, 112, 117, 119–122, 126, 142, 143
Final Destination (2000) 9, 25, 44, 45, 68, 88, 89, 116, 117, 132, 138, 142
Final Destination 2 (2003) 25, 139, 143
Final Destination 3 (2006) 25, 139, 143
The Final Destination (2009) 25, 139, 143
Final Destination 5 (2011) 25, 140, 143
Final Girl 12–14, 16, 25, 27–28, 30, 35, 44, 45, 50, 51, 60–64, 70, 71, 74, 76–82, 86, 93, 111–119, 121, 122, 130, 141–143
Final Woman 28, 70, 80, 81, 115, 142, 143
Form, Andrew 96
Francis, James 80
Frankenstein (1931) 21, 22
Frankenstein Meets the Wolf Man (1943) 106
Freddy vs. Jason (2003) 25, 43, 105, 106, 138, 142, 151
Freddy's Dead: The Final Nightmare (1991) 137, 142
Freddy's Nightmares (TV series) 62
Freud, Sigmund 21
Freud, Sophie 19
Friday the 13th (1980) 2, 32, 33, 35, 38, 48, 51, 56, 57, 62–64, 70, 76, 79, 135, 141, 151
Friday the 13th (2009) 43, 45, 108, 117–121, 123, 139, 143, 150, 151
Friday the 13th (TV series) 62
Friday the 13th Part 2 (1981) 135, 141, 151
Friday the 13th Part III (1982) 136, 141, 151
Friday the 13th: The Final Chapter (1984) 136, 151
Friday the 13th: A New Beginning (1985) 63, 136, 151
Friday the 13th Part VII: The New Blood (1988) 137, 142, 151
Friday the 13th Part VIII: Jason Takes Manhattan (1989) 137, 142, 151
The Fun House (1981) 136, 141

Gein, Ed 55
gender 2, 6, 12–15, 27, 28, 32, 44, 48, 56, 60, 61, 63, 66–69, 76–78, 89, 90, 94, 112, 113, 115–117, 119, 121, 123, 129, 130, 132, 133, 148
Ghostface 71, 72, 85, 86, 111
Gianni, Erin 126
Gledhill, Christine 7
Gomery, Douglas 20
Gothic 20, 22
Grand Guignol 5
Grease (1978) 49
Greenwood, Vaughn 1
Greven, David 28
Griffin, Sean 36
Grindon, Leger 6, 11
Gulf War 73

Haddonfield 49, 51, 91–94
Halloween (1978) 2, 3, 5, 9, 12, 13, 15, 19, 32, 35, 38, 41, 48, 49–52, 56–65, 73, 79, 83, 107, 123, 129, 135, 141, 145, 149
Halloween (2007) 33, 41, 43, 90, 92–94, 106–109, 113, 114, 119, 123, 139, 143, 149, 150
Halloween II (1981) 51–52, 65, 135, 141, 149
Halloween II (2009) 28, 44, 90, 93–95, 114, 139, 143, 149, 150
Halloween III: Season of the Witch (1982) 149
Halloween 4: The Return of Michael Myers (1988) 137, 142, 149
Halloween 5 (1989) 137, 142, 149
Halloween: The Curse of Michael Myers (1995) 40, 137, 142, 149
Halloween H20: 20 Years Later (1998) 69–71, 75, 76, 79, 80, 115, 138, 142, 149
Halloween: Resurrection (2002) 115, 138, 142, 149
Hand, Richard 103
Happy Days (TV series) 49
Harvey, Dennis 123
He Knows You're Alone (1980) 135, 141
Heba, Gary 57
Hegel, Georg Wilhelm Friedrich 22
Henkel, Kim 53, 96
Hills, Matt 62
The Hills Have Eyes (1977) 135, 141
The Hills Have Eyes (2006) 43, 96, 139, 143
Hitchcock, Alfred 78
Hollywood 33, 43, 86, 102
Hooper, Tobe 53, 54, 96, 100
Horror of Armageddon (horror category) 21
horror of double personality (subgenre) 8
Horror of Personality (horror category) 21, 65, 108
Horror of the Demonic (horror category) 21–22, 57, 65, 108
House of Wax (2005) 139, 143
The House on Sorority Row (1983) 136, 141
Hutcheon, Linda 37
Hutchings, Peter 79

I Know What You Did Last Summer (1997) 38, 40, 69, 75, 77, 82, 138, 142
I Still Know What You Did Last Summer (1998) 38, 39, 76, 138, 142
IMDb 7
intertextuality 37–40, 67–69, 71, 72, 88, 128, 132
Iraq 90, 96, 100
It (1990) 105

Jameson, Frederic 37
Jarrett, Murphy 42
Jason Goes to Hell: The Final Friday (1993) 137, 142, 151
Jason Lives: Friday the 13th Part VI (1986) 116, 141, 151
Jason X (2001) 151
Jeepers Creepers (2001) 25, 44, 138, 142

Jeepers Creepers 2 (2003) 139, 143
Jemmer, Patrick 26

Kahn, Paul 69
Kaklamanidou, Betty 145
Kawin, Bruce F. 122
Kellner, Douglas 96
Kendrick, James 57
knife 12, 14, 59, 95
Kristeva, Julia 22, 23, 101, 103
Krueger, Freddy (character) 12, 39, 55, 57, 63–64, 80, 81, 104–106, 120–122
Kvaran, Kara 68

Lacan, Jacques 22, 23, 26, 101
Lakoff, George 5
Langenkamp, Heather (character) 39, 63, 80, 81
Laverne and Shirley (TV series) 49
Leatherface (character) 12, 53–55, 97–101, 108–110, 113, 114
Leatherface: Texas Chainsaw Massacre III (1990) 150
The Leopard Man (1943) 6
Levinas, Emmanuel 22
Liebesman, Jonathan 108
location(s) 17, 18, 20–22
Loomis, Sam Dr. (character) 50–52, 59, 62, 81, 83, 92–95, 113, 114
Loth, Jean 14
Lowenstein, Adam 123

MacGregor Johnston, David 57
male gaze 59
Manning, David 96
Markovitz, Jonathan 64
Marriott, James 54
mask 16, 37, 38, 56–59, 62, 70, 71, 74, 75, 79, 85, 86, 107, 108, 111, 118
McDonald, Rick 127
McRoy, Jay 43
Metz, Christian 26, 60
middle class 5, 29, 35, 36, 44, 49, 91–94, 97, 98, 113
Modleski, Tania 64
Morrison, Cary 23
Mrs. Voorhees (character) 24, 32, 56, 118, 119
Munch, Edvard 38
My Bloody Valentine (1981) 136, 141
My Bloody Valentine 3D (2009) 43, 99, 139, 143
My Soul to Take (2010) 99
Myers, Michael (character) 12, 32, 35, 41, 49–52, 55, 58–62, 65, 70, 71, 75, 81, 90–95, 106–108, 113–115, 123
The Mysteries of Paris (1935) 1

Neale, Steve 11, 17, 61
Nelson, Andrew Patrick 109
New Line 10, 106

New Nightmare (1994) 39, 40, 67, 69, 80, 84, 137, 142, 151
Night School (1981) 56, 78, 136, 141
A Nightmare on Elm Street (1984) 2, 12, 19, 33, 35, 39, 48, 56, 57, 62, 63, 80, 83, 104, 129, 136, 141, 151
A Nightmare on Elm Street (2010) 28, 43, 90, 108, 117, 120, 121, 123, 139, 143, 150, 151
A Nightmare on Elm Street Part 2: Freddy's Revenge (1985) 116, 136, 141, 151
A Nightmare on Elm Street 3: Dream Warriors (1987) 136, 141, 151
A Nightmare on Elm Street 4: The Dream Master (1988) 136, 141, 151
A Nightmare on Elm Street: The Dream Child (1989) 137, 142, 151
9/11 42, 43, 96, 97
Nispel, Marcus 43, 96, 97, 117, 118
Nixon, Richard 52, 53

Obama, Barack 98
The Omen (2006) 43

Palmer, William J. 36
Paramount 10
parent(s) 16, 50, 57, 59, 82, 107, 120, 121
parody 37–40, 67–69, 73, 88, 102, 127, 128, 132
pastiche 37, 39, 70, 88, 102, 125, 132
Peeping Tom (1960) 6
Perkins, Claire 86
Pheasant-Kelly, Fran 72
Phillips, Kendall R. 50, 54, 65
Platts, Todd 53
point of view (POV) 16, 18, 22, 26, 51, 56, 58–60, 88, 92, 100, 107
police 16, 51, 72, 73, 92, 95, 99–101, 108, 114, 115, 118, 120
pop culture 5, 34, 37, 39, 62, 129–131
possession film 1, 57
post-apocalyptic 54, 55, 96–98, 100–102, 109, 110, 113
pragmatic approach 17
prequel(s) 43, 90, 94, 108, 110, 150
pre-slasher(s) 6, 8, 70, 72
Prom Night (1980) 41, 57, 135, 141
Prom Night (2008) 43, 139, 143
Psycho (1960) 6, 8, 12, 13, 20, 22, 55, 70, 72
Psycho (1998) 8
Psycho II (1983) 8
Psycho III (1986) 8

Reagan, Ronald 30, 35, 36, 42, 49, 73, 96
remakes 8, 25, 28, 43–45, 48, 62, 90, 91, 93–96, 114, 117, 118, 120, 127, 129, 150
The Return of the Texas Chainsaw Massacre (1994) 50
The Ring (2002) 127
Ringu (1998) 127
Robertson, David Brian 53
Rockoff, Adam 11, 16, 26, 145

Sartre, Jean-Paul 22
Savini, Tom 62
Schneider, Steven Jay 62
Schwartz, Russell 106
science fiction 8
Scream (1996) 3, 27, 33, 38–40, 51, 69, 71–77, 85, 102, 111, 115, 138, 142
Scream (TV series) 9
Scream 2 (1997) 24, 69, 74, 78, 87, 138, 142
Scream 3 (2000) 9, 68, 69, 74, 84, 86, 87, 89, 138, 142
Scream 4 (2011) 24, 25, 42, 74, 90, 110–112, 115, 124–126, 128, 140, 143
Scream Queens (TV series) 9
sequel(s) 8–10, 12, 25, 28, 36, 37, 43, 51, 62, 69, 74, 76, 77, 82, 85, 90, 93, 99, 108, 114, 150
sexuality 6, 19, 24, 30, 32, 36, 40, 44, 52, 61, 63, 78, 94, 96, 130, 132, 148
Sharrett, Christopher 54
Shary, Timothy 74
shock 12
shocker (1989) 137, 142
shot(s) 17, 18, 26, 38, 51, 56, 58–60, 92, 97, 99, 106, 107, 114
Sidney (character) 27, 71, 73–75, 85, 86, 111, 112, 115, 124, 125
The Silence of the Lambs (1991) 55, 71
Simon, David 53
The Sixth Sense (1999) 40
slash-and-chop 1
sleeper 49, 149
slice-'em-up films 1
Smith, Kathy 43
social consensus method 7
sociopolitical 2, 20, 33, 35, 36, 42, 44, 50, 52–54, 61, 90, 92, 98–100, 102, 122, 123
sorority 58
special effects 16, 62
splatter film 1, 8, 92
Staiger, Janet 7
stalker film 1, 15
Stam, Robert 38
Stephens, John 76
stereotypes 25, 41, 44, 48, 56, 62, 63, 66, 78, 83, 89, 91, 95, 98, 99, 103, 109, 111, 116–120, 126, 127, 132
Strait-Jacket (1964) 6
Strode, Laurie (character) 41, 49–52, 59–62, 64, 65, 70, 71, 75, 81, 82, 91–95, 107, 113–115
Student Bodies (1981) 8

teacher(s) 16, 87, 124
teeniekill 1
television 9, 40, 43, 62, 73, 89, 94, 129, 130
Telotte, J. 59
Texas Chainsaw 3D (2013) 43, 90, 99, 101, 108, 140, 143
The Texas Chainsaw Massacre (1974) 6, 12, 33, 48, 49, 52–55, 57, 90, 96, 102, 135, 141, 150

The Texas Chainsaw Massacre (2003) 43, 90, 96, 108, 112, 113, 117, 138, 143, 150
The Texas Chainsaw Massacre 2 (1986) 136, 141, 150
The Texas Chainsaw Massacre: The Beginning (2006) 43, 90, 108, 109, 114, 118, 119, 139, 143, 150
theory of prototype 5
Thirteen Women (1932) 6
Thomas, Kevin 22
3D (technology) 99
Tietchen, Todd 72
Tompkins, Joe 91
torture porn film 1, 43
trilogy 74, 85, 86
Tudor, Andrew 7

uncanny 21, 58
urban horror (subgenre) 8
Urban Legend (1998) 38, 40, 69, 75, 77, 78, 82, 83, 138, 142
Urban Legends: Final Cut (2000) 9, 38, 68, 69, 78, 79, 83, 86–89, 138, 142

Valentine (2001) 33, 42, 44, 138, 142
vampire film 1, 20
Vietnam War 53, 96, 98, 100, 114
Visiting Hours (1982) 57, 136, 141
Voorhees, Jason (character) 24, 32, 35, 56, 62, 64, 65, 70, 76, 105, 106, 117–120

War on Terror 42, 96
Warner Bros. 57
Watergate 53, 54, 98
weapon(s) 5, 12, 16, 18, 104
Wee, Valerie 39, 72, 124
Werewolf (character) 22
Western culture 20–22, 98, 101, 113, 123, 127, 130
Wetmore, Kevin J. 27, 43, 97
When a Stranger Calls (1979) 16, 58, 72, 135, 141
When a Stranger Calls (2006) 43, 139, 143
whodunit 34, 38, 68, 71, 74–78, 88, 129, 131, 132
Williams, Linda 14
Without Warning (1952) 1
Wittgenstein, Ludwig 7
The Wolfman (2010) 43
Wolgamott, Kent 118
Wood, Robin 18, 21, 22, 29, 53, 54
Woodsboro 85
Woofter, Kristopher 127
working class 44, 49, 91–95, 97, 109, 114
Worland, Rick 77
World Trade Center 42, 90
Wrong Turn (2003) 96
Wrong Turn 2: Dead End (2007) 96

Žižek, Slavoj 23, 43
Zombie, Rob 91

www.ingramcontent.com/pod-product-compliance
Ingram Content Group UK Ltd.
Pitfield, Milton Keynes, MK11 3LW, UK
UKHW042016140426
5217IPUK00015B/1199